Learning, Earning and Investing

Middle School

Learning, Earning and Investing

Middle School

The Moody's Foundation

This publication was made possible through funding from The Moody's Foundation,
a charitable foundation established by Moody's Corporation.

NCEE

National Council on Economic Education

AUTHORS

Jean Caldwell
Professor of Economics Emerita
University of Central Oklahoma, Edmond

James E. Davis
Executive Director
Social Science Education Consortium, Boulder, Colorado

Suzanne M. Gallagher
Professor of Economics and Director of the Center for Economic Education
Virginia Commonwealth University, Richmond

Jane S. Lopus
Professor of Economics and Director of the Center for Economic Education
California State University, Hayward

John S. Morton
Vice President for Program Development
National Council on Economic Education, Scottsdale, Arizona

Mark C. Schug
Professor of Curriculum and Instruction and Director of the Center for Economic Education
University of Wisconsin-Milwaukee

Mary Suiter
Director of the Center for Entrepreneurship and Economic Education
University of Missouri-St. Louis

Phillip J. VanFossen
Associate Professor of Social Studies Education and Associate Director of the Center for Economic Education
Purdue University, West Lafayette, Indiana

Donald R. Wentworth
Professor of Economics
Pacific Lutheran University, Tacoma, Washington

William C. Wood
Professor of Economics and Director of the Center for Economic Education
James Madison University, Harrisonburg, Virginia

Cover photos: **© Zoran Milich / Masterfile, © Ron Fehling / Masterfile, © David Muir / Masterfile, © Carl Valiquet / Masterfile and © Daryl Benson / Masterfile**

ISBN: 1-56183-569-2

CONTENTS

FOREWORD

Americans today are more responsible than ever for their financial futures. Yet survey after survey shows that American adults and children know little about even the most elementary principles and facts about money management, saving and investing. Schools have a critical role to play in helping parents and others to provide an overall economic education — including investor education — to our young people. In order to be successful, investor education must be taught early, often and well.

Learning, Earning and Investing introduces students to the world of investing, its benefits and risks, and the critical role it plays in fostering capital formation and job creation in our free market system. *Learning, Earning and Investing* is a comprehensive investor education program focusing on the benefits of and strategies for investing for the long term. Lessons cover basics such as the language of financial markets, reading the financial pages and financial institutions in the U.S. economy. There are lessons on stocks, bonds and mutual funds. The 16 lessons in the middle school volume and the 23 lessons in the high school volume provide students with the active-learning experiences which are an NCEE trademark. The author team led by Mark C. Schug of the University of Wisconsin-Milwaukee has created path-breaking activities.

Learning, Earning and Investing is much more than two publications. The companion Web site offers sample lessons, interactive simulations, downloadable PowerPoint visuals, a glossary and assessments. In addition, there are downloadable lessons, which are not included in the print publications, for fourth- and fifth-grade students. The Web site serves as a portal for a wide range of investor education Web sites and materials.

Because the National Council on Economic Education (NCEE) believes that knowledgeable and skilled teachers are the key to successful investor education, the NCEE state Councils on Economic Education and university Centers for Economic Education are conducting 150 workshops across the United States. More than 4,500 teachers will receive free copies of the publication at the workshops. We hope this will be just the beginning of an extensive program of workshops on investor education for teachers.

None of this would be possible without the generous financial support provided by The Moody's Foundation. NCEE thanks The Moody's Foundation for its commitment to this investor education initiative, which will provide long-term benefits to the nation and its future investors.

Robert F. Duvall, Ph.D.
President & Chief Executive Officer
National Council on Economic Education

ACKNOWLEDGMENTS

The National Council on Economic Education expresses its deepest gratitude to the many individuals who were involved with this project.

PROJECT DIRECTOR:

Mark C. Schug
Professor of Curriculum and Instruction and
Director of the Center for Economic Education
University of Wisconsin-Milwaukee

PROJECT EDITOR:

Richard D. Western
Editorial Consultant
University of Wisconsin-Milwaukee
Center for Economic Education

REVIEWER:

William C. Wood
Professor of Economics and
Director of the Center for Economic Education
James Madison University, Harrisonburg, Virginia

DESIGN TEAM:

James Chasey
College of DuPage
Glen Ellyn, Illinois

Dara Duguay
Jump$tart Coalition for Personal Financial Literacy
Washington, D.C.

Dave Fettig
Federal Reserve Bank of Minneapolis

Gale Glassy
Flagstaff Middle School
Flagstaff, Arizona

Mara Hilderman
Moody's Investors Service
New York

Frances G. Laserson
The Moody's Foundation
New York

FIELD TEST TEACHERS:

Andy Bosley
Homestead High School
Mequon Thiensville School District, Wisconsin

Susan Cloud
Cross Keys Middle School
Ferguson-Florissant School District, Missouri

Scott Hancock
Capital High School
Santa Fe Public Schools, New Mexico

Mike Holley
Nipher Middle School
Kirkwood, Missouri

Jeffrey Sroka
Milwaukee Urban League Academy of Business and Economics
Milwaukee, Wisconsin

Learning, Earning and Investing Web Site

Visit the Learning, Earning and Investing Web site today to find additional resources. You can reach the site at http://lei.ncee.net. Resources include:

- Interactives that demonstrate for teachers and students various concepts presented in the book.
- Web resources that support the lessons in the book and provide additional information for teachers and students.
- Lessons from National Council on Economic Education's library of publications that relate to each of the lessons in the book.
- Downloadable visuals in pdf and PowerPoint formats.

Correlation to National Standards

Middle School Correlation of *Learning, Earning and Investing* Lessons to the *Voluntary National Content Standards in Economics*

	1	2	3	4	5	6	7	8	9	10	11	12	13	14	15	16
1. Scarcity			X										X		X	
2. Marginal costs/marginal benefits	X						X					X	X	X	X	
3. Allocation of goods and services															X	
4. Role of incentives	X														X	
5. Gains from trade				X				X								
6. Specialization and trade																
7. Markets; price and quantity determination									X							
8. Role of price in market system					X				X							
9. Benefits of competition								X								
10. Role of economic institutions				X							X	X	X			
11. Role of money			X													
12. Role of interest rates						X						X				
13. Role of resources in determining income																
14. Profit and the entrepreneur																
15. Growth		X	X													
16. Role of government																
17. Costs of government policies																
18. Circular flow; interdependence																
19. Unemployment and inflation																
20. Monetary and fiscal policy																

Middle School Correlation of *Learning, Earning and Investing* Lessons to the *Principles and Standards for School Mathematics*

	1	2	3	4	5	6	7	8	9	10	11	12	13	14	15	16
1. Number and operations	X	X	X	X	X		X					X	X	X		
2. Algebra																
3. Geometry																
4. Measurement	X				X								X			
5. Data analysis and probability						X										
6. Problem solving																
7. Reasoning and proof																
8. Communication																
9. Connections																
10. Representation																

Middle School Correlation of *Learning, Earning and Investing* Lessons to the *National Standards in Personal Finance*

Standards	1	2	3	4	5	6	7	8	9	10	11	12	13	14	15	16
1. Income			X	X												
2. Money management															X	
3. Spending and credit														X	X	
4. Saving and investing	X	X		X	X	X	X	X	X	X	X	X	X			X

Lesson 1 Why Save?

Middle School

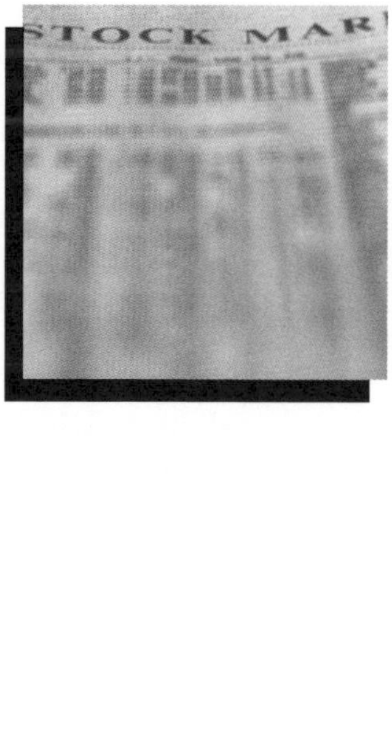

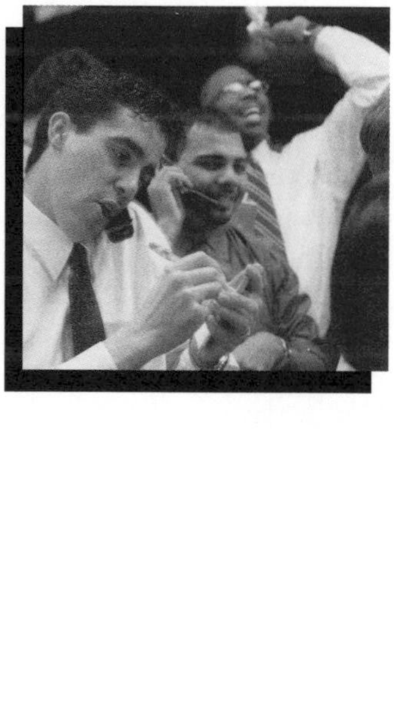

Lesson 1 Why Save?

Lesson Description

Following an introduction that defines *saving*, the students discuss the idea of "paying yourself first" and the reasons why people save. After reporting on their small-group discussions, the students simulate the accumulation of simple interest and compound interest. The lesson concludes with students calculating both simple interest and, using the Rule of 72, the amount of time it takes savings to double when interest is compounded.

Savings are disposable income (income after taxes) minus consumption spending. For younger students, disposable income is likely to come from an allowance, gifts of money or payments for doing jobs at home or in the neighborhood. Many older students are employed, and their paychecks reflect their net income after taxes (disposable income). "Paying yourself first" means saving before spending on consumer goods. Incentives to save may include a promise that money saved will be matched by an adult (a parent or uncle, perhaps), the satisfaction of buying a special gift for someone in the future or the desire to buy something for one's self in the future. Simple interest on savings is the annual interest paid on the initial amount saved (the principal). Compound interest is interest paid on both the principal and the interest added to the principal.

Concepts

- Compound interest
- Consumption
- Income
- Rule of 72
- Saving
- Simple interest

Objectives

Students will:

1. Define *saving*.
2. Identify reasons why people save.
3. Compare simple and compound interest.
4. Apply the formula for calculating simple interest.
5. Apply the Rule of 72 to determine how much time it takes for a given amount of savings to double.

Time Required

45 minutes

Materials

- A transparency of Visuals 1, 2, 3 and 4
- A copy of Visual 2 for each student
- A copy of Activity 1 for each student
- Four hundred lima beans (or other dried beans) and two small jars. The jars will be used to show annual simple and compound interest earned. Label one jar "simple interest" and the other jar "compound interest." (Alternatively, you may use cards or slips of paper, but these props are apt to be less effective.)
- Optional: calculators

Procedure

1. Tell the students that this lesson will focus on saving: what it is, why people save, and how interest is calculated on money saved. Many financial experts think Americans save too little. The U.S. Bureau of Labor Statistics reports that we spend (consume), on average, 97 percent of our disposable income (after-tax income). In other words, we save only three percent of our disposable income.

2. **Display Visual 1.** Explain that disposable income equals consumption plus savings. Point out that for younger students disposable income might include money from an allowance, money received as a gift or money earned for doing jobs at home or in the neighborhood. Explain that consumption is spending on goods and services. Define *saving* by explaining that saving equals disposable income minus consumption.

3. Divide the class into groups of about five students each. Ask each group to choose a reporter to take notes and report the group's work to the class.

4. **Distribute Activity 1 to each student.** Ask the students to read Activity 1 and, in their groups, discuss the two questions posed at the end of the handout. Give the students about 15 minutes to read Activity 1 and conduct their discussions.

5. Call upon the groups' reporters to report each group's results. Discuss the Questions for Discussion. ***Ask:***

A. What do you think is meant by this statement: "Pay yourself first"?
"Pay yourself first" means that a person saves before spending money on goods and services.

B. What are some reasons why people save?
People save money to gain the satisfaction of purchasing a special gift, to make large purchases, to meet emergencies that might arise, because the money will be matched by someone and for a college education.

6. Note that all savings decisions relate to some future use of money. Point out to the students that they should have their own reasons for saving. These reasons necessarily will derive from goals the students envision. Thinking about saving, in other words, involves thinking about goals.

7. **Display Visual 2** and explain the Simple Interest Adds column and the Compound Interest Adds column.

8. To illustrate the information provided in Visual 2, divide the class into two groups: Simple and Compound. Announce that the class will calculate the accumulation of simple and compound interest. Give 200 beans to each group. Announce that each bean represents $1. Tell the students in each group to put 100 beans ($100) in its jar. (Note: You can organize the students to count out and place the beans in the jars on your command, or they can organize themselves for this purpose.) The students in the Simple group should count out nine groups of eight ($8) beans each. The students in the Compound group should count out eight beans for Year 1, nine beans for Year 2 and so on through Year 9, according to Visual 2. Assign two students to act as accountants. The accountants keep running totals of the initial savings amount ($100), plus interest.

9. The simulation proceeds in rounds, with each round representing a year. Tell the students in the Simple group that they may place their beans in the jar (simulating each year of interest earned) in any order because each group of beans represents $8. Each interest payment carries the same value. The students in the Simple group are, in effect, spending the interest they earn each year. The Simple group does not receive the increased amount of beans on which the additional interest is calculated.

10. Tell the students in the Compound group that they must place their beans in the jar in the year-by-year order shown on Visual 2. Their interest payments remain in savings, and the value accumulates each year. The students in the Compound group are, in effect, saving the interest they earn each year.

11. Proceed with the simulation, which will go rapidly. After each round, the accountants are to add the total amount of savings and interest held by each group. After nine rounds, the simple interest total should be $172 and the compound interest total should be $200, as shown on Visual 2. (Note: Relatively small jars — pint-size, say — will begin to show the difference in simple and compound interest after about six rounds [years] of adding the beans.)

12. To conclude the simulation, **distribute a copy of Visual 2 to each student.** Review Visual 2, telling the students that the numbers shown in the visual reflect what happened in the year-by-year simulation. ***Ask:***

What did you notice about the accumulation of simple interest?
It increased by the same amount ($8) each year.

13. Tell the students that in each year, the $8 in simple interest was not put back into savings. This is why interest did not compound. ***Ask:***

What did you notice about the accumulation of compound interest?

It increased by more each year. The $100 initially saved doubled after nine years.

14. Tell the students that we can use arithmetic to understand how interest is calculated.

Display Visual 3. Explain that simple interest is calculated as follows:

> Interest (the amount of interest received on saving) = Principal (amount of initial saving) x Rate (of interest being paid on saving) x Time (in years).

Here is the calculation for the end of Year 3 in the simulation:

> Interest (the amount of interest received on saving) = Principal ($100 in initial saving) x Rate (8% rate of interest paid) x Time (3 years).

Plugging in the numbers yields this calculation:

> Interest = ($100) x (.08) x (3); $8.00 x 3 = $24.

You may want to provide some additional problems for the students to use in practicing applications of the simple-interest formula.

15. The Rule of 72 is a simple way to illustrate how compound interest works. **Display Visual 4.** The Rule of 72 states that we divide 72 by the interest rate paid to determine how many years it will take for savings to double when the interest is compounded. To apply this rule to the earlier simulation, divide 72 by the rate of interest paid (8 percent). The result is nine years. At the end of nine years, the initial savings had increased to $200 — double the amount of the initial savings. At an interest rate of 6 percent, it would take 12 years for savings to double (72 divided by 6 = 12).

Closure

1. ***Ask:*** What is saving?
Saving is disposable income minus consumption.

Remind the students that there are several reasons for saving, such as saving to make a large purchase, saving for emergencies or saving to pay for a college education. These reasons encourage many people to get an early start on saving.

2. Pose a practice problem for use with the simple-interest formula. Initial savings are $1,000; the interest rate is 5 percent. If you keep the initial savings for five years, how much simple interest will be paid?
$1,000 x 5% = $50 per year; $50 x 5 years = $250

3. Pose a practice problem for use with the Rule of 72. Initial savings are $500. At an interest rate of 3 percent, how long would it take to double your initial savings?
72 divided by 3 = 24 years

Assessment

Multiple-Choice Questions

1. Which of the following is the best definition of saving?
   a. The discount received from buying something on sale
   b. Disposable income minus consumption spending
   c. Putting your money under your mattress
   d. The interest paid on a savings account

2. Which of the following is a reason to save?
   a. Your parents place a dollar into your savings for every dollar you save.
   b. The penalty for taking your savings out of the bank
   c. Not being able to buy something right now
   d. Having to go to the bank before making a purchase

3. If you have $50 in savings for one year at an interest rate of 6 percent, how much interest will you earn at the end of the year?
   a. $5
   b. $4
   c. $3
   d. $2

4. If you divide the interest rate paid on savings into 72, the result tells you how many years it will take for your savings to double if you receive compound interest. At a compound interest rate of 10 percent, how many years will it take to double your money?
   a. 2.7 years
   b. 7.2 years
   c. 7.0 years
   d. 10.0 years

Essay Questions

1. Explain in your own words what this statement means: "Pay yourself first."
Paying yourself first means making saving a priority over spending. The decision on how much to save is made before the decision on how much to spend on consumption. Paying yourself first allows a person to more easily achieve goals for saving.

2. A friend asks you what sort of interest — simple or compound — is better. What would your answer be, and why?
When savings are allowed to accumulate with simple interest, savings grow more slowly than they do when they accumulate with compound interest. The rule of 72 explains how many years it will take for savings to double if you receive compound interest. Compound interest allows savings to grow dramatically over the long term.

Lesson 1 Visual 1

Disposable Income and Saving

Disposable income = consumption + saving

Saving = disposable income – consumption

Lesson 1 Visual 2

Interest Earned on an Initial $100 Saved at 8 Percent Interest Rate

Year	Simple Interest Adds	Total Saving Using Simple Interest	Compound Interest Adds	Total Saving Using Compound Interest
1	$8.00	$108.00	$8.00	$108.00
2	8.00	116.00	9.00	117.00
3	8.00	124.00	9.00	126.00
4	8.00	132.00	10.00	136.00
5	8.00	140.00	11.00	147.00
6	8.00	148.00	12.00	159.00
7	8.00	156.00	12.00	171.00
8	8.00	164.00	14.00	185.00
9	8.00	172.00	15.00	200.00

Note: All numbers are rounded using the previous number as the base.

LESSON 1 VISUAL 3

CALCULATING SIMPLE INTEREST

Interest = Principal (amount of initial saving)
x Rate (of interest being paid on savings) x Time (in years)

Example: Simple Interest at 8% for 3 years

Interest = ($100) x (.08) x (3); $8.00 x 3 = $24.

Lesson 1 Visual 4

The Rule of 72

The Rule of 72 is a simple way to illustrate the magic of compound interest.

Rule of 72

- 72 divided by the Rate (of interest being paid on savings) = the number of years it will take for savings to double when interest is allowed to compound.
- The Rule of 72 illustrates how compound interest doubles savings more quickly than simple interest.

Example: Compound Interest at 8% for 9 years

72 divided by 8% = 9 years

At the end of nine years, the initial savings of $100 have increased to $200 — double the amount of initial savings.

LESSON 1 ACTIVITY 1

A CONVERSATION AMONG FRIENDS

Amanda, Barbara, Duane, Joshua and Taylor are talking about money. Their teacher, Ms. Barnett, has asked them to think about saving money. Read their conversation. Then answer the questions that follow.

Joshua: Last week I bought this really cool basketball jersey for $28. The week before, the price had been $35. I saved $7.

Amanda: But Josh, you spent $28. I don't think this is what Ms. Barnett means by saving.

Duane: I think Ms. Barnett means that saving is not spending our money now.

Taylor: Yeah, I think Duane is right. But it is SOOO hard to save! I don't really have very much money. And I want a lot of stuff.

Barbara: Well, my parents want me to save some of my allowance. They said that if I have $100 saved at the end of the year, they would add $100 to it.

Amanda: Wow! That's pretty generous. Are you going to do it?

Barbara: I'm going to try. I started a savings account at the bank.

Duane: I don't have a savings account, but I try not to spend all the money I have because I want to buy a nice Christmas present for my mom.

Joshua: I've heard that you get interest on money you put into a savings account at a bank. Is that right, Barbara?

Barbara: Yeah, I think so, but I don't know much about it.

Taylor: I really do want a new bike, and my parents said I have to save my money for it. They won't buy it for me.

Amanda: I want a digital camera, and my parents told me the same thing.

Joshua: I just don't know how I can save any money. There are too many things to spend my money on now. I don't know if I want to give up spending.

Duane: You're right, Josh. It's hard to give up spending, especially when we don't have much money just now.

Taylor: I heard some guy on TV the other day say that people should pay themselves first. I wonder what he meant by this.

QUESTIONS FOR DISCUSSION

In your small group, choose a representative to take notes and report the results of your discussion to the class. Then discuss and record your responses to the following questions.

A. What do you think is meant by this statement: "Pay yourself first"?

B. What are some reasons why people save?

1 Why Save?

Lesson 2 Investors and Investments

Middle School

LESSON 2 INVESTORS AND INVESTMENTS

Lesson Description

In this lesson the students explore different types of investments, some of which are unconventional, in order to grasp the basic idea that investment involves trading off present benefits for future satisfaction. The students also apply the criteria of risk, return and liquidity to define more precisely the meaning of *investing.*

Investing means different things to different people. The term itself is often used imprecisely and for different reasons in different contexts. *Financial investing* refers to setting money aside in an effort to increase wealth over time. *Personal investing* is one type of financial investing. Personal investing also includes other actions (saving, for example) by means of which investors forgo benefits today in an effort to increase future wealth or satisfaction. *Economic investing* refers to the purchase of capital goods such as machinery, technology and buildings used to increase the production of consumer goods and services in the future.

The lessons in *Learning, Earning and Investing* address several aspects of investing; this introductory lesson is intended to help reduce confusion about the basic concept and the forms that investing can take.

Concepts

- Investing
- Investment
- Liquidity
- Return
- Risk

Objectives

Students will:

1. Analyze various investments to identify similarities and differences.
2. Define *risk, reward* and *liquidity.*
3. Distinguish between personal investment and other types of investment.
4. Apply criteria in considering an investment decision.

Time Required

45 minutes

Materials

- A transparency of Visuals 1 and 2
- A copy of Activities 1 and 2 for each student

Procedure

1. Explain that the words *investment* and *investing* mean different things to different people. In using these words or understanding other people's use of them, it is important to be alert to these differences.

2. Provide examples of misunderstandings caused by words that mean different things to different people. For example:
   - A father and his teenage daughter are having a conversation about shows. Dad is talking about movies. The daughter is talking about rock concerts.
   - Two people are watching an NBA basketball player play very well. One says, "He's bad!" The second person is confused because the player is playing very well.
   - One student says that she studies four hours a night as an investment. Her friend doesn't think that studying can be an investment, since no money is involved.

3. **Display Visual 1** and read the different definitions of *investing.* Explain that the definition under the heading of "Personal Investing" is the one most often used in newspaper and television business reports. The definition under "Economic Investing" is the one commonly used by economists and economics students.

4. **Distribute Activity 1** and ask the students to answer the questions. Discuss their answers.
1. Personal Investment, 2. Personal Investment,
3. Economic Investment, 4. Personal Investment,
5. Not an Investment, 6. Economic Investment,
7. Personal Investment, 8. Not an Investment,
9. Personal Investment, 10. Economic Investment.

5. ***Ask:*** What similarities can you find in these examples of investment?
Each involves risk and payment in money or effort now in order for the investor to receive a future benefit.

6. Explain that most investors set criteria to guide their investment choices. **Display Visual 2.** Discuss the criteria.

- **Liquidity.** Explain that *liquidity* refers to the ease with which savings or investments can be turned into cash. Financial investments are more liquid than other investments. Liquidity helps to explain why people value financial investments. It is not a simple task to turn an education, paper towels or helicopters into cash. It is relatively easy, however, to convert stocks and bonds into cash.

- **Risk.** For investors, *risk* refers to the chance of losing some or all of the money invested. Explain that some investments involve more risk than others. Investing money in a bank savings account involves almost no risk; investing money in stocks involves greater risk.
- **Return.** For investors, *return* refers to earnings from an investment. Some investments earn higher returns than others.

7. **Distribute Activity 2.** Ask the students to read the directions and complete the grid.

Answers to Activity 2

	Criteria		
Investments	***Liquidity***	***Risk***	***Return***
Household Supplies	*1*	*1*	*3*
Real Estate Group	*1*	*2*	*3*
Molly's Mutual Fund	*3*	*2*	*2*

A. Answers will vary.

B. Answers will vary according to the criterion students prefer for protecting their investment or gaining a return.

C. Students may be interested in criteria suggested by social issues: choosing not to invest in companies that harm the environment, for example, or in companies that encourage smoking.

8. Conclude by acknowledging that the concept of *personal investment* may have been new and unfamiliar to the students. They probably have had little or no experience with the financial investments that personal investors make. But they are familiar with personal investments in education and family investments in bulk purchases. Successful financial investment serves a goal similar to the goals served by investing in education and buying in bulk. The goal is to gain a greater return in the future by forgoing benefits today.

Closure

1. ***Ask:*** What is the difference between personal investing and economic investing?
Personal investing involves setting money aside to increase wealth over time and accumulate funds for long-term financial goals such as retirement. Personal investing may also involve spending time or effort with the expectation of gaining future satisfaction. Economic investing is different. It involves the purchase of capital goods — including machinery, technology or new buildings — used to make consumer goods and services.

2. ***Ask:*** What are the three criteria most often used by investors to judge personal investments?
Liquidity, risk and return.

3. Tell the students to evaluate the following statement about investing. Which of the three criteria for investing does it not address?

> "All investment choices — by a person buying discount paper towels to save future costs, a student learning skills for future employment or a person buying stocks and bonds to increase wealth in the future — are similar. They are choices that involve a willingness to forgo certain benefits now in order to gain a greater future return."
> *The statement is true as far as it goes. But it does not mention liquidity. Liquidity makes financial investing somewhat different because financial investments have relatively high liquidity; they can be turned readily into cash.*

Assessment

Multiple-Choice Questions

1. Which of the following is an example of investing?
   a. Putting money into a piggy bank at home.
   b. Saving spare change and using it to buy snacks.
   c. Buying a U.S. savings bond.
   d. Buying groceries for the family.

2. What is the difference between economic investment and personal investment?
   a. There is no difference.
   b. Economic investment involves risk; personal investment does not involve risk.
   c. Economic investment involves machines and technology; personal investment usually involves stocks and bonds.
   d. Personal investment involves the risk of losing the amount invested; there is no risk involved in economic investment.

3. In which of the following ways does personal investment differ from educational investment?
   a. Personal investment involves risk; educational investment always pay off.
   b. Personal investment can be easily turned into cash, while educational investment cannot.
   c. For personal investment only, costs must be paid in the present.
   d. For personal investment only, investors receive returns at some time in the future.

4. Which of the following is not an investment?
   a. Buying 100 shares of Microsoft Inc.
   b. Buying a bond from Microsoft, which promises to pay back the money plus interest.
   c. Buying a bond issued by the government of Mexico.
   d. Buying a hamburger for lunch.

Essay Questions

1. What is *personal investment?* Define the term, give two examples and explain the examples.
Personal investment refers to setting money aside in order to increase one's wealth over time and to accumulate funds for long-term financial goals such as retirement. Buying stocks and bonds is a good example because stocks and bonds involve current payment, future return, risk and liquidity. Personal investment may also involve spending time or effort with the expectation of gaining future satisfaction. Investing in education is a good example of this form of personal investing.

2. Read the following statement. Write a short comment in response to the statement that demonstrates your knowledge of investing and investment.

> "Buying paper towels is not investment! I don't care if you buy one or 100 rolls. Towels are just consumer items. Investment means buying stocks and bonds."

> *Using a narrow definition of* personal investment, *the statement is correct. But there are other types of behavior that meet the investment criteria of buying now and running the risk of not getting a future return. Buying paper towels a year in advance to reduce future costs constitutes an investment. The towels do not lose value, so using them in the future has positive benefits. Buying them separately in the future is more costly. Avoiding that higher, future cost has the same financial advantage as gaining a monetary return. The biggest problem with such an investment is the lack of liquidity. It is hard to convert paper towels into cash.*

LESSON 2 VISUAL 1

TWO TYPES OF INVESTING

When people invest, they spend something now (it can include time and effort as well as money) in an effort to gain something in the future. Not all investments are alike. Here is a distinction between two main types.

1. Personal Investing
Personal investing is one type of financial investing, practiced by individuals. It involves depositing or spending money in an effort to make a financial gain in the future. People who buy stocks or bonds are engaged in personal investing.

2. Economic Investing
Economic investing involves spending money to buy capital goods (including machinery, technology and new buildings) used to make consumer goods and services. When a company buys new computers or new delivery trucks, it is engaged in economic investing.

LESSON 2 VISUAL 2

CRITERIA FOR INVESTING

1. **Liquidity:** The ease with which savings or investments can be turned into cash.

2. **Risk:** The chance of losing some or all of the money invested.

3. **Return:** Earnings from an investment.

LESSON 2 ACTIVITY 1

WHO IS INVESTING?

Directions: Decide whether each of the following examples represents a personal investment (PI), an economic investment (EI) or is not an example of investment (NI).

1. A person buys a year's supply of paper towels and toilet paper at the discount grocery store. _____
2. A high school student studies advanced math and auto mechanics to prepare for a career as a race-car mechanic. _____
3. An owner of a helicopter service buys two new helicopters in order to serve more customers. _____
4. Parents with a five-year-old child prepay their child's college tuition by paying the current rate of tuition now. The college guarantees that the child's tuition is covered if the parents pay now. _____
5. A 90-year-old man declines the opportunity to buy stocks. He says, "I don't plan for the future anymore; why, I don't even buy unripe bananas!" _____
6. The owner of a printing company obtains a bank loan to build a new building and purchase state-of-the-art digital printing technology. _____
7. A couple puts $50 a month into a special savings fund to avoid current taxes and save for the future. _____
8. A student uses her savings to buy 10 popular-music CDs. _____
9. A student buys 20 blank CDs on sale, planning to use them to store data for a school project. _____
10. A student purchases a computer to start a Web site design company. _____

LESSON 2 ACTIVITY 2

CRITERIA FOR USE IN EVALUATING INVESTMENTS

Most investors develop criteria to guide their choices as they make investments. Here are three important criteria:

1. Liquidity: The ease with which savings or investments can be turned into cash.
2. Risk: The chance of losing some or all of the money invested.
3. Return: Earnings from an investment.

By reference to these criteria, rate the following investments on the grid below, using a rating from 1 to 3 (1 is low; 3 is high). Then decide which investment option you would prefer. You have $1,000 to invest.

- You can buy a year's worth of household goods like paper towels, toilet paper, soap and so forth for $1,000. This cost will be half the cost of the same household goods if you bought them in once-a-week shopping trips as you needed them over the next year.
- You can invest in a local real-estate investment group. This group buys houses and small office buildings, fixes them up and resells them. The group pays you a return of $150 per year. To get back their initial investments, investors in this group must find a willing buyer within the group to repay them so that they can leave the group. There are 20 people in the group.
- You can buy shares in Molly's Mutual Fund. A mutual fund is an investment company that pools money from investors to buy securities such as stocks or bonds. Investors in Molly's Mutual Fund have earned mixed returns over the last 10 years. For three years the fund lost 15 percent of its money; in another three years it made 19 percent; and in the other four years it made only a 2 percent return. Mutual fund investors can sell their shares at any time.

INVESTMENT GRID

		Criteria	
Investments	***Liquidity***	***Risk***	***Return***
Household Supplies	________	________	________
Real-Estate Group	________	________	________
Molly's Mutual Fund	________	________	________

QUESTIONS FOR DISCUSSION

A. Based on your rankings, which investment would you make with the $1,000?

B. Which criterion was most important to you, and why?

C. Are there other criteria that might influence your decision to invest? Explain.

Lesson 3 Invest in Yourself

Middle School

3 Invest in Yourself

Lesson 3 Invest in Yourself

Lesson Description

To explore the concept that people invest in themselves through education, the students work in two groups and participate in a mathematics game. Both groups are assigned mathematics problems to solve. One group is told about a special technique for solving the problems. The other group is not. The game helps the students recognize that improved human capital allows people to produce more in the same amount of time — in this example, more correct answers in the same time or less. Next, the students identify the human capital required for a variety of jobs. Finally, they learn about the connections among investment in human capital, careers and earning potential.

Investment takes many forms. One form is the development of human capital — the knowledge, skills, health and values that individuals possess. People develop their human capital through formal and informal education. To obtain education, people give up something in the short run (time, effort and money, for example) in order to gain larger returns (a good job, for example) in the future. This sort of exchange — giving up something now in order to realize gains later — is the essence of investment behavior, whether it involves putting money into a mutual fund or putting resources into education.

Concepts

- Human capital
- Income
- Investment in human capital
- Opportunity cost

Objectives

Students will:

1. Define and give examples of *human capital.*
2. Explain that human capital is related to career choices, opportunities and income.
3. Define and give examples of *opportunity cost.*

Time Required

90 minutes

Materials

- A transparency of Visuals 1, 2, 3 and 4
- A copy of Activity 1-A for half the class
- A copy of Activity 1-B for half the class
- A transparency of Activity 1-B
- A copy of Activity 2 for each student
- Classroom Material 1, cut apart
- 10 pieces of construction paper
- A glue stick
- A calculator for each student
- Classroom Material 2, cut apart to provide at least one card per student
- Graph paper for each student
- A watch or clock with a second hand
- Masking tape
- Markers

Procedure

1. Before class, glue the job signs from Classroom Material 1 on pieces of construction paper. Post job signs on the wall or chalkboard, leaving space below the sign where the students will place human capital cards. Have blank human capital cards available so that the students may add examples.

2. Tell the students that this lesson will help them understand an important economic term, *human capital. Human capital* refers to the knowledge, skills, health and values that individuals possess. Explain that developing human capital — through formal and informal education — is a form of investing. In devoting some resources to education, students give something up now in order to gain something important in the future.

3. Divide the class into two groups, A and B. Explain the following rules:

   - Each person in each group will receive some problems to solve.
   - Nobody in either group may begin to work on the problems until they are told to.
   - Everybody will have five minutes to solve the problems.
   - When a student has solved all of the problems, she or he should stand.

4. **Distribute a copy of Activity 1-A *face down*** to each student in group A and **a copy of Activity 1-B *face down*** to each student in group B.

5. Tell the students in group B that they may turn their papers over and read the instructions. They may ***not*** begin working on the problems; they may read only the instructions.

6. After several minutes, tell the members of group A to turn their papers over. Tell all the students that they may begin working to solve their problems. Keep track of time.

7. As the students finish and stand up, tell each student how much time it took him or her to solve the problems.

8. When all the students are standing, or after five minutes have elapsed, tell the students to stop working. Have them sit down. **Display Visual 1** and have the students check their answers.

9. Ask the following questions and record the answers on the transparency:

A. How many students in group A completed the problems in less than one minute? *Answers will vary.* How many correct answers did you have? *Answers will vary.* Add the number of correct answers for those who completed the problems in less than one minute and record the total.

B. How many students in group A took more than one minute but less than two minutes to complete the problems? *Answers will vary.* How many correct answers did you have? *Answers will vary.* Add the number of correct answers for those who completed the problems in more than one but less than two minutes and record the total.

C. How many students in group A took more than two minutes but less than three minutes to complete the problems? *Answers will vary.* How many correct answers did you have? *Answers will vary.* Add the number of correct answers for those who completed the problems in more than two but less than three minutes and record the total.

D. How many students in group A took more than three minutes but less than four minutes to complete the problems? *Answers will vary.* How many correct answers did you have? *Answers will vary.* Add the number of correct answers for those who completed the problems in more than three but less than four minutes and record the total.

E. How many students in group A took more than four minutes but less than five minutes to complete the problems? *Answers will vary.* How many correct answers did you have? *Answers will vary.* Add the number of correct answers for those who completed the problems in more than four but less than five minutes and record the total.

10. Repeat steps A through E for students in group B. Discuss the following:

A. In general, which students had more correct answers? *Most likely those in group B had more correct answers.*

B. In general, which students were able to complete the problems faster?
Most likely those in group B were able to complete the problems faster.

11. Ask a student from group A and a student from group B to go to the board and show their work for the first problem. Point out that the group A and group B students used different methods to solve the problem.

12. Ask the students in group B where they learned the method they used. *Instructions on the handout.* Tell a student from group A to read the directions on his or her handout. **Display a transparency of Activity 1-B** and tell the students these were the directions provided for group B.

13. Explain that the students in group B received knowledge and skills to help them solve the problems more quickly. The knowledge and skills improved the students' human capital. Human capital is the knowledge, skills, health and values individuals possess. With improved human capital, people can produce more and better products than other people can — in the same amount of time or less. In this example, the students in group B were able to produce more correct answers than those in group A — in the same amount of time or less — because students in group B had more human capital.

14. Point out the job signs posted on a wall or on a chalkboard. Explain that the students will identify the human capital associated with each of these jobs.

15. **Distribute at least one card from Classroom Material 2** to each student. Use all of the cards.

16. Tell the students that each card describes the human capital required for one of the jobs posted. Ask a student volunteer to read what is on his or her card, decide which job that human capital is associated with, and tape the card beneath that job on the wall or chalkboard.

17. Continue this process until all the students have placed their human capital cards beneath job signs. If the students have trouble deciding where to place their cards, allow them to ask classmates for assistance.

18. When all the students have placed their cards, read the human capital required for each job.
All the jobs require mathematics and communication skills. Some jobs require additional human capital: carpenter, trade school, apprenticeship, ability to use special tools and equipment; retail sales, none; mechanical engineer, college degree, ability to use special tools and equipment; graphic designer, community college/trade school or college, ability to use special tools and equipment; medical technician, community college/trade school, special certification, ability to use special tools and equipment; interpreter, college degree; auto mechanic, community college/trade school, ability to use special tools and equipment; bus driver, special classes, special license; fire fighter, college or community college, ability to use special tools and equipment; family doctor, medical school, internship, residency, ability to use special tools and equipment.

19. Discuss the following:

A. Can you think of other human capital required for the jobs posted?
Answers will vary.
As the students give examples, write each example on a blank human capital card and tape the card under the appropriate job sign. (The students may add that an interpreter must practice speaking and listening to languages, a graphic designer must learn to use many types of computer software, and so on.)

B. What similarities are there in the human capital required for all the jobs posted?
Communication skills, mathematics skills.

C. What mathematics abilities/skills would an automotive technician/mechanic need?
Convert from standard to metric measures, calculate costs of labor and parts.

D. Give examples of communication skills needed by a school bus driver.
Reading: maps, street signs, schedules, vehicle manual, safety manual, employment information; speaking: with students and co-workers; writing: completing safety evaluations, completing written portion of licensure test.

E. Give examples of mathematics skills needed by a retail sales clerk.
Understanding of decimals and percents, ability to count money and make change.

F. For the most part, how do people obtain basic mathematics and communication skills?
By going to school and staying in school until graduation.

G. What differences are there in the human capital required for the jobs posted?
Some require apprenticeships and special training; some require college degrees; some require advanced degrees.

H. How does a carpenter acquire the education and special skills needed for the job?
Carpenter training programs, apprenticeship programs.

I. How does a tailor or seamstress obtain the education and special skills needed?
Classes at a community college or trade school; apprenticeship.

J. How does a mechanical engineer obtain the education and special skills needed?
By attending college and earning a degree in mechanical engineering.

K. How does a doctor obtain the education and special skills needed?
Graduating from college, attending medical school, completing an internship and a residency.

20. ***Ask:*** what examples of human capital do you have?
Ability to read, write, work in groups, solve problems, play an instrument, use the computer, draw, sing, play a sport and so on.

21. Emphasize the point that when people go to school, attend special classes, obtain special licenses, and study or practice skills to improve, they are investing in their human capital. ***Ask:***

A. Why do people invest in their human capital?
To learn something new, to learn to do something better, to get a specific job, to start a new job.

B. For which of the jobs posted do people earn the highest income?
Answers will vary.

C. What connections or links are there among the human capital people have, the type of job they have and how much income they earn?
Answers will vary. Some students may recognize that people with more human capital are able to obtain jobs that require more skills and education, and these jobs usually pay higher salaries.

22. Explain that income is the payment people receive for selling or renting their productive resources. For example, people receive wage or salary payments for the work (labor) that they do.

23. **Display Visual 2** and explain that it shows the median yearly incomes for people holding certain jobs in 2001.

Explain that median means that half of the workers in a particular group earn more than the median income and half earn less than the median income. Thus some people working at a given job earned more and some earned less than the amount shown. Select students in the class, give them markers, and tell them to write the median income below the job name on the wall.

24. **Display Visual 3** and explain that it shows median annual wages for some additional occupations. Ask the students what type of human capital is required for each of these occupations.
Good communication skills, basic math skills, college education, professional degrees, special certification, apprenticeship and so on.

25. Point out that, in general, very high-paying occupations require more education and training than very low-paying occupations. For example, doctors earn higher incomes and require more education than retail sales clerks. Tell the students that, in general, investment in human capital leads to higher pay.

26. **Display Visual 4** and tell the students that it shows median weekly incomes for people by educational attainment level. Explain the following:

- Bachelor's degrees require four years of education or more at a college or university.
- Master's degrees require two or more years of additional education at a college or university.
- Professional degrees require additional years of study and, often, additional training. Lawyers, medical doctors, nurses and engineers are examples of people with professional degrees.
- Ph. D. degrees require additional study beyond a master's degree, plus the completion of a dissertation. College professors and research scientists usually have Ph. D. degrees.

27. Distribute calculators and tell the students to assume that workers at each attainment level work 50 weeks out of the year. Tell the students to calculate the yearly median income for each educational attainment level.
High school — $25,350; bachelor's degree — $41,700; master's degree — $49,150; professional degree — $58,700; and Ph. D. degree — $60,700

28. Distribute a piece of graph paper to each student. Tell the students to construct a bar graph to illustrate the data on Visual 4. Tell the students to put the educational attainment levels along the x-axis and the earnings along the y-axis. Tell the students to title their graphs to illustrate the idea that investment in human capital pays off.

29. Point out that there are costs associated with investment in human capital. For example, when people attend college, they must pay tuition and fees, they must buy books, and they give up the opportunity to earn income while they are in school. (Note: Room and board costs are not included here because they are costs people pay whether they attend school or not.)

30. Explain that these costs are the opportunity cost associated with attending college. An *opportunity cost* is the next-best alternative a person gives up when she or he makes a choice. If people choose to attend college full-time, they give up the income that they could have earned while working. When they use money to pay their tuition and fees and to buy books, they give up the other things they could have bought with that money (the next-best alternative use for the money). Discuss the following.

A. Sam can choose one elective course in his freshman year of high school. The options he prefers are woodworking, current events and art class. He chooses the art class. What is his opportunity cost?
It is either the woodworking class or the current events class: whichever is his next-best alternative. It is not both classes. Because he has the option of only one elective, he gives up the next-best alternative.

B. Sam has been taking art classes for some time. He hopes to continue to paint and may even choose a career in art. By taking an additional art class, what is Sam doing?
Investing in his human capital.

31. Tell the students that even though there are costs associated with attending college, the investment in human capital usually pays off. To demonstrate this point, have the students calculate the lifetime earnings of someone with a high-school degree working 54 years at the median income.
$25,350 x 54 = $1,368,900

Then ask the students to calculate the lifetime earnings of someone with a bachelor's degree working 50 years (four years less because of time spent in college).
$41,700 x 50 = $2,085,000

Then ask the students to calculate the difference between the two.
$2,085,000 - $1,368,900 = $716,100

Point out that even if people spent $120,000 for tuition, fees and books for college, in the long run they probably would be better off. Their earnings would be greater because their human capital and earning potential are greater.

Closure

Review the important points of the lesson by asking the following questions:

1. What is human capital?
The knowledge, skills, health and values individuals possess.

2. Give an example of human capital that you have.
Abilities to read, write, compute, work in groups, play a sport, play an instrument.

3. How do people invest in their human capital?
By going to school, finishing high school, going to college, attending training programs, practicing their skills, living a healthy lifestyle.

4. How could you invest in your human capital?
Practice to improve a skill you have, develop a new skill, finish high school, attend college.

5. Why do people invest in their human capital?
To learn new skills, to obtain a new job, to earn more income, to improve skills and talents they already have.

6. What is income?
Payments people receive for selling or renting the productive resources they own.

7. What is opportunity cost?
The next-best alternative that people give up when they make a choice.

8. Give an example of a decision you made and the opportunity cost of that decision.
Answers will vary.

9. What are the benefits associated with finishing high school and going on for additional education?
More career options, the possibility of earning more income.

10. **Distribute a copy of Activity 2** to each student. Have the students complete the skills inventory and answer the questions that follow the inventory.

Assessment

Multiple-Choice Questions

1. Which of the following is an example of human capital?

   a. Money

   b. A hammer

   c. Stocks

   d. The ability to read

2. Each day after school, Tom practices piano for an hour. Tom could spend this hour playing video games with his friends. Playing video games with his friends is Tom's

   a. income.

   b. opportunity cost.

   c. favorite thing to do.

   d. investment in human capital.

3. Payments people receive for selling or renting their productive resources are called

   a. cost.

   b. income.

   c. investment.

   d. human capital.

4. All of the following are investments in human capital except

   a. finishing high school.

   b. attending a trade school.

   c. practicing to improve a skill.

   d. buying a new computer.

Essay Questions

1. Your friend's older brother is a senior in high school. He has been working part-time for a local company. He enters data into the computer system and does other related work. He could work full-time for the company when he graduates. The idea of earning $18,000 a year is very appealing. He has also applied to a local college that offers a computer-systems degree. He would attend full-time. College is expensive; however, there is some financial aid available. Based on what you've learned about investment in human capital, income and opportunity cost, tell your friend's brother what you think he should do and why.
Use financial aid and go to college. The opportunity cost of this decision is the income given up over the four years and the cost of tuition, fees and books. Over a lifetime, the additional income earned will be greater than the costs of going to college. Investment in human capital — earning a degree in computer systems — will provide skills and knowledge for many different jobs, and allow for higher income in the future.

2. The high school you attend offers students who take foreign language classes an opportunity to travel to a country in which one of the foreign languages is spoken. Students with the best ability to communicate in the second language are selected. You want to participate in the program. You have been taking German in middle school, but you want to make sure your written and oral communication skills in German are the very best. In terms of investment in human capital, what could you do improve your ability to write and speak in German?
Students might suggest the following: Ask the German teacher to tutor you. Practice speaking in German with others in the class. Enroll in German class during the summer. Listen to German tapes obtained from the library.

Lesson 3 Visual 1

Human Capital Production Report

Answers to the problems on Activity 1-A and 1-B.

1. 180 dimes
2. 18,986 dimes
3. 15 dimes
4. 5,958 dimes
5. 360 dimes

Time	Group A		Group B	
	Number of Students	Number of Correct Answers	Number of Students	Number of Correct Answers
0 to 59 seconds				
60 to 119 seconds				
120 to 179 seconds				
180 to 239 seconds				
240 to 299 seconds				

Lesson 3 Visual 2

Jobs and Wages

Occupation	Median Annual Wage
Automotive technician/mechanic	$ 24,315
Carpenter	$ 33,467
Family doctor	$118,394
Graphic designer	$ 36,026
Interpreter	$ 31,990
Mechanical engineer	$ 61,443
Medical technician	$ 27,300
Retail sales clerk	$ 17,139
School bus driver	$ 21,986

Source: Table 1. National Employment and Wage Data from the Occupational Employment Statistics Survey by Occupation, 2001. www. bls.gov. Annual wages have been calculated by multiplying the hourly wage by a year-round, full-time hour figure of 2080.

LESSON 3 VISUAL 3

MORE INFORMATION ABOUT JOBS AND WAGES

Occupation	Median Annual Wage
Cafeteria cook	$17,326
Chef	$26,790
Child, family and school social worker	$32,947
Fire fighter	$34,674
Floral designer	$19,282
Janitor	$17,493
Lawyer	$88,774
Nurses' aide	$19,282
Paralegal	$36,670
Petroleum engineer	$75,171
Pharmacist	$74,880
Sound engineer	$35,152
Waitress/waiter	$13,728

Source: Table 1. National Employment and Wage Data from the Occupational Employment Statistics Survey by Occupation, 2001. www. bls.gov. Annual wages have been calculated by multiplying the hourly wage by a year-round, full-time hour figure of 2080.

Lesson 3 Visual 4

Median Incomes by Educational Attainment Levels

Educational Attainment Level	Median Weekly Earnings, 2000
High school diploma or equivalent	$ 507
Bachelor's degree	$ 834
Master's degree	$ 983
Professional degree	$1,174
Doctoral degree (Ph.D.)	$1,214

LESSON 3 ACTIVITY 1-A

BUYING WITH DIMES

Determine how many dimes you would need to buy each item listed below. Please show your work.

1. A new compact disc (CD) that sells for $17.99

2. A top-of-the-line CD player with surround-sound speaker system that sells for $1,898.59

3. Three candy bars that sell for $1.50

4. Three front-row tickets to a play-off game, snacks at the game and parking, for a total of $595.78

5. A new pair of jeans priced at $35.99

LESSON 3 ACTIVITY 1-B

DIMES FOR DOLLARS

For each problem below, determine how many dimes you would need to buy the item. Use the following information.

- Write the price as a number without decimals. For example, $18.95 becomes 1895.
- Erase the last digit. So, 1895 becomes 189.
- Add a 1. So, 189 + 1 = 190
- It would take 190 dimes to buy the item.
- There is one exception to this rule. If the number erased is zero, don't add the extra dime. For example, if the price is $18.90, simply eliminate the decimal and erase the zero. It would take 189 dimes to buy the item.

Please show your work.

1. A new compact disc (CD) that sells for $17.99

2. A top-of-the-line CD player with surround-sound speaker system that sells for $1,898.59

3. Three candy bars that sell for $1.50

4. Three front-row tickets to a play-off game, snacks at the game and parking, for a total of $595.78

5. A new pair of jeans priced at $35.99

Lesson 3 Activity 2

Human Capital Review

What human capital do you have? Probably more than you think. Review the list of skills below and check those that apply to you. In the blank spaces at the bottom of the table, add skills you have that aren't included in the list.

Check here if you have the skill described in the next column.	**Human Capital**
	I like to work with people.
	I like to work in groups.
	I like to work with computers.
	I read well.
	I write well.
	I am a good listener.
	I am able to follow directions.
	I like to solve problems and puzzles.
	I can play an instrument.
	I am well organized.
	I like to organize things.
	I have a positive attitude.
	I am a hard worker.
	I can add, subtract, multiply and divide.
	I can compute using decimals, fractions and percents.
	I like to play board games.
	I like to play team sports.
	I can sing.
	I like physical activity.
	I have good hand-eye coordination.
	I like to work with younger children.
	I like to cook.
	I draw and paint well.
	I like to work with numbers.
	I like to build things.
	I like to read fiction, plays and poetry.
	I like to give talks or speeches.
	I like to work independently.

LESSON 3 ACTIVITY 2 (CONTINUED)

HUMAN CAPITAL REVIEW

Select one of the skills listed on the previous page and identify three things that you could do to invest in (improve your mastery of) this skill.

1. ____

2. ____

3. ____

Lesson 3 Classroom Material 1

Job Signs

CARPENTER

MECHANICAL ENGINEER

RETAIL SALES PERSON

SCHOOL BUS DRIVER

LESSON 3 CLASSROOM MATERIAL 1 (CONTINUED)

JOB SIGNS

GRAPHIC DESIGNER

MEDICAL TECHNICIAN

INTERPRETER

AUTOMOTIVE TECHNICIAN/MECHANIC

LESSON 3 CLASSROOM MATERIAL 1 (CONTINUED)

JOB SIGNS

FIRE FIGHTER

FAMILY DOCTOR

LESSON 3 CLASSROOM MATERIAL 2

HUMAN CAPITAL CARDS

Communication Skills	Communication Skills
Communication Skills	Communication Skills
Communication Skills	Communication Skills
Communication Skills	Communication Skills
Communication Skills	Communication Skills
Mathematics Skills	Mathematics Skills
Mathematics Skills	Mathematics Skills
Mathematics Skills	Mathematics Skills
Mathematics Skills	Mathematics Skills

Lesson 3 Classroom Material 2 (continued)

Human Capital Cards

Mathematics Skills	Mathematics Skills
College Degree	College Degree
College Degree	College Degree
Community College or Trade School	Community College or Trade School
Community College or Trade School	Community College or Trade School
Medical School	Apprenticeship
Apprenticeship	Special License
Residency	Internship
Special Certification	Ability to Use Special Tools and/or Equipment

LESSON 3 CLASSROOM MATERIAL 2 (CONTINUED)

HUMAN CAPITAL CARDS

Ability to Use Special Tools and/or Equipment	Ability to Use Special Tools and/or Equipment
Ability to Use Special Tools and/or Equipment	Ability to Use Special Tools and/or Equipment
Ability to Use Special Tools and/or Equipment	Ability to Use Special Tools and/or Equipment
Ability to Use Special Tools and/or Equipment	

Lesson 4 What is a Stock?

Middle School

Lesson 4 What Is a Stock?

Lesson Description

The students work in small groups that represent households. Each household answers mathematics and economics questions. For each correct answer, a household earns shares of stock. At the end of the game, the groups that answered all questions correctly receive a certificate good for 150 shares of stock in The Economics and Mathematics Knowledge Company. They also receive dividends based on their shares. Those who answered fewer questions correctly receive fewer shares and smaller dividends. Finally, the students participate in a role play to learn more about stocks.

Stocks are sometimes called equities. *Equity* means ownership. If you own stock, you have equity in, or own, a portion of the company that issued the stock. When a corporation decides to sell shares of its stock to the public, it hires an investment banker to sell the stock. This is called an *initial public offering* (IPO). In return, the company receives money. After the shares are sold in the primary market, stocks are bought and sold by the public in secondary stock markets such as the New York Stock Exchange, the American Stock Exchange and NASDAQ.

People buy stock because they hope to earn a return. They can earn a return if they sell the stock at a higher price than the price for which they bought it. They may also seek an annual return in the form of dividends. Since 1926, people who have held a portfolio of stocks through any 15-year period have typically earned higher returns than those holding other financial instruments.

Concepts

- Dividend
- Income
- Saving
- Stocks
- Stockholders

Objectives

Students will:

1. Define *income*, *saving*, *stock* and *dividend.*
2. Explain why people buy stock.
3. Identify some advantages and disadvantages of owning stocks.
4. Explain ways in which stockholders can reduce risk.

Time Required

50 minutes

Materials

- A transparency of Visual 1
- A copy of Activity 1 for each group
- A transparency of Activity 1
- Three copies of Activity 2
- A copy of Activity 3 for each student
- An envelope, one sheet of plain white paper, one marker and one sheet of construction paper for each group of 3-4 students
- A roll of transparent tape for each group of 3-4 students
- A large supply of small, wrapped candies — a minimum of 30 pieces per group of 3-4 students.

Procedure

1. Before class, write your name on the line labeled Teacher's Name on Activity 1. Make a copy of Activity 1 for each group of 3-4 students. Cut each copy of Activity 1 on the perforation lines and place the strips in an envelope. Label the envelopes Shares of Stock Group 1, Shares of Stock Group 2, Shares of Stock Group 3 and so on. There should be an envelope for each group in the classroom.

2. Ask the students what they have heard about stocks. *Answers will vary.* Explain that stocks represent ownership shares or equity in a corporation.

3. Tell the students they will participate in a group activity. Each group represents a household. Households earn *income.* Income is payments earned by households for selling or renting their productive resources. Households usually spend some of their income and save some of it. *Saving* is income not spent on consumption or taxes. Some households use their savings to purchase stocks.

4. Explain that each group will have an opportunity to earn stock by correctly answering mathematics and economics questions. Tell the students that for each correct answer, a household will receive a strip of paper worth 15 shares of stock in The Economics and Mathematics Knowledge Company. If the group answers all questions correctly, the

strips can be taped together to create a stock certificate that represents 150 shares of The Economics and Mathematics Knowledge Company. Groups that answer only some of the questions correctly will own fewer shares of stock.

5. Explain that people who own shares of stock are called investors or *stockholders*. Stockholders are partial owners of a company. The households will be partial owners of The Economics and Mathematics Knowledge Company.

6. Divide the class into groups of three or four students. Assign each group a number corresponding to the numbers written on the envelopes containing the strips. Distribute a piece of plain white paper and a marker to each group.

7. Tell each group to appoint a spokesperson. Tell the spokesperson to write a large "T" with the marker on one side of the paper and a large "F" on the other side of the paper. Explain that when a question is asked, members of the group will have a few moments to discuss the question and decide whether the answer is true or false. When told to "Show the answer," the spokesperson should hold up the side of the paper displaying the "T" if the group thinks the answer is true or the "F" side if the group thinks the answer is false.

8. Tell each group to appoint a stockholder. This person will hold the envelope containing the shares of stock and will take the correctly-numbered strip from the envelope when the group answers a question correctly. Each time the group answers a question correctly, it will receive a stock strip representing 15 shares of stock. These stock strips will be important when the game is over.

9. **Display Visual 1**, revealing only the first question. Read the question and allow the groups to decide on answers. Tell the groups to hold up their answers all together when told to. Tell the shareholders for the groups that answered the question correctly to take stock strip 1 from the envelope. Continue revealing one question at a time.
Answers to questions: 1. T, 2. F, 3. T, 4. F, 5. F, 6. F, 7. F, 8. T, 9. T, 10. F.

(Note: If a group answers question 1 incorrectly but answers question 2 correctly, the group would receive its first strip for its answer to question 2. If the group answers question 3 correctly, it would receive its second strip, and so on.)

10. When the game is over, distribute a piece of construction paper and a tape dispenser to each group. Tell group members to tape the pieces together. Point out that if they missed questions, they will not have all of the strips needed to complete the certificate.

11. Allow time for the groups to tape their shares together. **Display a transparency of Activity 1** and explain that this is a certificate of stock ownership. If a group answered all the questions correctly, it will have a complete certificate.
Ask:

A. If your group answered all the questions correctly, how many shares of stock would the group own? *150*

B. How many shares does your group own?
Answers will vary but could include 15, 30, 45, 60, 75, 90, 105, 120, 135, 150.

C. Of the 150 shares your group could have purchased, what percent does your group in fact own?
Answers will vary but could include: 15 shares = 10% [15/150 = .1; .1 X 100 = 10%], 30 shares = 20%, 45 shares = 30%, 60 shares = 40%, 75 shares = 50%, 90 shares = 60%, 105 shares = 70%, 120 shares = 80%, 135 shares = 90%, 150 shares=100%.

12. Tell the students that the groups will earn dividends based on the number of shares they own. Dividends are a part of a company's profits that may be distributed to shareholders. For this activity, dividends will be paid in candy. Explain that the dividend paid on each share of The Economics and Mathematics Knowledge Company stock is one-fifth of a piece of candy. Tell each group to determine its dividends.
15 shares =3 pieces of candy (1/5 X 15 = 3), 30 shares = 6, 45 shares = 9, 60 shares = 12, 75 shares = 15, 90 shares =18, 105 shares =21, 120 shares = 24, 135 shares =27, and 150 shares = 30

When the groups have calculated their dividends, distribute the candy to each group.

13. ***Ask:*** How do you think this game is different from occasions when dividends are distributed in real life?
In real life, obviously, dividends are distributed in money, not candy. More important, in real life, households don't have an opportunity to "win" stock by answering questions. Instead, they have to decide to save some of their income and use it to buy stocks.

14. Select three students to participate in a role play about stocks. **Give each of these students a copy of Activity 2** and allow them a few minutes to read the play.

15. **Distribute a copy of Activity 3** to each of the remaining students. Tell them they will listen to a short play that takes place at dinnertime in the Navarro house. Tell the students to read the questions on Activity 3. As they watch the play, they should listen for answers to the questions.

16. Tell the three cast members to come to the front of the room and read the play. When the play is over, discuss the following:

A. What is a stock?
Part ownership in a corporation.

B. Why do corporations issue stock?
To raise money to pay for equipment, buildings and operating expenses.

C. When the shares of stock are first issued, to whom are they sold?
To investment bankers.

How does the corporation get money from the stocks?
Investment bankers pay for the stocks.

D. Why do investment bankers buy the stock?
They expect to resell the stocks to the public for a higher price in the secondary market.

E. What are stock markets?
Places or ways in which people can buy and sell stocks.

F. Why do people buy stock?
They expect to earn money.

G. How do people earn money from stocks?
To make a capital gain by selling the stock at a higher price than the price they paid for the stock. They may also receive dividends.

H. What are dividends?
Part of the company's profits, distributed to owners.

I. When people buy stock, is there a guarantee that they will receive dividends or that they will be able to sell the stock at a price higher than the price they paid for it?
No.

J. If there's no guarantee, why are people willing to buy stock?
Because the stocks they buy might provide them with a higher return than the return they could get by putting money into other financial investments or a savings account.

K. What determines the price of a stock?
The value of a stock depends on whether stockholders want to keep or sell the stock and on how much those who want to buy the stock are willing to pay for it.

L. What is the main advantage of owning stock?
Sharing in the company's profits as the company grows; having a chance to get an above-average return on a financial investment.

M. What is the main disadvantage of owning stock?
The chance of losing all or part of the investment.

17. Ask the students if they know what a portfolio is and what it means to diversify.
Answers will vary.

Tell one student to find the meaning of *diversify* in the dictionary. Tell another student to find the meaning of *portfolio*. Have the students read the definitions
Portfolio: an itemized list of investments; diversify: to spread out or vary investments.

18. Explain that stockholders can reduce the chance of losing their financial investment and increase the chance of earning an above-average return if they diversify their portfolios. This means that they must buy various types of stocks — for example, stock in an electric company, a computer company, a company that sells prepared foods and an entertainment company. Investors also can buy stocks from different asset classes such as large-cap, mid-cap and small-cap. And stockholders can diversify by buying shares in mutual funds. A mutual fund is a pool of money collected from different people and invested by a manager with the goal of increasing the value of each share of the fund for its investors. (Note: For additional information about mutual funds, see Lesson 7.)

Closure

Review the lesson by asking the following questions:

1. What is income?
Payments earned by households for selling or renting their productive resources.

2. What is saving?
Income not spent on consumption or taxes.

3. What are stocks?
Part ownership or equity in a corporation.

4. Why do corporations issue stock?
To raise money to pay for things needed to operate the business and earn a profit.

5. Why do people buy stocks?
They expect to earn a return on their financial investment.

6. When stockholders sell their stock, do corporations receive the money? *No.* Who does? *The stockholder.*

7. How do stockholders earn money on their financial investment?
By selling the stock they own at a higher price than the price they paid for it, and by receiving dividends.

8. What are dividends?
A part of a company's profits that may be distributed to shareholders.
9. What can a corporation do with its profits besides pay dividends?
Put the profit back into the business.
10. What is the main disadvantage of being a stockholder?
The chance of losing all or part of the investment.
11. What is the main advantage of being a stockholder?
Sharing in the company's profits as the company grows; having a chance to get an above-average return on a financial investment.
12. What influences the value of a stock?
Whether the shareholders want to keep or sell it; how much buyers are willing to pay for it.
13. Are stockholders guaranteed a return on their financial investment? *No.*
14. How can stockholders reduce their chance of loss?
They can diversify and invest in mutual funds.

Assessment

Multiple-Choice Questions

1. What is a stock dividend?
   a. A capital gain
   b. Part of a company's profit that is paid to owners
   c. The price for which the stock is sold in stock markets
   d. The price for which the stock is sold to investment bankers

2. People buy stocks because
   a. there is no chance of loss.
   b. they expect to earn a return.
   c. the government encourages them to buy stock.
   d. they are guaranteed interest payments each year.

3. One way people can earn money from stocks is by
   a. buying stock from an investment banker.
   b. selling the stock for the same price as the price they paid for the stock.
   c. selling the stock for a lower price than the price they paid for the stock.
   d. selling the stock for a higher price than the price they paid for the stock.

4. When people buy stock on a stock market,
   a. the corporation loses money.
   b. the corporation receives money.
   c. the people buying the stock receive money.
   d. the people selling the stock receive money.

Essay Questions

1. What can people do to reduce their chance of loss in the stock market?
They can diversify their portfolio — buy many different types of stocks or buy mutual funds.

2. Explain the advantages of owning stocks.
Stockholders have a chance of earning money through dividends and by selling the stock at a higher price than the price they paid for the stock.

Lesson 4 Visual 1

Mathematics and Economics Questions

1. Stocks represent ownership in a corporation.
2. 50% written as a decimal is 5/100.
3. Mark bought 100 shares of Nike stock, and each share sold for $35.50. If no fees were involved, Mark paid $3,550 for the shares.
4. If Jenny has $100 in a savings account and earns 2 percent interest this month, she has earned $20 in interest.
5. The closing price for a share of Wal-Mart stock was 37.25. This means that the price of the share was $37 and one-quarter of a dollar. One-quarter of a dollar is .20.
6. People who own stocks are guaranteed a return on the money they have invested in stocks.
7. The only way stockholders make money is through dividend payments while they own the stock.
8. One way stockholders make money is to sell their stock for more than they paid for it.
9. Stockholders can reduce the risk on their stock investment by diversifying their portfolios.
10. The New York Stock Exchange is the only place where people can buy and sell stocks.

Lesson 4 Activity 1

Certificate of Ownership

1	2	3	4	5	6	7	8	9	10

Certificate of Ownership

The Economics and Mathematics Knowledge Company

Students in

Class

(Teacher's name)

Own 150 Shares of Stock

in

The Economics and Mathematics Knowledge Company

15 Shares	15 Shares	15 Shares	15 Shares	15 Shares	15 Shares	15 Shares	15 Shares	15 Shares	15 Shares

Lesson 4 Activity 2

Stock Tips

Maria, Michael and their mom are talking about stocks and business expansion. Read their conversation as it is acted out in front of the class.

Mom: How was school today?

Maria: Okay.

Michael: Yeah, it was okay. How was work, Mom?

Mom: My corporation really needs to expand. Our new line of software is very popular and we have many orders, but we need more equipment and a larger building to keep up. We could raise some money by issuing more stock.

Michael: Mom, what is stock, and how can your company get money from stocks?

Mom: Stocks represent part-ownership in a corporation. Our corporation could work with investment bankers to issue stock. We would sell that stock to the investment bankers, and they would give us money in return. We could use the money from the sale of the stocks to pay for equipment, buildings and operating expenses.

Maria: Mom, why do the investment bankers want stock?

Mom: The investment bankers buy the stock and try to resell it at a higher price to the public.

Michael: Some of the kids at school play a stock market game. What is a stock market, anyway?

Mom: A stock market is a way for people to buy and sell stocks. There is a New York Stock Exchange, an American Stock Exchange and the NASDAQ market. There are stock markets in other countries too. A lot of the buying and selling occurs on computers or by phone.

Maria: Aren't stocks just pieces of paper? Why do people want to buy stocks?

Mom: People buy stock because they expect to earn a return — to make money.

Michael: How do people who buy stock make money?

Mom: One important way they may earn money is by selling the stock at a price higher than the price they paid for it. The difference between the price they paid for the stock and the higher price they receive for the stock is called a capital gain. Stockholders can also make money if the company pays dividends.

Maria: What are dividends? Sounds like something we talk about in math class.

Mom: Dividends are paid to people who own stocks. Here is how it works. Stockholders are owners of corporations. They get to make decisions about who runs the corporation. If a company earns a profit, it may pay dividends. Dividends are a part of a company's after-tax profit that may be distributed to shareholders — the owners. Companies can also put the profit back into the business.

Michael: Who decides the price for a stock? I mean, if I want to sell it at a higher price than the price I paid for it, how can I be sure the price will go up?

Mom: The value of a stock depends on whether stockholders want to keep it or sell it and on how much those who want to buy the stock are willing to pay for it. If the stock is very popular and many people want to buy it, the price would go up. Prices can go down, too. There's no guarantee.

LESSON 4 ACTIVITY 2 (CONTINUED)

STOCK TIPS

Maria: If there's no guarantee that you can sell stock for a higher price than you paid, you could lose money. Wouldn't it be better to keep your money in the bank?

Mom: Well, it is always good to keep some money in the bank. It is safe there, and the bank pays interest. But people have a chance to earn an above-average return — more than they would earn in interest at the bank or through other financial investments — if they buy stock. Usually, people who buy stock and keep it for a long period of time receive a higher return than they would with another financial investment. And you know, stockholders can reduce the chances of loss by diversifying their portfolios.

Michael: Mom, I have an art portfolio at school. But I don't know what a portfolio is and I don't know what diversify means.

Mom: Hmmm. Those might be a couple of good words for you to look up in the dictionary.

Lesson 4 Activity 3

Noting Stock Tips

A. What is a stock?

B. Why do corporations issue stock?

C. When the shares of stock are first issued, to whom are they sold? How does the corporation get money from the stocks?

D. Why do investment bankers buy the stock?

E. What are stock markets?

F. Why do people buy stock?

G. How do people earn money from stocks?

H. What are dividends?

I. When people buy stock, is there a guarantee that they will receive dividends or that they will be able to sell the stock at a price higher than the price they paid for it?

J. If there's no guarantee, why are people willing to buy stock?

K. What determines the price of a stock?

L. What is the main advantage of owning stock?

M. What is the main disadvantage of owning stock?

LESSON 5 READING THE FINANCIAL PAGES: IN PRINT AND ONLINE

MIDDLE SCHOOL

Lesson 5 Reading the Financial Pages: In Print and Online

Lesson Description

The students learn how to read and understand information presented in the financial pages of newspapers and online sources. Working in pairs, they examine entries for stocks, mutual funds and corporate bonds. They participate in a scavenger hunt for financial information, using a local newspaper. They learn how to follow stocks online.

In newspapers and online sources, financial pages provide basic information about stocks, mutual funds and bonds, including daily reports of stock prices, dividends, yield and trading volume. The financial pages also carry more general articles about the world of business and finance, reporting on stock-price trends, government activities related to regulation, and the activities of companies and industries.

Concepts

- Closing price
- Dividend
- Net asset value
- Percentage change in fund value
- Price/earnings ratio (P/E ratio)
- Stock symbol
- Trading volume
- Yield

Objectives

Students will:

1. Read stock, mutual fund and corporate bond tables presented in newspaper financial pages.
2. Demonstrate an understanding of the data presented in the tables.
3. Follow a security online.

Time Required

60 minutes; time in subsequent weeks for students to track stocks; 60 minutes at the close of the tracking period for reports

Materials

- A transparency of Visuals 1, 2 and 3
- A copy of Activities 1, 2, 3, 4 and 5 for each student
- Access to the Internet

Procedure

1. Explain that in order to make informed financial decisions, people need to follow and understand certain information provided in newspapers and on the Internet. The purpose of this lesson is to introduce the background knowledge and skills people must have in order to read and understand basic financial information.

2. **Distribute a copy of Activity 1** to each student. Ask the students to read the *Overview of the Financial Pages*. ***Ask:*** What sort of information is found in the financial pages?
Articles on the markets, news about corporations, and graphs and charts summarizing information about stocks, bonds, and currencies. A key feature is the listing of daily trading activity in stocks, bonds and mutual funds.

3. Refer to the section of Activity 1 titled *Examples from a Stock Table*. Call attention to the list of three stocks: Boeing (BA), IBM (IBM) and ExxonMobil (XOM). **Display Visual 1.** Using the information presented in Activity 1, explain how to read a stock table, column by column.

4. Divide the class into pairs. Assign the students to read *Examples from a Stock Table* and answer the Questions for Discussion. When they have finished, discuss the answers:

A. What is the 52-week high stock price for Boeing? *$46.03*

B. What is the 52-week low stock price for IBM? *$29.75*

C. What is the annual dividend for IBM? *$0.60*

D. What is the percentage yield for ExxonMobil? *2.6%*

E. What is the price/earnings ratio for ExxonMobil? *21*

F. On April 21, 2003, how many shares of Boeing stock were traded? *3,540,700*

G. What was the closing price of IBM stock on April 21, 2003? *$83.36*

H. Did the closing price of IBM stock represent a gain or a loss? How much? *A loss of $0.90*

5. Ask the students to read the section of Activity 1 titled *Behind the Numbers: Understanding More about a Stock Table* and answer the Questions for Discussion in writing. ***Ask:***

A. What is revealed about a company by the 52-week high and low?
Numbers denoting the 52-week high and low provide the range of the share price of the stock for the past year. Some investors use this information for hints about how well a company has been performing in the short term.

B. Why might dividends be important to some people?
Dividends are portions of a company's profits paid to stock holders. Some investors count on dividend payments as a source of income.

C. What do investors expect to happen when the P/E ratio of a company is high for its industry?
Investors expect the company to earn higher profits in the future.

6. Tell the students that many investors invest by purchasing mutual funds. Explain briefly that a mutual fund is a pool of money invested by a manager on behalf of fund shareholders. The goal is to increase the value of each share of the fund for its shareholders. A mutual fund offers investors certain advantages including professional management and the reduction of risk through diversification. (Lesson 7 deals with mutual funds in more detail.)

7. Keep the students in pairs and **distribute a copy of Activity 2 to each student. Display Visual 2.** Use the information in Activity 2 to explain the mutual fund column headings.

8. Assign the students to read Activity 2 and answer the Questions for Discussion in writing. When they have finished, discuss the answers.

A. What is the net asset value of the Magellan Fund? *$82.55*

B. What is the year-to-date percentage rate of return of the Magellan Fund? *4.5%*

C. What is the net change in the fund price of the Janus Fixed Income Fund? *$0.04*

D. What is the three-year percentage rate of return on the Janus Fixed Income Fund? *8.2%*

E. If an individual purchased 100 shares of the Vanguard Index Fund at the close of the trading on April 24, how much would he or she pay? *$1,609.00*

9. **Distribute a copy of Activity 3 to each student. Display Visual 3** and use the information in Activity 3 to explain the bond column headings.

10. Assign the students to read Activity 3 and answer the Questions for Discussion in writing. When they have finished, discuss the answers.

A. What is the coupon rate of interest on Lucent Technologies bonds? *7.25%*

B. What is the maturity date of the Sprint bonds? *2028*

C. What is the closing price of the Lucent Technologies bonds? *$88.25*

D. What was the net change in the Sprint bond price on April 20, 2003? *$0.50*

11. For Activity 4, the students will track stocks online, following selected companies for 10 business days. It would be ideal if they could use a computer lab with Internet access. But the Activity can also work in a regular classroom if the classroom has a few computers connected to the Internet.

12. Choose a Web site to be used by the students for finding information about stocks. Possibilities include Quicken (www.quicken.com), MSNBC (www.msnbc.com) and USA Today (www.usatoday.com).

13. The students will need to know both the name of the company and its stock symbol. They can find company names and symbols on a newspaper's financial pages or online.

14. Show the students how to enter the company name or stock symbol at the financial Web site.

15. **Distribute a copy of Activity 4** to each student. It asks the students to enter basic information about the company they are following and to answer questions about the company. Tell the students that each pair of students will be asked to present a report on the performance of the stock they followed at the end of two weeks.

16. At the end of the tracking period, ask the students to report to the class on the company they have been tracking. Allow each pair five minutes for its presentation.
Answers will vary. Students should describe the basics of the company (name, exchange, changes in the stock price) and comment on what trends they have been able to observe by responding to the Questions for Discussion.

Closure

1. **Display Visual 1** and review the symbols from the stock pages. Ask the students to explain what they mean. Do the same with Visuals 2 and 3.
2. Emphasize the importance of understanding how to read the three kinds of tables introduced in this lesson. In many respects, knowing how to read the tables is demonstrating basic knowledge of the language of investment.
3. Distribute a copy of Activity 5 to each student. Ask the students to answer the questions, using the financial pages of a newspaper. Discuss the answers.

   A. *Answers will vary.*

   B. *The New York Stock Exchange (NYSE), the NASDAQ and the American Stock Exchange (AMEX).*

   C. *See chart below for answers.*

Stock Name	Stock Market	Stock Symbol
Microsoft	NASDAQ	MSFT
Wal-Mart	NYSE	WMT
Badger Meter Inc.	AMEX	BMI
Coca-Cola	NYSE	KO

   D. *1. The symbol for Nike is NKE.*
   Answers for 2 to 6 are in the daily newspaper.

   E. *Answers are in the daily newspaper.*

Assessment

Multiple-Choice Questions

1. In a stock table, **DIV** stands for the dividend, which is
   a. a daily payment made to a stockholder.
   b. a measure of company diversification.
   c. an annual payment per share of stock to stockholders.
   d. the closing stock price.

2. In a stock table, **YLD** stands for yield, which is
   a. the opening stock price for the trading day.
   b. the dividend as a percentage of the price.
   c. the percentage of stock owned by the investor.
   d. the ratio of price to earnings.

3. If you invest in a mutual fund, you
   a. become a shareholder in the fund.
   b. become a shareholder in a stock.
   c. become a shareholder in bonds.
   d. become a shareholder of a non-stock corporation.

4. In a bond table, AT&T 5.5 13 means
   a. AT&T stock sells for $5.50 per share.
   b. the AT&T bond coupon rate is 5.5 percent and the bond maturity year is 2013.
   c. The AT&T bond coupon rate is 13 percent and the bond matures in 5.5 years.
   d. The AT&T bonds are a good investment.

Essay Questions

1. In your own words, describe what a price/earnings (P/E) ratio is.
One term in the ratio is P, for price; it refers to the price of a single share of stock. The other term is E, for earnings per share of the stock over the last four quarters. The price divided by earnings per share yields the P/E ratio. A high P/E ratio for a given stock means investors pay a relatively high price for that stock per dollar of reported earnings.

2. What are the differences between a stock, a mutual fund and a bond?
All three are investment options. A stock represents a share of ownership in a company. A mutual fund is a pool of money used to purchase stocks, bonds or money market instruments on behalf of fund shareholders. A bond is a certificate of indebtedness issued by a corporation or a government, promising to repay borrowed money to the lender at a specified rate of interest.

LESSON 5 VISUAL 1

READING A STOCK TABLE

The table below shows three stocks listed on the New York Stock Exchange on April 22, 2003.

Col. 1		Col. 2	Col. 3	Col. 4	Col. 5	Col. 6	Col. 7	Col. 8
52-WK HI	52-WK LO	STOCK (SYM)	DIV	YLD %	P/E	VOL 100S	CLOSE	NET CHG
46.03	24.73	Boeing **BA**	.68	2.5	9	35407	26.78	0.13
42.65	29.75	IBM **IBM**	.60	.7	38	66675	83.36	-0.90
90.03	29.75	ExxonMobil **XOM**	.92	2.6	21	81584	34.87	-0.16

Lesson 5 Visual 2

Reading a Mutual Fund Table

Below is information about three mutual funds traded on April 24, 2003.

Column 1	Column 2	Column 3	Column 4	Column 5
FUND	**NAV**	**NET CHG**	**YTD % RET**	**3-YR % RET**
Vanguard Index Funds Sm Cap	16.09	-0.11	2.7	-3.9
Fidelity Investment Magellan Fund	82.55	-0.84	4.5	-13.1
Janus Fixed Income	9.75	0.04	2.7	8.2

LESSON 5 VISUAL 3

READING A BOND TABLE

The table below shows the status of bond trading for three companies at the end of the trading day, April 20, 2003.

Column 1	Column 2	Column 3	Column 4	Column 5
BOND	**CUR YLD**	**VOL**	**CLOSE**	**NET CHG**
IBM 6.5 28	5.9	12	109.50	–
Lucent 7.25 06	8.2	226	88.25	0.25
Sprint 6.75 28	7.7	241	89.00	0.50

LESSON 5 ACTIVITY 1

READING A STOCK TABLE

1. Overview of the Financial Pages

Many newspapers publish financial pages that provide readers with a great deal of information about the world of stocks, mutual funds and bonds. One excellent source is *The Wall Street Journal* (often called "The Journal" or "WSJ"). *The Wall Street Journal* section on Money and Investing, for example, carries articles on changes in the financial markets and news about corporations. It often uses charts or graphs to show movement in the prices of stocks, bonds, the dollar and other currencies and commodities. It also reports the prices of stocks listed on the New York Stock Exchange (NYSE) and other stock exchanges. The Personal Journal section of *The Wall Street Journal* reports mutual fund prices. Other newspapers provide similar information.

2. Examples from a Stock Table

The table below shows three stocks listed on the New York Stock Exchange on April 22, 2003.

Col. 1		Col. 2		Col. 3	Col. 4	Col. 5	Col. 6	Col. 7	Col. 8
52-WK HI	52-WK LO	STOCK (SYM)		DIV	YLD %	P/E	VOL 100S	CLOSE	NET CHG
46.03	24.73	Boeing	**BA**	.68	2.5	9	35407	26.78	0.13
42.65	29.75	IBM	**IBM**	.60	.7	38	66675	83.36	-0.90
90.03	29.75	ExxonMobil	**XOM**	.92	2.6	21	81584	34.87	-0.16

Column 1: This column reports the highest and lowest price of the stock in the most recent 52-week period.

Column 2: This column provides the name of the company and its stock symbol on the New York Stock Exchange. Boeing, the aircraft manufacturer and aerospace company, has the symbol **BA**. IBM, the computer hardware and software company, has the symbol **IBM**. ExxonMobil, the oil company, has the symbol **XOM**.

Column 3: DIV stands for dividend, an annual payment per share to owners of the stock. Stock dividends are usually paid quarterly (every three months).

Column 4: The yield (**YLD**) is the dividend calculated as a percentage of the closing price. For Boeing, the .68 dividend divided by the $26.78 closing price equals .025, or a yield of 2.5 percent.

Column 5: P/E stands for the ratio of price to earnings. The P/E ratio is obtained by dividing the stock's price by the company's latest twelve-month earnings per share.

Column 6: VOL is shown in 100s of shares traded on the previous day. For Boeing, the number of shares traded on April 21, 2003, was 3,540,700.

Columns 7 & 8: Column 7 shows the price at which the stock closed at the end of the previous trading day, April 21, 2003. Boeing's closing stock price was $26.78. Column 8 shows the net change from the previous trading day's close. Boeing had a positive net change or a gain of $0.13.

LESSON 5 ACTIVITY 1 (CONTINUED)

QUESTIONS FOR DISCUSSION

Directions: Use information from the Stock Table to write answers to the following questions.

A. What is the 52-week high stock price for Boeing?

B. What is the 52-week low stock price for IBM?

C. What is the annual dividend for IBM?

D. What is the percentage yield for ExxonMobil?

E. What is the price/earnings ratio for ExxonMobil?

F. On April 21, 2003, how many shares of Boeing stock were traded?

G. What was the closing price of IBM stock on April 21, 2003?

H. Did the closing price of IBM stock represent a gain or a loss? How much?

3. Behind the Numbers: Understanding More about a Stock Table

Here are some hints to help you better understand the information provided in a stock table.

52-Week High and Low. Study the difference represented by these two numbers. If there is a large difference, you will want to gather more information to explain why the difference is large. Is the company's stock trading near its high? Is there any reason to think the price may go higher? Is the company's stock trading near its low? If so, why has the share price declined?

Stock Symbol and Name. Commit the stock symbol and name to memory. This will help you find the stock quickly in the financial pages and when you are online.

Dividend. The annual dividend is quoted as if you owned one share of the stock. A company that is doing well usually tries to pay shareholders a regular dividend. Some people use dividends as a source of regular income. Also, healthy companies try to increase their dividends from year to year.

Yield. The yield is the return on your invested money that comes from dividends. Yield changes daily as a stock's price changes. If you are interested in income from a stock investment, yield becomes important. If a company does not report a dividend (and some do not), the yield cannot be calculated.

Price/Earnings Ratio. This ratio is often referred to as the P/E ratio. The P/E ratio is calculated by dividing a stock's last price by its annual earnings per share. The higher the P/E ratio, the more profit growth stock holders expect from the company. The lower the P/E ratio, the more closely the price of the stock is

Lesson 5 Activity 1 (continued)

expected to reflect the current earnings of the stock. If no P/E ratio is reported for a stock, the company had a loss during the last four quarters. Since rates of growth in profit vary by industry, P/E ratios for a given company should be compared to those for other companies in the same industry.

Volume. For a given stock, you need to watch the volume traded over time. Soon you will learn what the normal trading volume of a stock is. If that trading volume increases or decreases significantly, find out why.

Close and Net Change. These two numbers tell you the closing price of the stock on the trading day reported and the change in dollars and cents compared to the previous trading day. If you follow these two figures over time, you can track what is called the stock-price trend.

Questions for Discussion

A. What is revealed about a company by the 52-week high and low?

B. Why might dividends be important to some people?

C. What do investors expect to happen when the P/E ratio of a company is high for its industry?

LESSON 5 ACTIVITY 2

READING A MUTUAL FUND TABLE

1. What Is a Mutual Fund?

A mutual fund is a pool of money used by a company to purchase stocks, bonds or money market assets on behalf of fund investors. The fund is managed by a fund manager. Mutual funds allow the investor to diversify — to invest in many different companies and industries. When a person invests in a mutual fund, she or he becomes a shareholder in (an owner of) the fund. The fund manager's duty is to make sound decisions about where to put the shareholders' money.

2. Examples from a Mutual Fund Table

The table below shows three mutual funds traded on April 24 and listed on April 25, 2003.

Column 1	Column 2	Column 3	Column 4	Column 5
FUND	**NAV**	**NET CHG**	**YTD % RET**	**3-YR % RET**
Vanguard Index Funds Sm Cap	16.09	-.011	2.7	-3.9
Fidelity Investment Magellan Fund	82.55	-0.84	4.5	-13.1
Janus Fixed Income	9.75	0.04	2.7	8.2

Column 1: Funds from three fund families are listed: Vanguard, Fidelity and Janus. One fund within each family is listed: the Vanguard Small Cap (SmCap) Index Fund, the Magellan Fund within Fidelity and the Janus Fixed Income Fund within Janus.

Column 2: NAV stands for net asset value per share of the fund at the close of the trading day, April 24, 2003. NAV is calculated by adding up the value of the stocks, bonds or other assets of the fund, subtracting the fund's liabilities and dividing the result by the number of fund shares available. NAV represents the value of a share of the fund.

Column 3: NET CHG stands for the change in the **NAV** from the previous trading day, in this case April 23, 2003.

Column 4: YTD % RET means the year-to-date percentage change in the fund value, including reinvestment of fund proceeds, less annual expenses paid by investors.

Column 5: 3-YR % RET means the percentage change in the fund value over the previous three-year period.

Lesson 5 Activity 2 (continued)

Questions for Discussion

Directions: Use information from the Mutual Funds Table to answer the following questions.

A. What is the net asset value of the Magellan Fund?

B. What is the year-to-date percentage rate of return of the Magellan Fund?

C. What is the net change in the fund price of the Janus Fixed Income Fund?

D. What is the three-year percentage rate of return on the Janus Fixed Income Fund?

E. If an individual purchased 100 shares of Vanguard Index Fund at the close of trading on April 24, how much would he or she pay?

LESSON 5 ACTIVITY 3

READING A BOND TABLE

1. What Is a Bond?

Unlike stocks, corporate bonds do not represent shares of ownership in a company. In buying a corporate bond, the buyer lends money to the corporation. The bond itself is a certificate acknowledging the debt incurred by the bond issuer. In exchange for the loan, the corporation agrees to pay the bondholder a specified amount of interest each year up to the maturity date of the bond. For example, suppose you buy a $1,000 bond in Xerox Corporation with a 10-year maturity date at 6 percent interest. This means that the corporation guarantees to pay you $60 interest per year for 10 years. Upon the bond's maturity date, Xerox Corporation repays you the $1,000.

Bonds are traded in financial markets, much the same as stocks. A 6 percent fixed-interest bond pays $60 annually. In trading, however, the price of the bond may change. If the price of the bond goes up to $1,200, the bondholder still earns $60 — only 5 percent of $1,200 ($60 divided by $1,200). If the price of the bond falls from $1,000 to $800, the annual interest rate increases to 7.5 percent ($60 divided by $800). Bond prices change when interest rates change. Higher market interest rates decrease the prices of existing bonds. Lower market interest rates increase the prices of existing bonds.

2. Examples from a Bond Table

The table below shows the status of bond trading for three companies at the end of the trading day, April 20, 2003.

Column 1	Column 2	Column 3	Column 4	Column 5
BOND	**CUR YLD**	**VOL**	**CLOSE**	**NET CHG**
IBM 6.5 28	5.9	12	109.50	–
Lucent 7.25 06	8.2	226	88.25	0.25
Sprint 6.75 28	7.7	241	89.00	0.50

Column 1: Three corporate bonds are listed: IBM; Lucent Technologies, a high tech communications company; and Sprint, a telephone company. The numbers following the name of the company state the coupon (or interest) rate of the corporate bond and its maturity date. For example, the IBM coupon (interest) rate is 6.5 percent, and its maturity date is 2028.

Column 2: CUR YLD stands for current yield. The current yield column shows the annual interest payment as a percentage of the current bond price. At the trading-day price of $109.50 for the IBM bond, the current yield is 5.9 percent, not the 6.5 percent interest of the initial bond issue.

Column 3: VOL stands for trading day volume multiplied by 10,000. On April 20, 120,000 IBM bonds were bought and sold (12 x 10,000).

Column 4: CLOSE provides the closing price of the bond. The quote is given in $100 units. So, a closing price of $109.50 is actually $1,095.00.

Column 5: NET CHG stands for the net change in bond price in dollars and cents. In the case of the IBM bond, there was no change in bond price from the previous trading day.

Lesson 5 Activity 3 (continued)

Questions for Discussion

Directions: Use information from the Bond Table to answer the following questions.

1. What is the coupon rate of interest on Lucent Technologies bonds?

2. What is the maturity date of the Sprint bonds?

3. What is the closing price of the Lucent Technologies bonds?

4. What was the net change in the Sprint bond price on April 20, 2003?

LESSON 5 ACTIVITY 4

TRACKING A STOCK ONLINE

The Internet provides a means by which investors may keep track of stocks, mutual funds or bonds easily and quickly. Internet sources can provide stock and mutual fund quotes that are accurate within 20 minutes of the actual trading time. The quotes include all the information readers could find on the financial pages of the newspaper, and often much more.

With a partner, select a stock you want to track for several days. Choose a Web site for finding information on the stock. You will need to memorize the symbol of the stock and enter it at the Web site to find your company.

You and your partner will be responsible for planning how to keep track of the quotes. Complete the information requested below and the questions that follow.

Name of Company ____________________

Symbol ___________ Exchange __________

Day and Date	Today's Close	Net Change	Volume	Yield

Lesson 5 Activity 4 (continued)

Questions for Discussion

1. Where is the company located?

2. What does the company produce?

3. Who are its customers?

4. What are its plans for the future?

5. What have recent news stories reported about the company?

6. Do you think there will be a growth in demand for this company's products? Why or why not?

7. If you were interested in investing in a growth-oriented company over the long term, would you want to own this company? Why or why not?

LESSON 5 ACTIVITY 5

SCAVENGER HUNT

Directions: Use the financial tables of a daily newspaper to answer each of the questions below.

A. The stock prices in your newspaper are from the previous trading day.
So the stock prices in the newspaper you are using now are actually for what date?

B. There are three major stock markets in the United States.
What are the names of the three major stock markets?

C. Complete the following table by finding each stock in the stock tables of your newspaper.

Company	Stock Market	Stock Symbol
Microsoft		
Wal-Mart		
Badger Meter Inc.		
Coca-Cola		

D. Find the stock listing for Nike. Answer the following questions:

1. What is the stock symbol for Nike?
2. What is the highest price paid for Nike during the last year?
3. What was the dividend paid for Nike during the last year?
4. How many shares of Nike stock were traded?
5. What was the lowest price paid for Nike stock on this trading day?
6. How much did the closing price of Nike stock change from the day before?

LESSON 5 ACTIVITY 5 (CONTINUED)

SCAVENGER HUNT

E. Besides listing stocks, most newspapers also present various tables and other information related to the stock markets. For example, newspapers often summarize events in the stock markets by showing the number of shares traded in each stock market. They also show the most actively traded stocks in the three stock markets. Find these tables and answer the following questions:

1. How many shares of stock were traded on the New York Stock Exchange on this trading day?

2. Which stock was the most actively traded stock on the American Stock Exchange on this trading day?

Lesson 6 What is a Bond?

Middle School

Lesson 6 What Is a Bond?

Lesson Description

In this lesson the students learn what bonds are and how bonds work. They learn the basic terminology related to bonds and participate in a simulation activity aimed at showing that bonds are certificates of indebtedness, similar to an IOU note. Finally, the students explore credit ratings and calculate average coupon rates for various bond ratings in order to determine the relationship between ratings and bond coupons.

Corporations and local, state and federal governments often raise additional money to operate, buy new equipment, pay off debts or finance general operations. To get the money they sometimes borrow money from the public by selling bonds. A bond is an "I owe you" certificate given to a lender (the holder of the bond) by a borrower (the bond seller). The bond states the terms of this special kind of loan: that the borrower will pay back the entire amount borrowed (called the principal) and will pay the lender something additional (an interest payment) for the use of his or her money. The purchase price of a bond is known as its face value. The borrower promises to pay back the loan on a particular day (the bond's maturity date) at a predetermined rate of interest (the bond's coupon rate).

An important difference between stocks and bonds is that stocks make no promises about paying the stockholder dividends or returns. For example, Company X may generate profits that result in an expected dividend for all shareholders in the company, but Company X is under no obligation to pay out such a dividend. Also, it is possible that the price of Company X stock might fall over time. If Company X issues a bond, however, the company promises to pay back the principal (the face value of the bond) plus interest. If you purchase a bond from Company X and hold it to maturity, you can calculate how much you're supposed to be paid back by the company. Government-issued bonds (particularly those issued by the U.S. government) carry very little risk; bonds issued by corporations carry more risk. Part of this risk is measured by the credit rating of the bond's issuer. Such ratings are indicators of the ability of a corporation or a state or local government to repay its debts. For example, Moody's Investor Services rates bonds on a scale from Aaa (highest quality) to C (no interest being paid, bankruptcy filed or in default). These ratings help investors make decisions about which bonds to buy.

Concepts

- Bond
- Bond rating
- Coupon
- Coupon bond
- Coupon rate
- Default
- Face value
- Maturity date
- Par value
- Risk
- Zero-coupon bond

Objectives

Students will:

1. Explain what a bond is and how bonds are used by governments and corporations.
2. Define *face value*, *coupon* and *maturity date.*
3. Distinguish between coupon bonds and zero-coupon bonds.
4. Identify the relationship between a bond's rating, risk and rate of return.

Time Required

90 minutes

Materials

- A transparency of Visuals 1, 2 and 3
- Activity 1: Investor Dollars. Photocopy and cut out enough $100 slips so that, on average, each lender (one-half of the students) has $200. That is, if there are 13 lenders, cut out no more than 26 $100 slips.
- Activity 2: Role Cards. Photocopy and cut out enough role cards and IOU slips for one-half of the students.
- A copy of Activities 3, 4 and 5 for each student

Procedure

1. Ask the students to describe situations in which they have borrowed something. **Display Visual 1.** Ask the students to read the quotations and state what they have in common. Guide the discussion to the question, "If borrowing is such a bad thing, why do people borrow so often?" Ask the students

to list several reasons why people might choose to borrow.
To buy a car, buy a house, pay for college, pay for medical care and so on.

2. Ask the students if they have ever lent something to someone and, if so, to describe what it was and why they lent it. Guide the discussion to the question, "Would you be more likely to lend to people who promised to pay you back with more than you lent them?" Explain that the students will play a short game that involves the concepts of *lending* and *borrowing*.

3. Divide the class in half. Assign half of the students to be lenders. Distribute $100 slips (Activity 1) to the lenders so that, on average, each lender has $200. Do not give everyone $200; give some lenders $100 and some $300. Tell the students that the goal for lenders is to get the greatest return on their money. Tell the lenders that they need to seek out the borrowers who offer the best terms.

4. Assign the other half of the class to be borrowers. Distribute one role card and three IOU slips (from Activity 2) to each borrower. Tell the borrowers that their goal is to sell all their IOU slips to the lenders.

5. Tell the students they will have five to ten minutes to sell and buy IOU slips.

6. When time has elapsed, have the students return to their seats. Ask the following questions:

- How many lenders lent all their money?
  All should have.
- How many borrowers sold all their IOU slips?
  There should be several students who were not able to sell all, or any, of their slips.
- Why were the lenders willing to buy some IOUs and not others?
  While answers will vary, the lenders should state that some borrowers seemed unlikely to be able to pay back the loan — for example, the borrower who wanted to open the ice cream stand at the skating rink.

7. Tell the lenders to assume that a year has passed; now it is time to collect on their IOUs. **Display Visual 2.** Ask the lenders to write down the payments they received from their borrowers. Ask for a show of hands of lenders who received at least the amount they lent, who received a payment in excess of the amount they lent and who received less than the amount they lent. Ask why some lenders made a return while others did not.

8. Tell the students that, like individuals, governments and corporations often money for equipment, expansion or operations. Governments and corporations often borrow using something called a *bond*. Explain that a bond is a certificate of indebtedness — that is, an IOU certificate given to a lender (the purchaser of the bond) by a borrower (the corporation or government issuing the bond).

9. **Distribute a copy of Activity 3** to each student. Tell the students to read the first three sections of Activity 3.
Ask: What are the main differences between government bonds and corporate bonds?
U.S. government bonds are backed by the government and thus are less risky than corporate bonds.

10. Have the students read the section of Activity 3 titled *How Bonds Work*. At the same time, **display Visual 3.** Point out the difference between a coupon and a zero-coupon bond. Explain that a coupon bond pays out interest (the coupon) at set intervals, with a final payment that includes the original principal (or par value) at the maturity date. A zero-coupon bond, on the other hand, pays all the interest and the principal of the bond at the maturity date. ***Ask:*** Why would a person purchase a coupon bond rather than a zero-coupon bond?
Someone who wants a steady income stream, such as a retiree, might prefer a coupon bond.

11. Have the students complete their reading of Activity 3. Ask them to list several reasons why investors would buy bonds, particularly in light of the fact that, over time, stocks have outperformed bonds.
Less risk and the certainty of fixed income over time may make bonds attractive to retired people and others who want the income that bonds generate; also, some bonds generate lower tax liability than stocks.

12. Ask the students to quickly review the terms at the end of the reading. **Distribute a copy of Activity 4** to each student and have the students complete the Bond Quiz. Discuss their answers.
Answers: 1 c, 2 a, 3 c, 4 b, 5 b.

13. Ask the students to recall the IOU activity. Ask how many students received less than their promised payment. Ask if knowing more about the borrower would have changed their decisions. Explain that bonds are often rated; the ratings are intended to provide information to investors. **Distribute a copy of Activity 5** to each student. Have the students read the introduction and examine the Moody's Investor Service bond-rating categories. Explain that Moody's and other third-party rating services provide valuable information about the likelihood that corporations or governments will be able to pay off their bond obligations. The lower the rating, the more likely a firm or government

will default on the bonds and not be able to pay the interest and principal back to investors.

14. Ask the students to examine the table with selected coupon rates across various Moody's ratings. Tell them that these are real data drawn from actual bonds that had a one-year maturity date. Ask them to complete the table by calculating the average coupon rates for the selected Moody's ratings categories.
Average coupons: Aaa: 4.50, Aa: 6.60, Baa: 8.42, Caa: 9.79, C: 12.08.

Once the students have calculated these, have them plot the average coupon rate for each rating on the figure titled *Average Coupon Rates for Sample Bonds by Selected Moody's Ratings.* Upon completion, have the students answer the follow-up questions.
1. an inverse relationship: as bond ratings fall, coupon rates rise; 2. corporations with poor ratings must offer higher rates in order to overcome investor concern about the risk of default; 3. investors who buy C-rated bonds do so because, for these investors, the hope of high returns outweighs the potential risks involved.

Closure

1. Review the main points of the lesson. ***Ask:***

- What is a bond?
  A bond is a certificate acknowledging a loan from the lender to a government or corporation.
- Why would someone buy a bond?
  To earn income. The bond's issuer promises to pay a specified rate of interest during the life of the bond and to repay the original loan. For capital gains if interest rates fall.
- Which type of bond is the least risky for investors? Why?
  U.S. governments bonds are the least risky; they are backed by the U.S. government.
- What is a U.S. savings bond?
  U.S. savings bonds are issued by the U.S. government and are available in smaller denominations than other U.S. bonds. They are issued at half the face value and mature at face value at a date determined by the interest rate.
- What is a municipal bond?
  A bond issued by a state or local government.
- What is a major tax benefit of holding municipal bonds?
  The bondholder does not have to pay a federal tax on the interest.
- If corporate bonds are riskier than U.S. government bonds, why do people buy corporate bonds?
  Corporate bonds pay a higher interest rate.
- What is the difference between a coupon bond and a zero-coupon bond?
  A coupon bond pays interest at fixed intervals; a zero-coupon bond pays accumulated interest at the bond's maturity date.

2. Suggest that the students visit the following Web sites to learn more about bonds:

- More detailed overview of bonds:
  <http://www.investinginbonds.com>
- Bond ratings: Moody's Investor Service
  <http://www.moodys.com/>
- U.S. savings bonds:
  <http://www.publicdebt.treas.gov/sav/sav.htm>
- Buying bonds:
  <http://www.bondpage.com>

Assessment

Multiple-Choice Questions

1. What is a bond?
   a. A certificate representing a loan from an investor to a corporation or government entity that makes fixed payments for a set time and eventually pays back the loan in full.
   b. A certificate of ownership in a corporation, with the right to a percentage of the earnings.
   c. A payment from an investor to a corporation for the rights to future profits.
   d. A group of stocks sold together for a set price.

2. A bond that pays all of its interest and principal at the bond's maturity date is called a
   a. coupon bond.
   b. zero-coupon bond.
   c. bond fund.
   d. par-value bond.

3. Generally speaking, the relationship between a bond's coupon rate and its credit rating is
   a. as the bond's rating improves, the coupon rate increases.
   b. as the bond's rating declines, the coupon rate decreases.
   c. as the bond's rating improves, the coupon rate decreases.
   d. unable to be determined.

4. All of the following are reasons to buy bonds except

   a. bonds may outperform the stock market in certain periods of time.

   b. bonds pay out interest at set intervals, allowing people to live off the income.

   c. bonds generally have outperformed the stock market over the last 100 years.

   d. investing in bonds may generate less tax liability (some bond returns are even tax-free) than investing in stocks.

Essay Questions

1. Explain why bond ratings, such as those provided by Moody's Investor Service, are important for investors.
Bond ratings address the risk of default and the relationship between credit rating and the coupon rate. These services save investors time and resources that they might otherwise spend researching bonds on their own.

2. Describe the difference between a coupon bond and a zero-coupon bond.
Coupon bond: purchased at face (par) value, coupon (interest) payments set at fixed intervals, final payment at maturity includes the principal plus the final coupon. Zero-coupon bond: purchased below face (par) value, no interest payments until maturity when principal and accumulated interest are paid.

Lesson 6 Visual 1

To Borrow or Not to Borrow? That Is the Question

Neither a borrower nor a lender be;
for loan oft loses both itself and friend…

***William Shakespeare,* Hamlet**

Who goes a borrowing, goes a sorrowing.

Proverb

I wish it were possible to [amend our] constitution with... an additional article taking from the federal government the power of borrowing.

Thomas Jefferson, letter to John Taylor

Borrowing is not much better than begging; just as lending with interest is not much better than stealing.

Doris Lessing, British author

LESSON 6 VISUAL 2

ONE YEAR LATER

BORROWER	*AFTER ONE YEAR...*
You are trying to raise $300 to buy a new bike in order to expand your already successful paper route.	The bike helped double the size of the paper route. Pay each bearer of this bond $110.
You are trying to raise $300 to buy a new bicycle in order to hang out with your friends in a bike club.	The bike club detracted from your school-work, forcing you to quit your after-school job. Pay each bearer of this bond $100.
You are trying to raise $300 for tuition payments to the local art school. Once you finish school, you plan to put your talents to work for Disney Studios as an animator.	You finished art school and took a job at MGM Studios. Pay each bearer of this bond $110.
You are trying to raise $300 for tuition payments to the local art school. Once you finish school, you plan to put your talents to work as a graffiti artist, "tagging" buildings at night.	You are arrested and spend six months in juvenile hall. Pay each bearer of this bond $0.00.
You are trying to raise $300 to buy a new lawn-mower for your landscaping business. Business has been so good that you need another mower to meet the demand.	Business improves after the addition of the new mower. Pay each bearer of this bond $110.
You are trying to raise $300 to start a hot chocolate stand you want to open this summer in front of the local pool. You are convinced that, even in the heat of summer, people want the "heart-warming feeling that a good cup of hot cocoa brings."	Bad idea! No one wants hot cocoa in 100° heat! Pay each bearer of this bond $50.
You are trying to raise $300 to start an ice cream stand this winter in front of the local outdoor ice skating rink. You are convinced that, even in the cold of winter, people want the "feeling of summer that an ice cream cone covered with sprinkles brings."	Bad idea! No one wants ice cream in the middle of winter! Pay each bearer of this bond $50.
You are trying to raise $300 to start a CD rental business at your school. You have conducted a survey of your classmates and are convinced that students will pay to rent CDs for a week.	Great idea! The rental business is a hit with your classmates! Pay each bearer of this bond $110.

Lesson 6 Visual 3

How a Bond Works

Coupon Bonds

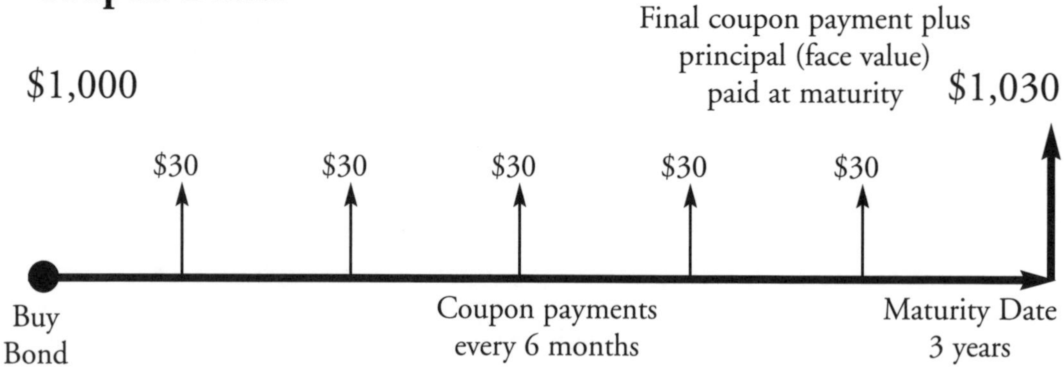

A 3-year coupon bond with a coupon rate of 6.0% and a face (par) value of $1,000

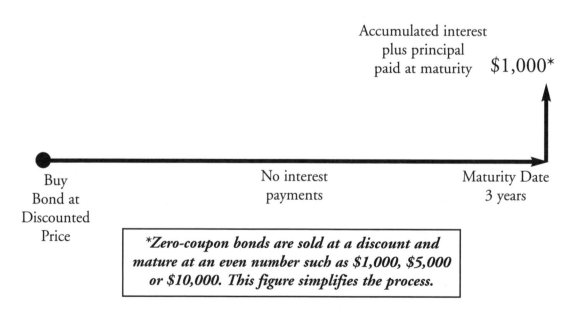

Zero-Coupon Bonds

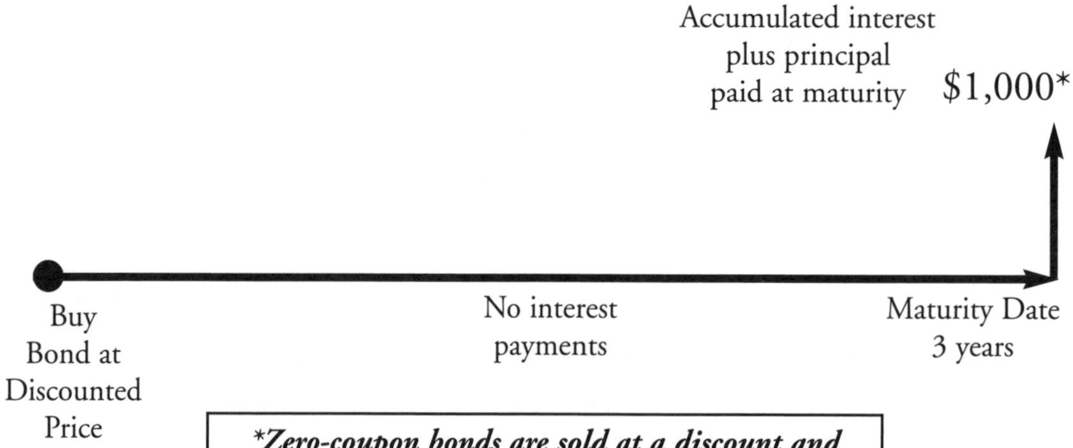

****Zero-coupon bonds are sold at a discount and mature at an even number such as $1,000, $5,000 or $10,000. This figure simplifies the process.***

LESSON 6 ACTIVITY 1

INVESTOR DOLLARS

100 $ 100	100 $ 100	100 $ 100
100 $ 100	100 $ 100	100 $ 100
100 $ 100	100 $ 100	100 $ 100
100 $ 100	100 $ 100	100 $ 100
100 $ 100	100 $ 100	100 $ 100
100 $ 100	100 $ 100	100 $ 100
100 $ 100	100 $ 100	100 $ 100

Lesson 6 Activity 2

Role Cards

You are trying to raise $300 to buy a new bike in order to expand your already successful paper route. ***Role Card***	**IOU:** For lending me **$100**, I agree to pay you **$110** at the end of the year. Signed, *Paper route mogul*
IOU: For lending me **$100**, I agree to pay you **$110** at the end of the year. Signed, *Paper route mogul*	**IOU:** For lending me **$100**, I agree to pay you **$110** at the end of the year. Signed, *Paper route mogul*
You are trying to raise $300 to buy a new bicycle in order to hang out with your friends in a bike club. ***Role Card***	**IOU:** For lending me **$100**, I agree to pay you **$120** at the end of the year. Signed, *Future bike club member*
IOU: For lending me **$100**, I agree to pay you **$120** at the end of the year. Signed, *Future bike club member*	**IOU:** For lending me **$100**, I agree to pay you **$120** at the end of the year. Signed, *Future bike club member*
You are trying to raise $300 for tuition payments to the local art school. Once you finish school, you plan to put your talents to work for Disney Studios as an animator. ***Role Card***	**IOU:** For lending me **$100**, I agree to pay you **$110** at the end of the year. Signed, *Future Disney animator*
IOU: For lending me **$100**, I agree to pay you **$110** at the end of the year. Signed, *Future Disney animator*	**IOU:** For lending me **$100**, I agree to pay you **$110** at the end of the year. Signed, *Future Disney animator*

Lesson 6 Activity 2 (continued)

Role Cards

You are trying to raise $300 for tuition payments to the local art school. Once you finish school, you plan to put your talents to work as a graffiti artist, "tagging" buildings at night. ***Role Card***	**IOU:** For lending me **$100**, I agree to pay you **$120** at the end of the year. Signed, *Future graffiti vandal*
IOU: For lending me **$100**, I agree to pay you **$120** at the end of the year. Signed, *Future graffiti vandal*	**IOU:** For lending me **$100**, I agree to pay you **$120** at the end of the year. Signed, *Future graffiti vandal*
You are trying to raise $300 to buy a new lawn-mower for your landscaping business. Business has been so good that you need another mower to meet the demand. ***Role Card***	**IOU:** For lending me **$100**, I agree to pay you **$110** at the end of the year. Signed, *Lawn maintenance mogul*
IOU: For lending me **$100**, I agree to pay you **$110** at the end of the year. Signed, *Lawn maintenance mogul*	**IOU:** For lending me **$100**, I agree to pay you **$110** at the end of the year. Signed, *Lawn maintenance mogul*
You are trying to raise $300 to start a hot chocolate stand you want to open this summer in front of the local pool. You are convinced that, even in the heat of summer, people want the "heart-warming feeling that a good cup of hot cocoa brings." ***Role Card***	**IOU:** For lending me **$100**, I agree to pay you **$110** at the end of the year. Signed, *Hot cocoa entrepreneur*
IOU: For lending me **$100**, I agree to pay you **$110** at the end of the year. Signed, *Hot cocoa entrepreneur*	**IOU:** For lending me **$100**, I agree to pay you **$110** at the end of the year. Signed, *Hot cocoa entrepreneur*

Lesson 6 Activity 2 (continued)

Role Cards

You are trying to raise $300 to start an ice cream stand this winter in front of the local outdoor ice skating rink. You are convinced that, even in the cold of winter, people want the "feeling of summer that an ice cream cone covered with sprinkles brings." ***Role Card***	**IOU:** For lending me **$100**, I agree to pay you **$120** at the end of the year. Signed, *Ice cream entrepreneur*
IOU: For lending me **$100**, I agree to pay you **$120** at the end of the year. Signed, *Ice cream entrepreneur*	**IOU:** For lending me **$100**, I agree to pay you **$120** at the end of the year. Signed, *Ice cream entrepreneur*
You are trying to raise $300 to start a CD rental business at your school. You have conducted a survey of your classmates and are convinced that students will pay to rent CDs for a week. ***Role Card***	**IOU:** For lending me **$100**, I agree to pay you **$110** at the end of the year. Signed, *Future music mogul*
IOU: For lending me **$100**, I agree to pay you **$110** at the end of the year. Signed, *Future music mogul*	**IOU:** For lending me **$100**, I agree to pay you **$110** at the end of the year. Signed, *Future music mogul*

LESSON 6 ACTIVITY 3

THE ABCs OF BONDS

What Are Bonds?

Imagine that you are in the ice cream store with a friend on a Thursday evening and want to get a hot fudge sundae, but you realize you don't have any cash. You know you'll be getting your paycheck the next day, so you ask your friend to lend you a few dollars so you can have the sundae now. In return for the loan, you agree to pay your friend back tomorrow *and* buy lunch on Saturday as well. Your friend, finding these terms to his liking, lends you the money, and you enjoy a delicious sundae.

Governments and corporations often find themselves short of cash, just as you were on Thursday. One way to generate these needed resources is to issue *bonds*. A bond is similar to an I.O.U. When you purchase a bond, you are lending money to a government, a corporation or some other entity, known as the bond *issuer*. In exchange for this loan, the issuer promises to pay you a specified rate of interest during the life of the bond and to repay the original loan (referred to as the *face value* or *par value* of the bond) when it comes due at its *maturity date*.

U.S. Government Bonds

When the U. S. government spends more than it collects in taxes, it borrows money by issuing bonds to cover the difference. The bonds issued by the U. S. government are called Treasury bonds. A special type of Treasury bond is a U.S. savings bond. U.S. savings bonds are issued in smaller amounts than other Treasury bonds. They are issued at half the face value and mature at face value at a date determined by the interest rate. Treasury bonds and U.S. savings bonds are widely regarded as the safest bond investments because they are backed by "the full faith and credit" of the U.S. government; an investor is therefore nearly certain to get paid back. In addition, the interest paid on U.S. government bonds cannot be taxed by state or local governments.

Municipal bonds are issued by states, counties, cities, towns, villages and other units of local government. These bonds are considered fairly safe but are riskier than U.S. government bonds. The risk level for a municipal bond depends on the financial condition of the state or local government that issued it. The interest paid on most municipal bonds is not taxed by the federal government.

Corporate Bonds

As corporations grow, they often don't generate enough money to pay for the supplies necessary to keep growing. Many corporations issue bonds to pay for new capital equipment or to cover operating expenses. When a company issues bonds, it borrows money from investors in exchange for agreeing to pay them interest on their money at a set date in the future. Corporate bonds are generally riskier than government bonds because even large, stable companies are much more likely to go out of business than the U.S. government. Corporate bonds can also be the most lucrative bonds to invest in, as the investor is generally rewarded for the extra risk undertaken.

6 What is a Bond?

How Bonds Work

The most basic bond is called a *coupon bond.* Coupon bonds pay out an interest payment (called the *coupon*) to the investor every six months. The *principal* (also called the *face value* or *par value* of the bond) is paid to the investor at a specified *maturity date*, which can range from a few months to 30 years. These bonds are said to be *fixed-income* securities because the amount the investor receives is set, or fixed, by the coupon rate. Figure 1 presents a timetable graph showing how coupon payments work.

Figure 1. A Sample Coupon Bond

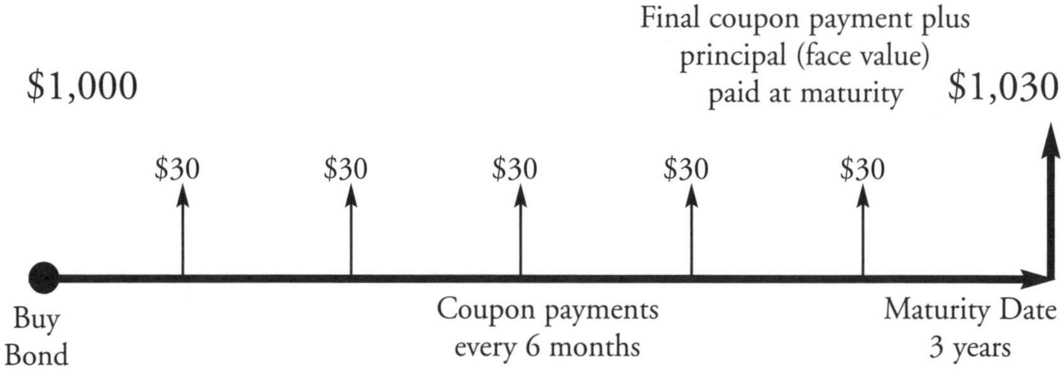

A 3-year coupon bond with a coupon rate of 6.0% and a face (par) value of $1,000

The other common bond is called a *zero-coupon bond.* Unlike coupon bonds, zero-coupon bonds do not make periodic interest payments to the investor. Rather, investors buy the bond at a reduced face value; then, at the maturity date, investors receive one payment. The payment is equal to the principal of the bond plus the interest that has accumulated during the time the bond has been held by the investor. A U.S. savings bond is an example of a zero-coupon bond. Figure 2 presents a timetable graph showing how zero-coupon bonds work.

Figure 2. A Sample Zero-Coupon Bond

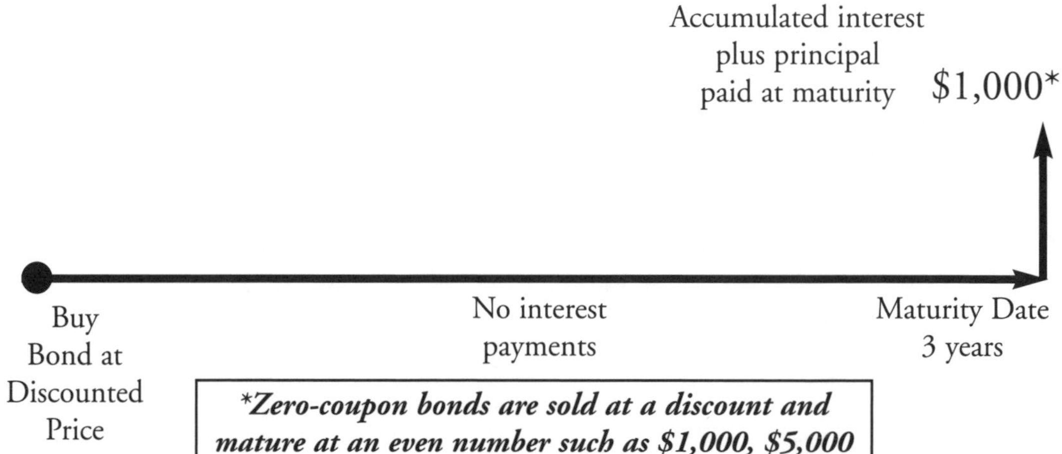

****Zero-coupon bonds are sold at a discount and mature at an even number such as $1,000, $5,000 or $10,000. This figure simplifies the process.***

Why Buy a Bond?

Over the last 100 years, the stock market has provided the greatest return to investors. So why not just invest in stocks? Although they do not provide the same return as stocks in the long run, bonds have several characteristics that investors value.

First, many bonds provide investors with relatively safe investments. Treasury bondholders can be almost certain that they will receive the amount they originally invested, plus interest, and corporate bondholders can have nearly the same certainty. By contrast, investors can lose their entire investment in individual stocks; in fact, that outcome occurs frequently — as it did recently, for some investors, in the so-called "dot.com" bubble of 2000-2001.

Second, bonds pay interest to investors at set intervals, and this arrangement can provide valuable income for those who need a regular cash flow — retirees, for example. If someone owned $100,000 worth of coupon bonds that paid 8 per cent interest annually (that would be $8,000 per year), one-half of that interest would be sent to the bondholder every six months, providing income or money to invest elsewhere.

Some people buy bonds to earn capital gains. Bond prices tend to change with interest rates. When interest rates fall, bond prices rise. When interest rates rise, existing bond prices fall. Some people buy bonds to make capital gains when interest rates fall. To do this, you must sell a bond before the maturity date.

Finally, bonds can also provide a tax advantage. When a government issues bonds to raise money to build bridges or roads, the interest investors earn can be tax-exempt. U.S. Treasury bonds are exempt from state and local taxes. Municipal bonds are exempt from federal taxes. Tax exemption can be an important factor for those who are eager to reduce the amount they pay in taxes.

A Review of Bond Terminology

Bond	Bonds are similar to an I.O.U. When you buy a bond, you make a loan to a government or a corporation in return for promised repayment at a specified rate of interest.
Coupon bond	A bond that pays out interest at fixed intervals (usually six months) over the time the bond is held by the investor.
Coupon	The interest payment on a coupon bond.
Face value	The price an investor pays for a bond (also called par value or principal).
Fixed-income security	An investment in which the amount of income an investor receives is set, or fixed, by the issuer.
Issuer	The entity (government or corporation) that writes the bond purchased by investors.
Maturity date	The date at which the bond matures and the final payment is made to the investor.
Municipal bond	A bond issued by state or local governments.
Par value	The price an investor pays for a bond (also called face value or principal).
Principal	The initial cost of the bond (also known as the par value or face value of the bond).
Zero-coupon bond	A bond whose purchase price is below face value. One payment is made at maturity that includes the principal plus accumulated interest.

Lesson 6 Activity 4

A Bond Quiz

1. What is a bond's coupon?
   a. The value of a bond at its issue date
   b. The value of a bond at its maturity date
   c. The rate of interest to be paid by the bond issuer
   d. The purchase price of a bond

2. A bond's face value may also be called the
   a. par value.
   b. coupon.
   c. maturity.
   d. final payment.

3. Which of the following is the least risky investment?
   a. Corporate bonds
   b. Stocks
   c. U.S. Treasury bonds
   d. Mutual funds

4. A bond's interest rate is called its
   a. par value.
   b. coupon rate.
   c. face value.
   d. principal.

5. A zero-coupon bond pays interest
   a. periodically.
   b. at the maturity date.
   c. at the time of purchase.
   d. never.

Lesson 6 Activity 5

Bond Ratings

Bonds are generally less risky than stocks. U.S. Treasury bonds carry very little risk for the investor because the U.S. government is unlikely to go bankrupt and default on its bonds. Defaulting means the issuer is unable to make further interest and principal payments to the bond holder. Because corporations can and sometimes do go into bankruptcy, the default risk for corporate bonds is higher than the risk for government bonds.

In order to help individual investors make better decisions about their investments, many corporate bonds are rated by a third-party source such as Moody's Investor Service to help describe the creditworthiness of the issuer. The higher the rating, the less the likely the corporation will go into default. Moody's ratings for bonds are as follows:

Moody's Investor Service Bond-Rating Codes

Aaa	Highest quality
Aa	High quality
A	Upper-medium quality
Baa	Medium grade
Ba	Somewhat speculative
B	Low grade, speculative
Caa	Low grade, default possible
Ca	Low grade, partial recovery possible
C	Default, recovery unlikely

Lesson 6 Activity 5 (continued)

Bond Ratings

A strong relationship exists between the credit rating of a corporate bond and its coupon rate. This relationship can be determined by examining a few sample cases. The following table reports the coupon rate for three corporate bonds in several of Moody's rating codes. Each of these bonds has a one-year maturity date. First, calculate the average coupon rate for each Moody's category. Enter the average in the third column.

Moody's Bond Rating (1)	Coupon rate (2)	Average (3)	
Aaa	Bond 1: 4.125		Average coupon for **Aaa** rated bonds
Aaa	Bond 2: 5.125		
Aaa	Bond 3: 4.250		
Aa	Bond 1: 6.625		Average coupon for **Aa** rated bonds
Aa	Bond 2: 6.250		
Aa	Bond 3: 6.923		
Baa	Bond 1: 8.250		Average coupon for **Baa** rated bonds
Baa	Bond 2: 8.875		
Baa	Bond 3: 8.125		
Caa	Bond 1: 10.125		Average coupon for **Caa** rated bonds
Caa	Bond 2: 9.750		
Caa	Bond 3: 9.500		
C	Bond 1: 11.500		Average coupon for **C** rated bonds
C	Bond 2: 12.875		
C	Bond 3: 11.875		

Source: Bond coupon rates for coupon bonds with one-year maturity dates issued by corporations; obtained using a search at http://www.bondpage.com/.

Lesson 6 Activity 5 (continued)

Bond Ratings

Now plot these results on the diagram below.

Average Coupon Rates for Sample Bonds by Selected Moody's Ratings

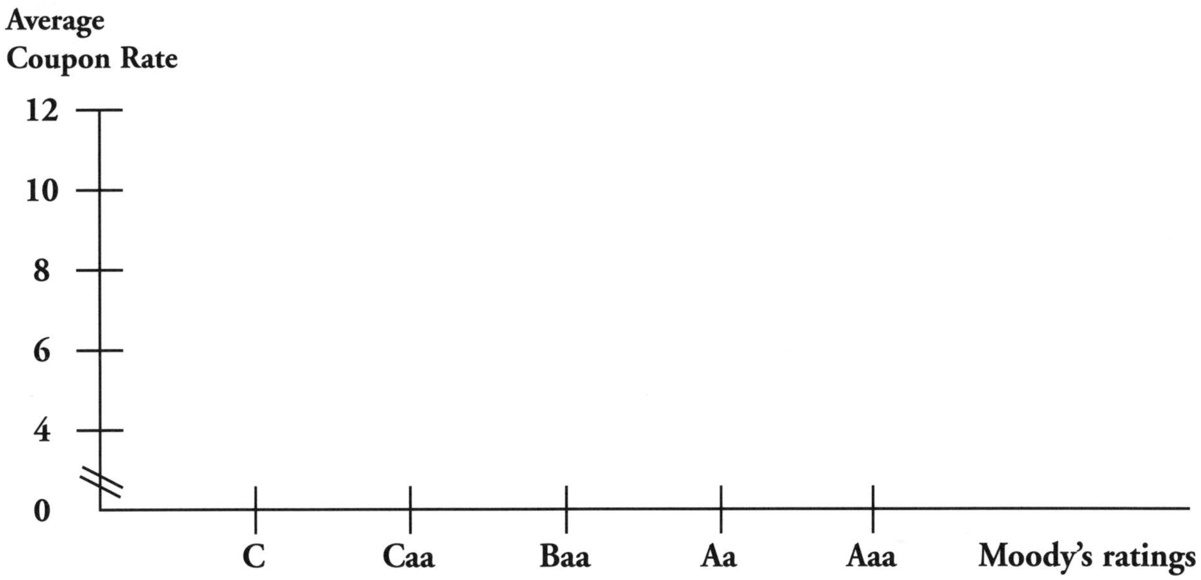

Answer the following questions.

Questions

1. What is the relationship between bond rating and coupon rate?

2. Why do corporations with lower credit ratings offer higher coupons or interest rates on their bonds?

3. Why would investors buy a bond rated Caa or C?

Lesson 7 What are Mutual Funds?

Middle School

Lesson 7 What Are Mutual Funds?

Lesson Description

The students form class investment clubs that work much in the way mutual funds do. They invest $3,000 (300 shares at $10 a share) in up to six stocks. One year later they revalue their shares and determine whether a share in their class investment clubs has increased or decreased in value. Finally, they read about mutual funds and learn that the concept behind mutual funds is similar to the concept behind their class investment clubs.

A mutual fund is a pool of money invested by a manager with the goal of increasing the value of each share of the fund for its investors. A mutual fund provides diversification, spreads risk and provides the convenience of buying and selling shares in the fund on any business day. These are the reasons why more Americans invest through mutual funds than directly in the stock, bond or money markets.

Concepts

- Diversification
- Liquidity
- Load
- Mutual fund
- Net asset value
- Risk and reward

Objectives

Students will:

1. Describe how mutual funds work.
2. Evaluate the advantages and disadvantages of investing in mutual funds.
3. Use the terminology of mutual funds.
4. Calculate the value of an investment on a per-share basis.

Time Required

75 minutes

Materials

- A transparency of Visuals 1 and 2
- A copy of Activities 1, 2, 3 and 4 for each student

Procedure

1. Explain to the students that they are going to learn about mutual funds. More Americans invest in stocks and bonds through mutual funds than in any other way.

2. Tell the students that a mutual fund is like an investment club with thousands of members. An investment club is any group of people who pool their money, invest and share the profits or losses. The class is now going to form investment clubs with just a few members.

3. Divide the class into groups of no more than five members each. Tell the students that each group is an investment club, and members will have to make some decisions about where to invest their money.

4. **Distribute a copy of Activity 1** to each student.

5. Go over Activity 1 and make sure the students understand these major points:

- Each club has $3,000 to invest.
- The club sold 300 shares at $10 each to members to raise the money that they will invest.
- They may buy any of six stocks. They must buy at least three stocks, but they may divide their money among all six stocks if they wish to do so.
- They must invest the entire $3,000.
- They must fill out the chart at the end of Activity 1. The investment value must be $3,000 (total of the last column). The price per share will be $10 ($3,000 / 300).

6. Give the groups about 15 minutes to make their investment decisions and fill out the charts. Be sure to check their math because the rest of the activity will not work unless their math is correct.

7. **Distribute a copy of Activity 2** to each student. Explain that it is now one year later. The value of the shares of stock they could have bought has changed. Column 2 of Activity 2 shows the new per-share price of the stocks. How well did their selected stocks perform?

8. **Display Visual 1** as an example of how the chart should be completed. Make sure the students understand that this is an example; their charts will differ depending on which stocks they purchased and how many shares they purchased.

9. Ask the groups to complete their charts and check the math. The amount invested will still be $3,000, and the number of shares of stock owned will be the same as in Activity 1. The price of the stocks and the investment value of the fund will have changed.

10. Ask questions about what happened to the clubs' investments:

A. Did the price per share of the investment club increase or decrease?
Answers will vary.

B. What determined whether the price per share of the investment club increased or decreased?
The investment value one year later, which is determined by the price of the stocks purchased.

C. If you had a real investment club and bought stocks, what would increase the value of the investments one year later?
Choosing stocks that increase in price or pay high dividends.

D. Assume that more students want to join your investment club and purchase shares. What price would you charge them? Why?
The price per share one year later or the price per share on the day they want to buy shares. At that price, they buy shares equal to what the shares are worth on that day.

11. Explain that mutual funds work like their investment clubs — but with more investors. In a mutual fund:

A. The price per share changes every day and depends on the value of the investments.

B. The value of the investments depends on the performance of the assets chosen by the fund manager. Unlike members of an investment club, mutual fund investors do not decide which stocks or bonds the fund will buy or sell. The fund manager does that.

C. A mutual fund charges investors for the financial management it provides. The investor may also pay brokers' fees and other costs. These costs are deducted from the value of the investments. The lower these costs, the higher the investors' returns from a set of holdings.

D. Some mutual funds charge a sales commission called a load. The higher the load, the less the actual investment made on behalf of the investor. Lower loads are better for investors, other things being equal.

12. **Distribute a copy of Activity 3** to each student. The students should read it and answer the questions at the end.

13. **Display Visual 2**. Make the point that mutual funds are not all the same. They have different investment objectives. Some mutual funds come with greater risks than others. Some offer greater potential rewards.

14. Discuss the answers to the questions at the end of Activity 3:

A. What is a mutual fund?
A pool of money used by an investment company to buy a variety of stocks and bonds.

B. A friend tells you, "All mutual funds are the same." How do you reply to your friend?
Your friend is wrong. Mutual funds have different investment objectives and buy different stocks and bonds. Different funds have different managers and different styles.

C. What is an advantage of buying a load fund? What is a disadvantage?
Advantage: A salesperson or investment advisor provides help in choosing a fund. Disadvantage: A load fund costs more because the investor must pay a sales commission.

D. What is an advantage of buying a no-load fund? What is a disadvantage?
Advantage: There is no sales commission, and therefore the cost is less. Disadvantage: The investor must select the fund without advice from a fund representative. The investor must do his or her own research.

E. What should you consider when deciding which mutual fund to buy?
Performance, cost and convenience. Have the students elaborate on these considerations.

F. More Americans own mutual funds than individual stocks and bonds. Why do you think this is so?
Mutual funds provide diversification, professional management and ease of buying and selling. It is safer to have money invested in 200 stocks or bonds than in only a few; investors spread the risk.

G. If your class participates in a stock market simulation that allows you to buy mutual funds, what type of fund should you buy? Why?
Because stock market simulations are for a short time period, you would probably buy a high-risk, high-reward fund.

H. What are the advantages and disadvantages of buying index mutual funds rather than actively managed funds?
Index funds provide more diversification and lower management fees. Index funds are designed to provide returns similar to returns from an unmanaged market index. Actively managed funds can provide higher returns although studies show most actively managed funds have under-performed index funds.

I. If you want to buy a mutual fund so you will have money to buy a house 10 years from now, what type of fund should you buy? Why?
You would buy a fund that you think would increase the most in value over the 10 years; you would look for funds with consistently good long-term records.

Closure

1. Tell the students that every mutual fund must provide potential investors with a prospectus. Tell them that they will now apply their knowledge by reading some statements from a prospectus.

2. **Distribute a copy of Activity 4** to each student. Have the students read the activity and answer the questions.

3. Discuss the answers:

A. You worry a lot about the stock market and want to limit the risk of losing your money. Would you buy this fund?
No. It is an aggressive growth fund specializing in small companies.

B. Does this fund charge a sales commission? *No.*

C. Is it good or bad that this fund charges no 12b-1 fees?
It is good. Some funds charge up to an additional 1.25 percent, which is used to advertise the fund.

D. How much does this fund charge in fees?
.91 percent

E. In your opinion, how does the fund's past performance look?
It did well last year, losing less money than most indexes, which are averages of groups of stocks or funds. During the 10-year period, it beat all averages. A fund should compare its performance not only to the general market but to indexes that track stocks it buys and other similar stocks. The Russell 2000 is a small-company index, and the Lipper index is for funds specializing in small stocks.

F. Does this mean the fund will perform well in the future?
Not necessarily. Past performance does not guarantee future performance. Nevertheless, the fund's track record is good. A prospective investor should check to see if the fund's investment manager has changed.

Assessment

Multiple-Choice Questions

1. A mutual fund without a sales charge is called
   a. a load fund.
   b. a no-load fund.
   c. a 12b-1 fund.
   d. an aggressive growth fund.

2. Which of the following statements about mutual funds is true?
   a. All mutual funds are the same.
   b. Mutual funds allow investors to spread risk among several stocks and bonds.
   c. Load funds do not charge a sales commission but invest in lower-quality stocks.
   d. Many mutual funds do not charge management fees.

3. A 12b-1 fee is a
   a. sales commission.
   b. management fee.
   c. fee to pay for fund advertising.
   d. fee to pay the fund's brokerage commissions.

4. The price per share that you can buy a fund for is called the
   a. net asset value.
   b. management fee.
   c. load.
   d. 12b-1 charge.

Essay Questions

1. Which factors should an investor consider before purchasing a mutual fund?
Students should discuss performance, cost, goals and convenience.

2. Your grandparents gave you $1,000 to help pay for your college education. You will graduate from high school in four years. What type of mutual fund should you buy?
Although answers will vary, students should evaluate risk and reward. Since four years is a short time to save the $1,000, students might argue that lower-risk sorts of mutual funds such as a bond fund or an income fund might be appropriate, but much will depend on each student's tolerance for risk and other circumstances.

LESSON 7 VISUAL 1

ONE YEAR LATER: AN EXAMPLE

This is an example of what might have happened to a class investment club's shares of stock.

Company	Price per Share	No. of Shares Owned	Amount Invested	Investment Value 1 Year Later
American Cellular	$ 8	100	$ 500	$ 800
Big Box Stores	$23	50	$1,000	$1,150
Biotech Industries	$ 8	0	0	$ 0
General Grocery	$22	0	0	$ 0
Giant Auto	$11	100	$1,000	$1,100
Gold Mining Group	$ 4	100	$ 500	$ 400
Total Investment Value (add last column)			$3,000	$3,450

Number of Shares 300 *Price per share $11.50

**The price per share is the total investment value (one year later) divided by the number of shares.*

Lesson 7 Visual 2

Types of Mutual Funds

Low Risk and Low Potential Reward				**High Risk and High Potential Reward**
Money-market funds (short-term securities)	Bond funds (corporate or longer-term government bonds)	Income funds (high-yield stocks and bonds)	Growth funds (larger company stocks; long-term capital gains)	Aggressive growth funds (smaller company stocks; short- and long-term capital gains)

Lesson 7 Activity 1

Class Investment Clubs

The members of your class have decided to form investment clubs. Class members may buy as many shares in a club as they like, for $10 per share. Each club sold 300 shares and collected $3,000. Now it's time to invest the money.

Your club held its first meeting and decided to invest in stocks. The club members proposed different stocks to buy. Here is a rundown on the stocks proposed.

1. **American Cellular, $5 per share**
   This is a new cellular company that features high-tech services such as phones that send streaming video. So far, the company has not made a profit but expects to do very well soon.
2. **Big Box Stores, $20 per share**
   Big Box Stores is one of the leading discount retailers in the country. Same-store sales have increased steadily in each of the last five years.
3. **Biotech Industries, $10 per share**
   Biotech Industries is a pharmaceutical company that specializes in developing cutting-edge drugs. It has some profitable products, but so far its profits are small.
4. **General Grocery, $20 per share**
   This is a leading grocery store chain. Sales are generally steady and do not change much with the economy's ups and downs. However, some experts predict that the growing trend toward eating out in restaurants will hurt future sales.
5. **Giant Auto, $10 per share**
   Giant Auto is one of the three leading automobile manufacturers in the world. The company's profits depend on economic conditions. Profits are high in times of strong economic growth and poor in bad times or recessions.
6. **Gold Mining Group, $5 per share**
   GMG is a gold-mining company. The price of gold often rises in bad times or recessions and falls in good times.

Your club decided to invest all 300 shares or $3,000 in at least three of these companies. Decide how to invest the money, and record your investments on the following worksheet.

Company	Price per Share	No. of Shares Owned	Amount Invested
American Cellular			
Big Box Stores			
Biotech Industries			
General Grocery			
Giant Auto			
Gold Mining Group			
Total Investment Value (add last column)			

Number of Shares <u>300</u> ***Price per Share <u>$10</u>**

**The price per share is the amount invested divided by the number of shares.*

LESSON 7 ACTIVITY 2

A CLASS INVESTMENT CLUB ONE YEAR LATER

One year later the prices of your investments have changed. The price per share of each investment is listed in the chart below.

Complete the chart to determine how well your investment club did. The value of your investment depends on the companies in which you invested.

Company	Price per Share	No. of Shares Owned	Amount Invested	Investment Value 1 Year Later
American Cellular	$ 8			
Big Box Stores	$23			
Biotech Industries	$ 8			
General Grocery	$22			
Giant Auto	$11			
Gold Mining Group	$ 4			
Total Investment Value (add last column)				

Number of Shares 300 *Price per share ______

**The price per share is the total investment value (one year later) divided by the number of shares.*

LESSON 7 ACTIVITY 3

MUTUAL FUND FACTS

A mutual fund is a pool of money similar to the money collected by a class investment club. A fund manager decides how to invest the money, with the goal of increasing the value of each share of the fund for the investors. That will happen only if the value of the investments chosen by the fund manager increases.

Investors may buy shares of open-end mutual funds each business day for the net asset value (NAV in the newspaper listing), the investment value of each share. The net asset value is calculated each day by dividing the total value of the investments by the number of shares. This is how you calculated the value of the shares of your investment club. You may also sell your shares in an open-end mutual fund any business day and receive the NAV.

There were about 6,000 mutual funds in early 2003. More Americans invest through mutual funds than by any other investment method. There are stock mutual funds, bond mutual funds, stock and bond mutual funds and money-market funds. There are mutual funds that specialize in almost any type of stock or bond. Some mutual funds which are called index funds buy the stocks that allow investors' returns to match a particular index. Index funds can provide more diversification than actively managed funds. In addition, the management fee (discussed later) should be lower because the fund manager does not have to research which stocks to buy and sell. For this reason, many experts advise buying a fund that tracks a broad market index if only one fund is bought. Some funds buy high-risk investments and some buy low-risk investments. How can you choose the right fund? Here are some factors to consider.

1. Performance. Buy mutual funds that you believe will perform well. Performance is the most important factor to consider. However, your consideration of performance must be tempered by how much risk you are willing to take. A mutual fund prospectus lists the stocks or bonds a fund owns and provides information on the fund's performance. However, past performance does not guarantee that the fund will do as well in the future. The fund manager is a key to performance. It is a good thing if the fund manager has had favorable results and has worked for the fund for a significant period of time.

2. Cost. A mutual fund company makes money by charging investors various fees. These fees are a cost to investors. The lower the costs, the better it is for investors — as long as performance is good. Here are some typical costs of mutual funds:

- Some funds charge a load. A load is a sales commission. It is usually a percentage of the price and can be as high as 8 percent. A front-end load is paid when you buy shares, and a back-end load is paid when you sell shares. A no-load fund does not charge a sales commission. If you need help in choosing a fund, you might consider paying an investment advisor a load or commission for advice. If you do not need help, choose a no-load fund.
- All funds charge a management fee and have expenses. The lower the management fee and the expenses, the better it is for investors.
- Some mutual funds charge a 12b-1 fee. This fee, which can be as high as 1.25 percent of the fund's value, is used by the company to advertise the fund to the public. Unless the fund has great performance, avoid funds with 12b-1 fees.

3. Convenience. A fund that provides good service is very helpful to investors. Are the statements easy to read? Are the fund's telephone representatives knowledgeable and helpful? Is it easy to make additional investments in the fund? Can you buy small amounts of the fund? Can you exchange shares in the fund for shares in another of the company's funds? Some fund families have dozens of different funds for different investment objectives.

Lesson 7 Activity 3 (continued)

Advantages of Investing in Mutual Funds

Why buy a mutual fund? After all, you can buy stocks and bonds directly. Mutual funds have several advantages over buying individual stocks and bonds. These advantages can make the extra costs worthwhile.

1. Professional management. A professional money manager chooses your stocks. The performance of your investment club depended on which stocks you bought. A professional manager might be able to do this better than you can. If you don't think this is true, you can buy an index fund. An index fund follows a stock average such as the Dow-Jones Industrial Average. You get average performance. Over the years, a majority of actively managed funds have failed to beat average performance.

2. Diversification. Diversification means you spend your money on several stocks and bonds rather than just a few. If one or two stocks or bonds in your mutual fund decrease sharply in value, your loss will be less than if you own only a few stocks or bonds. If a class investment club bought only one stock, it could have a greater loss or greater gain than if the club bought several stocks. Your risk is greater the fewer stocks you buy. A mutual fund may own 500 different stocks.

3. Liquidity. Liquidity means you can turn your investment into cash easily. You can sell a mutual fund at the net asset value (NAV) on any business day. Of course, you may need to sell the fund for less per share than what you paid for it, and lose money.

4. Investment objective. There is a mutual fund for almost any objective or goal. When you determine your goals and the risks you are willing to take, you can probably find a mutual fund that matches them.

LESSON 7 ACTIVITY 3 (CONTINUED)

QUESTIONS FOR DISCUSSION

A. What is a mutual fund?

B. A friend tells you, "All mutual funds are the same." How do you reply to your friend?

C. What is an advantage of buying a load fund? What is a disadvantage?

D. What is an advantage of buying a no-load fund? What is a disadvantage?

E. What should you consider when deciding which mutual fund to buy?

F. More Americans own mutual funds than individual stocks and bonds. Why do you think this is so?

G. If your class participates in a stock market simulation that allows you to buy mutual funds, what type of fund should you buy? Why?

H. What are the advantages and disadvantages of buying index mutual funds rather than actively managed funds?

I. If you want to buy a mutual fund so you will have money to buy a house 10 years from now, what type of fund should you buy? Why?

Lesson 7 Activity 4

A Mutual Fund Prospectus

All mutual funds must supply potential investors with a prospectus that provides information including the investment objectives, investment strategy, past performance, costs and other charges. Below are some excerpts from a fund's prospectus. See if you can interpret what the excerpts mean.

- The fund is an aggressive stock fund seeking long-term capital growth primarily through investments in small, rapidly growing companies.
- Investing in smaller companies generally involves greater risk than investing in larger companies. Stocks of small companies are subject to more abrupt or erratic price movements than the stocks of larger companies.
- The fund is 100 percent no-load. There are no 12b-1 fees.
- The fund's annual management fee and other expenses are .91 percent. These expenses are deducted from the fund's assets.
- The table below summarizes the fund's average annual returns for one year, five years and 10 years.

Average Annual Total Returns

The Fund	1 year	5 years	10 years
Returns before taxes	-2.84%	8.07%	13.75%
Returns after taxes on distributions	-3.33	6.37	11.03
Returns after taxes on distributions and sale of fund shares	-1.30	6.27	10.56
Russell 2000 Growth Index	-9.23	2.87	7.19
Russell 2000 Index	2.49	7.52	11.51
S&P 500 Stock Index	-11.89	10.70	12.94
Lipper Small-Cap Fund Index	-9.32	6.45	10.29

Lesson 7 Activity 4 (continued)

Questions

A. You worry a lot about the stock market and want to limit the risk of losing your money. Would you buy this fund?

B. Does this fund charge a sales commission?

C. Is it good or bad that this fund charges no 12b-1 fees?

D. How much does this fund charge in fees?

E. In your opinion, how does the fund's past performance look?

F. Does this mean the fund will perform well in the future?

Lesson 8 How to Buy and Sell Stocks and Bonds

Middle School

Lesson 8 How to Buy and Sell Stocks and Bonds

Lesson Description

In this lesson the students learn about the financial markets in which stocks and bonds are bought and sold. They read about the high transaction costs that individual investors would experience if there were no financial markets. They perform a play that illustrates how an individual stock transaction is made in an organized financial market. Finally, the students discuss the options available for buying and selling stocks and bonds.

Financial markets bring buyers and sellers of stocks and bonds together. These markets provide information about available trading partners and competitive prices. Today, investors have several alternative ways of buying and selling in financial markets.

Concepts

- Bond
- Broker
- Dividend reinvestment plan (DRIP)
- Financial markets
- Investor
- Stocks

Objectives

Students will:

1. Explain how financial markets help investors.
2. Describe how a transaction is made in an organized stock market such as the New York Stock Exchange.
3. Evaluate options available to investors for buying and selling stocks and bonds.

Time Required

45 minutes

Materials

- A transparency of Visual 1
- A copy of Activity 1 for each student
- A copy of Activity 2 for each of the 8 actors in the play
- Optional: Props for the play (newspaper, 4 telephones, 2 order forms and 4 computers)

Procedure

1. Tell the students that they are going to learn how investors buy and sell stocks and bonds. Stocks and bonds are bought and sold in financial markets. For example, at the New York Stock Exchange (NYSE), the oldest and largest stock exchange in the United States, about a billion shares of stock are traded each day. In the United States, about half of the publicly traded stocks are listed on exchanges such as the NYSE or other exchanges with a physical location. The other half are traded through a network of brokers throughout the country. This network is referred to as the over-the-counter (OTC) market. Bonds normally trade on the OTC market. Individuals who want to buy or sell stocks or bonds use the services of brokers to trade their securities in these markets.

2. Tell the students that without financial markets individuals would find it very difficult to trade their stocks and bonds. **Distribute a copy of Activity 1** to each student. After allowing time for reading, ***ask:*** How do financial markets help sellers like Veronica and buyers like Ron? *These markets reduce the costs of trading for sellers like Veronica and buyers like Ron. Markets provide information about potential trading partners and supply more than one buyer or seller so that competition can establish a price satisfactory to both parties in the transaction.*

3. Tell the students that they will act out a play; the play shows how an actual stock market trade is made. Select students to play the following roles: Moderator, Veronica Vargas, Veronica's Stockbroker, Ron Rosenthal, Ron's Stockbroker, two Order Room Clerks and the Johnson & Johnson Specialist. Give each actor a copy of the play (Activity 2). Set the stage in five areas from left to right: one area each for Veronica, Veronica's stockbroker, the Johnson & Johnson trading post, Ron's stockbroker and Ron. In Veronica's area and Ron's area, place a chair and a telephone. In each stockbroker's area, place a chair and computer for the stockbroker and, a short distance away, a chair and computer for the order room clerk. At the Johnson & Johnson trading post, place a chair and a computer for the specialist. Have the students perform the play.

4. When the play ends, tell the students that consumers today have a number of options for buying stocks and bonds. **Display Visual 1.** Tell the students that in the play, Ron Rosenthal's broker was a full-service broker. He advised Ron on what stock to buy. Ron told the broker about his investment objectives — he wanted a stock that was relatively safe and stable — and the broker suggested a stock that met those objectives. The broker had access to the invest-

ment research done by the research department of the firm. Investors who use a full-service brokerage firm usually can get copies of the firm's research reports. Also, full-service brokerage firms usually have other financial products for sale, such as various types of bonds. These brokerage firms charge a commission on every purchase or sale.

Veronica Vargas may have used either a full-service broker or a discount broker. Discount brokers take buy and sell orders from customers, but they provide little or no investment advice. Consequently, discount brokerage firms do not maintain research departments. Compared to full-service brokers, discount firms charge a lower commission for each transaction they make. Many firms charge a flat fee for making a transaction, rather than a percentage of the value of the stock.

When the Internet emerged, buyers gained a new option for buying stocks and bonds. Many discount brokers have now opened online offices. Commissions on these transactions are even lower than the charges of a conventional discount broker, since the transaction can now be made without directly involving a broker.

Many large companies offer dividend reinvestment plans, called DRIPs. A stockholder can choose to take his or her dividends in the form of shares of the company's stock rather than receive a dividend check. Shares of stock can be acquired in this way without paying a commission, although the shares will be taxed, just as a dividend check would be.

5. ***Ask:*** What kind of investor would benefit most from dealing with a full-service broker?
Someone who is not very knowledgeable about what stocks to buy and does not want to take the time to research individual stocks.

Closure

1. To review the lesson, ***ask:***

- What is the New York Stock Exchange?
  The New York Stock Exchange is the oldest and largest stock exchange in the world.
- Less than half of all stocks are traded on exchanges like the New York Stock Exchange. How are the rest traded?
  The other stocks are traded on the over-the-counter market, which is a network of brokers rather than a physical location.
- What role do brokers play in buying and selling stocks?
  Brokers assist their clients in making transactions in organized financial markets. Brokers charge fees for providing their services. Full-service brokers provide investment advice.
- What are DRIPS? What is the advantage of a DRIPS program?
  DRIPS stands for dividend reinvestment plans. Some large companies offer these plans. They allow shareholders to receive dividends in the form of company stock rather than cash. This allows shareholders to acquire more stock without paying broker fees.

2. Tell the students to imagine that they have money they would like to invest in stocks or bonds. Ask each student to write one or two paragraphs telling what method he or she would use to make the investment, and to give reasons for his or her decision.

Assessment

Multiple-Choice Questions

1. An order to buy or sell a stock at the market means to buy or sell the stock
   a. at an organized financial market, such as the New York Stock Exchange.
   b. as long as the price does not exceed a certain limit.
   c. at whatever price is currently set by the market.
   d. in the over-the-counter market.

2. The over-the-counter market
   a. handles about half of publicly traded stocks.
   b. only handles bonds.
   c. is located in Chicago, Illinois.
   d. can be used directly to buy or sell stocks or bonds by any investor who has access to the Internet.

3. In stock market trading, a specialist in McDonald's stock is
   a. an investor who only owns McDonald's stock.
   b. a McDonald's employee responsible for issuing shares of McDonald's stock.
   c. a broker on the floor of a stock exchange who matches buy and sell orders for McDonald's stock.
   d. any broker who buys or sells McDonald's stock for clients.

4. What does a full-service broker do that a discount broker does not do?
   a. Makes transactions in organized financial markets
   b. Charges a commission
   c. Makes transactions in the over-the-counter market
   d. Gives investment advice

8 How to Buy and Sell Stocks and Bonds

Essay Questions

1. How do financial markets like stock exchanges and the over-the-counter market help investors?
Such markets help buyers and sellers locate other buyers and sellers who want to exchange with them. By providing competition, markets establish prices that are satisfactory to both buyers and sellers.

2. Explain the advantages and disadvantages of using a full-service broker to buy stocks and bonds.
Full-service brokers provide information and advice, saving the investor the time needed to acquire expertise in selecting investments. However, the investor must pay higher commissions than those paid to a discount broker to obtain these services.

LESSON 8 VISUAL 1

WHERE TO BUY STOCKS AND BONDS

Full-service brokerage firms:

- Give investment advice
- Offer a wide variety of financial products and services
- Charge higher commissions

Discount brokerage firms:

- Do not give investment advice
- Offer a limited number of financial products and services
- Charge lower commissions

Buying online:

- Buyers pay lower commissions
- Buyers can more easily compare brokerage services

Dividend reinvestment plans (DRIPS):

- Many large companies offer DRIPs
- Stockholders are paid dividends in the form of stock
- No commission fee is charged

Lesson 8 Activity 1

How to Buy and Sell Stocks and Bonds

What Would We Do Without Stock Markets?

A market brings people who have something to sell together with people who want to buy. People who have pumpkins to sell need to connect with people who want to buy pumpkins. Buyers of automobiles have to get together with sellers of automobiles. A market is not always one physical location; it's any kind of organization or arrangement that makes it easier for buyers and sellers to contact each other.

People who want to buy and sell stock find ways to use organized stock markets. These are places where buyers and sellers meet to trade securities or where buyers and sellers trade securities through electronic networks.

The New York Stock Exchange (NYSE) and the American Stock Exchange (AMEX) are places where stocks are bought and sold at a physical location. Only members of these exchanges may buy and sell stock for the public. The members and the corporations listed on the exchange must follow certain rules. The NYSE is the oldest, largest and most prestigious of these markets. About 2,800 companies trade on the NYSE.

Increasingly, people trade stocks over sophisticated electronic networks known as the over-the-counter market (OTC). The NASDAQ Stock Market is the world's largest electronic network. It lists approximately 3,700 companies and trades more shares per day than any other U.S. equity market. Like the NYSE, AMEX and other exchanges, NASDAQ-listed companies must meet certain requirements.

Imagine a stockholder — let's call her Veronica Vargas — who owns 100 shares of Johnson & Johnson stock. (Johnson & Johnson is a company that makes baby powder and many other products.) Veronica has owned these shares for several years, but now she wants to sell them to get cash that she'll apply toward a down payment on a house.

Since we are imagining that there are no stock markets, Veronica has to find a buyer herself. She also has to figure out how much to charge for her shares, since she can't look the price up in the stock market pages of her local newspaper. First she calls her Aunt Elida, who is quite well off, but Aunt Elida isn't interested. Then she tries her next-door neighbor. He is interested, but he will pay only $20 per share, and Veronica is sure that the stock is worth more than that.

Meanwhile, just a few blocks from where Veronica lives, Ron Rosenthal would love to buy some Johnson & Johnson stock. He has money to invest, and he considers Johnson & Johnson to be a highly profitable company. He'd be willing to pay at least $60 a share. But he doesn't know Veronica, and he has no idea that she has Johnson & Johnson stock to sell. In fact, he doesn't know anyone who owns Johnson & Johnson stock.

Question for Discussion

How do financial markets help sellers like Veronica and buyers like Ron?

LESSON 8 ACTIVITY 2

THE STOCK MARKET PLAY

Cast of Characters: Moderator, Veronica Vargas, Veronica's Stockbroker, Ron Rosenthal, Ron's Stockbroker, Two Order Room Clerks, Johnson & Johnson Specialist

Props: Newspaper for Veronica; telephones for Veronica, Ron and the two Stockbrokers; order forms for the two Stockbrokers; computers for Veronica's Stockbroker, the two Order Room Clerks and the Johnson & Johnson Specialist

Moderator: Most individuals buy stocks and bonds through brokerage firms. These firms are members of exchanges that trade stocks or bonds at physical locations like the New York Stock Exchange or through computer networks such as the NASDAQ. Let's see how Veronica Vargas, who has 100 shares of Johnson & Johnson to sell, makes a connection with Ron Rosenthal, who wants to buy 100 shares of Johnson & Johnson.

Veronica: *(Reading the financial pages of a newspaper)* The price of Johnson & Johnson looks good. Yesterday it closed at $59.75. If I sell 100 shares now, I can combine it with my savings at the bank and have enough money to make a down payment on a house. I'm going to call my stockbroker and find out what the stock is selling for right now. *(Enters the number on telephone)* Hello, Stockbroker? Would you please tell me the current price of Johnson & Johnson?

Veronica's Stockbroker: *(Answering the telephone)* Certainly, Ms. Vargas. Let me check for you. *(Looks at computer)* The last sale of Johnson & Johnson was $60.

Veronica: Great! Please sell 100 shares for me.

Veronica's Stockbroker: Do you want to sell at the market or do you want me to enter a limit order?

Moderator: An order to buy or sell at the market tells the broker to take the best price being offered on the trading floor of the New York Stock Exchange. A limit order tells the broker to buy or sell at a given or better price.

Veronica: Sell it at the market.

Veronica's Stockbroker: I should be able to confirm the sale right away. I'll call you back in a few minutes.

Moderator: Meanwhile, Ron Rosenthal has decided that he has more cash than he needs in his money-market savings account. It's good to have some cash for emergencies, but money in the stock market is likely to earn a higher rate of return in the long run.

Ron: *(Enters the number on telephone)* Hello, Stockbroker. I'm interested in buying shares of a company that's stable and will grow in the future. I have about $6,000 to invest. Can you give me a recommendation?

Ron's Stockbroker: Well, one good idea is Johnson & Johnson, which is selling right now for about $60 a share. This company has been around a long time and it sells products that consumers buy in good times and bad.

Ron: That sounds like just what I want. Please buy 100 shares for me.

Ron's Stockbroker: Do you want to buy at the market price or should I enter a limit order?

Ron: Buy it as long as the price is $61 or less.

Lesson 8 Activity 2 (continued)

The Stock Market Play

Ron's Stockbroker: All right. I'll call you back as soon as the order goes through.

(Both brokers begin to write on forms.)

Moderator: Veronica's stockbroker fills out an order to sell 100 shares of Johnson & Johnson and takes it to the firm's order room. At the same time, Ron's stockbroker fills out an order to buy 100 shares of Johnson & Johnson and takes it to the firm's order room.

(Both brokers take the forms they have filled in to their respective order rooms.)

Veronica's Stockbroker: *(To the order room clerk)* Please make this trade.

Order Room Clerk: Johnson & Johnson trades on the New York Stock Exchange. I'll send this order on the electronic brokerage system to the Johnson & Johnson specialist.

Ron's Stockbroker: *(To the firm's order room clerk)* Please send this order to the Johnson & Johnson specialist.

(Both order room clerks type on their computers.)

Moderator: Stock exchanges have various locations, called trading posts, where different stocks are traded. Each post has a specialist assigned to it. One of the jobs of a specialist is to match buy and sell orders at current market prices. The specialist in Johnson & Johnson sees Veronica's and Ron's orders on the electronic workstation.

Specialist: I see that I have an order to sell 100 shares of Johnson & Johnson and also an order to buy 100 shares of the same stock. The last sale of Johnson & Johnson was at 60 and 20 cents. I'll make that transaction and send confirmation to both brokers. *(Types on computer keyboard)*

Moderator: Large trades are usually made by representatives of member firms called floor brokers. Floor brokers go to the specialist's post to bargain, but small purchases and sales go directly to the specialist's computer.

Veronica's Stockbroker: *(Enters the number on telephone)* Hello, Ms. Vargas?

Veronica: *(On the telephone)* Yes.

Veronica's Stockbroker: I've just received confirmation of your sale at $60.20. I'll send you a confirmation of the sale and a check for $6,020, less my broker's commission.

Veronica: That's wonderful. I can start shopping for a house now.

Ron's Stockbroker: *(Enters the number on phone.)* Hello, Mr. Rosenthal. This is your stockbroker. We bought 100 shares of Johnson & Johnson for you at $60.20. I'll get confirmation in the mail to you today. You'll need to pay us $6,020, plus my broker's commission.

Ron: That's great. I'm sure I've made a wise investment. I'll send you a check immediately.

Lesson 9 What is a Stock Market?

Middle School

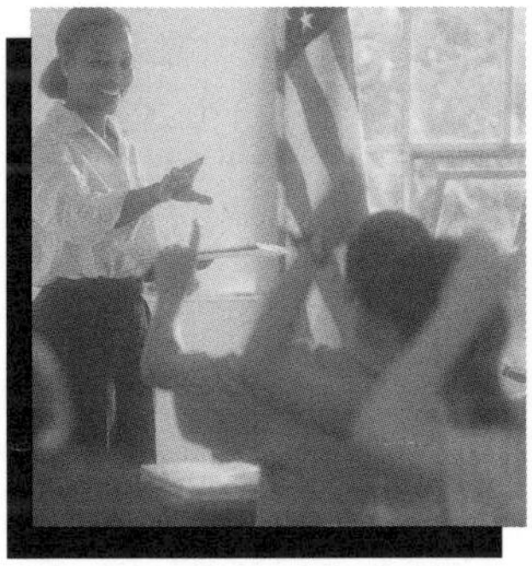

Lesson 9 What Is a Stock Market?

Lesson Description

The students are introduced to the key characteristics of a market economy through a brief simulation and a discussion of several examples drawn from their own experiences. Then they learn about differences among the three major stock markets in the United States and place sample stocks in each of the three markets using this knowledge.

Throughout history societies have faced the fundamental economic questions of what to produce and for whom to produce it in a world of limited resources. In the second half of the twentieth century, two very different economic systems evolved in response to these questions. Command economies are directed by a centralized government and characterized by limited choices on the part of buyers and sellers. Market economies are based on private enterprise and consumer and producer choice.

For many people, the word *market* may be closely associated with an image of a place — perhaps a local farmer's market. For economists, however, *market* need not refer to a physical place. Instead, a market may be constituted by any organization that allows buyers and sellers to communicate about and arrange for the exchange of goods, services or resources. Stock markets provide a mechanism whereby people who want to own shares of stock can buy from people who want to sell shares of stock.

The three major stock markets in the United States are the New York Stock Exchange (NYSE), the American Stock Exchange (AMEX) and the NASDAQ Stock Market. Although these markets differ from one another, especially in the kinds of stock traded and the mechanisms used for trading, all three are known as secondary markets. They are different from a primary market in which the company sells shares and receives money in an initial public offering (IPO).

Concepts

- Characteristics of a market
- Market
- Primary market
- Secondary market
- Stock market

Objectives

Students will:

1. List and describe the key characteristics of a market economy.
2. Describe the stock market as an example of a market.
3. Differentiate among the three major stock markets and predict on which market certain stocks might be listed.

Time Required

45 - 60 minutes

Materials

- 2 candy bars
- A transparency of Visuals 1 and 2
- A copy of Activity 1, 2 and 3 for each student
- 6-8 newspapers with recent stock market reports (e.g., *USA Today, The Wall Street Journal*)

Procedure

1. Display two candy bars. ***Ask:*** How many students would like to have one of the candy bars. Then ***ask:*** What problem has developed?
Scarcity condition: not enough candy bars to go around.

2. Tell the students that this situation is one faced by every society: how to allocate scarce resources among unlimited wants. ***Ask*** the students to suggest ways in which you might divide the two candy bars among the class; also ask them to identify problems associated with each method.
Teacher decides (not all students have an equal chance for a candy bar); cut each candy bar into 15 pieces (pieces now too small to satisfy students); hold a raffle (not all students have an equal chance for the candy bar); throw the candy bars into the middle of the room and let students grapple for them (too dangerous); sell the candy bars to the highest bidder (students with no money cannot get a candy bar)

3. Discuss the candy-bar example as it relates more generally to our economic system. How do we answer the basic question about allocating scarce resources?
Resources are sold to those willing to pay market prices for goods and services.

4. Tell the students that today they will look more closely at markets in general and at the stock market in particular.

5. Ask the students to list several markets they have participated in over the last week.
Examples might include farmer's market, supermarket, retail clothing market and gasoline market.

6. Ask the students to name the characteristics these markets share; list these characteristics on the board. Then **display Visual 1**. Make the following points for each characteristic:

- *Private property.* Markets depend on an individual's ability to own and sell property. In market transactions, people can choose to sell property to others and transfer the right of ownership with the sale.
- *Self interest.* Markets are based on individual, self-interested behavior. When a transaction occurs, both parties believe they will benefit.
- *Competition.* Markets foster competition because they allow the entry of many producers striving to meet the demands of consumers. Competition pressures these firms to satisfy consumer demand or be forced from the market by firms who can.
- *The profit motive.* Profits act as incentives for firms. Those firms that satisfy consumer desires and produce efficiently are rewarded with profits.
- *Voluntary exchange.* Because consumers have choices in a market, all exchanges are voluntary. This allows consumers and producers to focus on what they do best and to trade surplus production or wealth. Markets encourage trade and thus create wealth.
- *Limited role of government.* In a command economy, the government is the primary economic decision maker, producing or directing the production of goods and services. In a market economy, government's role is limited to protecting the integrity of the market by enforcing property rights and correcting market failures.

7. **Distribute a copy of Activity 1** to each student. Have the students read the introductory passage and then complete "Market or Not?" Discuss the students' answers.
Answers: 1 M (Car market is very competitive, with lots of advertising, etc.; dealership motivated by profit; dealer transfers ownership to consumer upon purchase); 2 NM (No competition; government provides this good; the day pass is a user fee paid to the U.S. government that provides this service; government not motivated by profit; ownership of Yellowstone cannot be transferred to visitors); 3 NM (Government provides this service; consumers must register vehicle if they wish to drive); 4 M (New carrier provides competition, gives consumers choice; Web site presents information for consumers; consumers look to get the best phone deal they can); 5 M (People are acting in their own interest; doughnut chain provides competition to other fast-food outlets); 6 NM (Government provides this good; not motivated by profit; no competition)

8. **Distribute a copy of Activity 2.** Have the students read the paragraph and complete the data-retrieval chart.
Suggested responses:

	You	***Straight-as-an-Arrow Records (Britainia Arrows' record company)***
Private property	*Once you purchase the CD, no one can take it from you without your permission; you are allowed to make copies for your personal use.*	*Holds the copyright on the music on the CD. Copyright means that only those who have purchased the CD can use it or copy it.*
Competition		*Britainia's record company knows that pop music is one of the most highly competitive businesses.*
Profit motive		*Straight-as-an-Arrow produces music for one reason – to sell it to consumers. The more the company satisfies its consumers, the more CDs it sells.*
Self-interest	*You want to get the most pleasure out of your listening experience, and you may also want to impress your friends by having the latest, most popular CDs.*	*Straight-as-an-Arrow produces acts that it believes will earn money. If it didn't think Britainia's CD would top the charts, it would not produce it.*
Voluntary exchange	*You would not buy the CD unless you believed you would like it.*	*Straight-as-an-Arrow may specialize in one type of music (e.g., pop, rap, etc.) or in one artist (e.g., Britainia).*
Limited role of government	*Little role for government beyond urging disclosure of offensive lyrics.*	Enforce copyrights held by Straight-as-an-Arrow.

9. Tell the students that they will now learn where they can go to buy stocks: the stock market. Ask the students where they go to buy DVDs or jeans or books. *Music or media store; department store or jeans shop; bookstore.* Explain that, just as with CDs, jeans and books, there is a market for stocks.

10. Tell the students that a stock is a share of ownership in a company and that people buy stocks for two main reasons: (1) they expect to share in company profits (called dividends) paid out to shareholders, or (2) they believe the price of the stock will rise above the purchase price.

11. Ask the students if they have ever seen a stock store at the mall. Where can you go to buy stocks? Explain that almost all stock sales and purchases — often called stock trades — are handled by a specialized salesperson called a broker. In addition, almost all stocks are sold by these brokers in secondary markets.

12. **Display Visual 2.** Explain that companies such as Company X often need additional resources to expand or run their business. One way to generate these resources is to offer all, or a portion, of the company for sale to the public-at-large ("take a company public"). This is done in the primary market through an initial public offering (IPO) in which stocks are sold to large investment banks. Investment bankers then sell the shares to brokerage houses, and brokers offer the shares for sale on the secondary market through one of the major stock exchanges: the New York Stock Exchange, the American Stock Exchange or the NASDAQ Stock Market.

13. **Distribute a copy of Activity 3** to each student. Have the students read the introduction. Briefly review the overview of market mechanics, using Visual 2 as appropriate.

14. Have the students read the descriptions of the three major stock markets. Call on students to identify the distinctive characteristics of each of the three markets; record their responses on the board or an overhead. Sample responses:

NYSE	AMEX	NASDAQ
Founded in 1792 *About 2,800 companies listed* *Home of the Dow Jones and S&P 500 indexes* *Listed companies must have at least $100,000,000 in outstanding stock and trade an average of at least 100,000 shares per day* *1,366 member seats*	*Founded after Civil War* *More than 800 companies listed* *Listed companies must have more than 500,000 shares outstanding and trade an average of more than 1,000 shares per day* *807 member seats*	*Founded in 1971* *More than 3,700 companies listed* *Considered the home of tech stocks* *No physical location; trades done via computer network* *Largest market in terms of stocks traded* *No fixed number of members*

15. Have the students complete the *Place the Stock* activity. Answers:

Market	Stock		
New York Stock Exchange (NYSE)	*Con Ed*	*Eastman Kodak*	*McDonald's*
American Stock Exchange (AMEX)	*Puradyn*	*The Rowe Cos.*	*TagIt Pacific*
NASDAQ Stock Market	*Atari*	*Intel*	*Telekom Austria*

Closure

1. Tell the students that they have learned about the characteristics of a market economy and characteristics of stock markets. Review these characteristics with the students; remind them that the stock market is simply a specialized market where shares of stock are bought and sold. Quickly review the three major stock markets.

2. Place the students in groups of four. Ask them to look at the clothing and shoes they are wearing, their backpacks or book bags and any other items they have brought with them to class. Can they determine the companies that made these items? If so, have them list several of these on a blank sheet of paper. In addition — or if they cannot determine who manufactured these items — ask the students to list the retail stores where the items were purchased, and add these stores to the list. Again, review the characteristics of a market, noting how the students' purchases reflect the characteristics of a market economy. Finally, have the students predict which of the three markets the companies that made their items (or sold them) might be listed on. For example, if students have a Palm™ Pilot PDA, they might predict that Palm, Inc. is listed on the NASDAQ (it is), as Palm is a technology-based corporation. If students are wearing Nike™ brand shoes, they might predict that Nike is listed on the NYSE (it is), because it is such a large corporation. Once students have made their predictions, distribute copies of recent stock market reports from the local paper or *USA Today* or *The Wall Street Journal*. Were their predictions correct? Why or why not? If the class has access to the Internet, students can also use the following sites to check predictions:

http://www.nyse.com

http://www.amex.com

http://www.nasdaq.com

http://money.cnn.com/

Assessment

Multiple-Choice Questions

1. All of the following are characteristics of a market economy except

   a. the government controls production and consumption decisions.

   b. private property of individuals is well defined and protected.

   c. competition puts pressure on businesses to satisfy consumer desires.

   d. profits are an incentive for producers to respond to consumer choices.

2. In the case of stock trades, the secondary market consists of

   a. the purchase of a company's stock by investment banks.

   b. the first offering of a company's stock to the public.

   c. the trading of a company's stock in a stock market through brokers.

   d. all trading that occurs in the initial public offering of a stock.

3. All of the following are true of the New York Stock Exchange except

   a. it is the oldest of the major stock markets.

   b. it has a fixed number of memberships called "seats."

   c. it is the home of the S & P 500 stock index.

   d. it is the largest market in terms of stock trade volume.

4. Which of these is an accurate statement about the NASDAQ and the NYSE?

   a. The NASDAQ is a secondary market; the NYSE is a primary market.

   b. Trading on both the NASDAQ and the NYSE is limited to one physical location.

   c. Membership on the NYSE is limited; the NASDAQ has an open membership.

   d. The NASDAQ was founded before the NYSE.

Essay Question

Briefly explain the role profits play in a market economy. Then explain how investors in the stock market are driven by the desire to earn profits when they buy stocks. Describe two ways in which investors can earn profits from investing in stocks.

Profits act as incentives for firms. Those firms that satisfy consumer desire, and produce efficiently, are rewarded with profits. Investors in stocks seek profit in the form of returns on their investments. Successful investors receive greater returns. Investors can profit through dividends paid out by companies or through the appreciation of stock prices.

Lesson 9 Visual 1

Characteristics of a Market

1. Private property
2. Self-interest
3. Competition
4. The profit motive
5. Voluntary exchange
6. Limited role of government

Lesson 9 Visual 2

Overview of the Market for Stocks

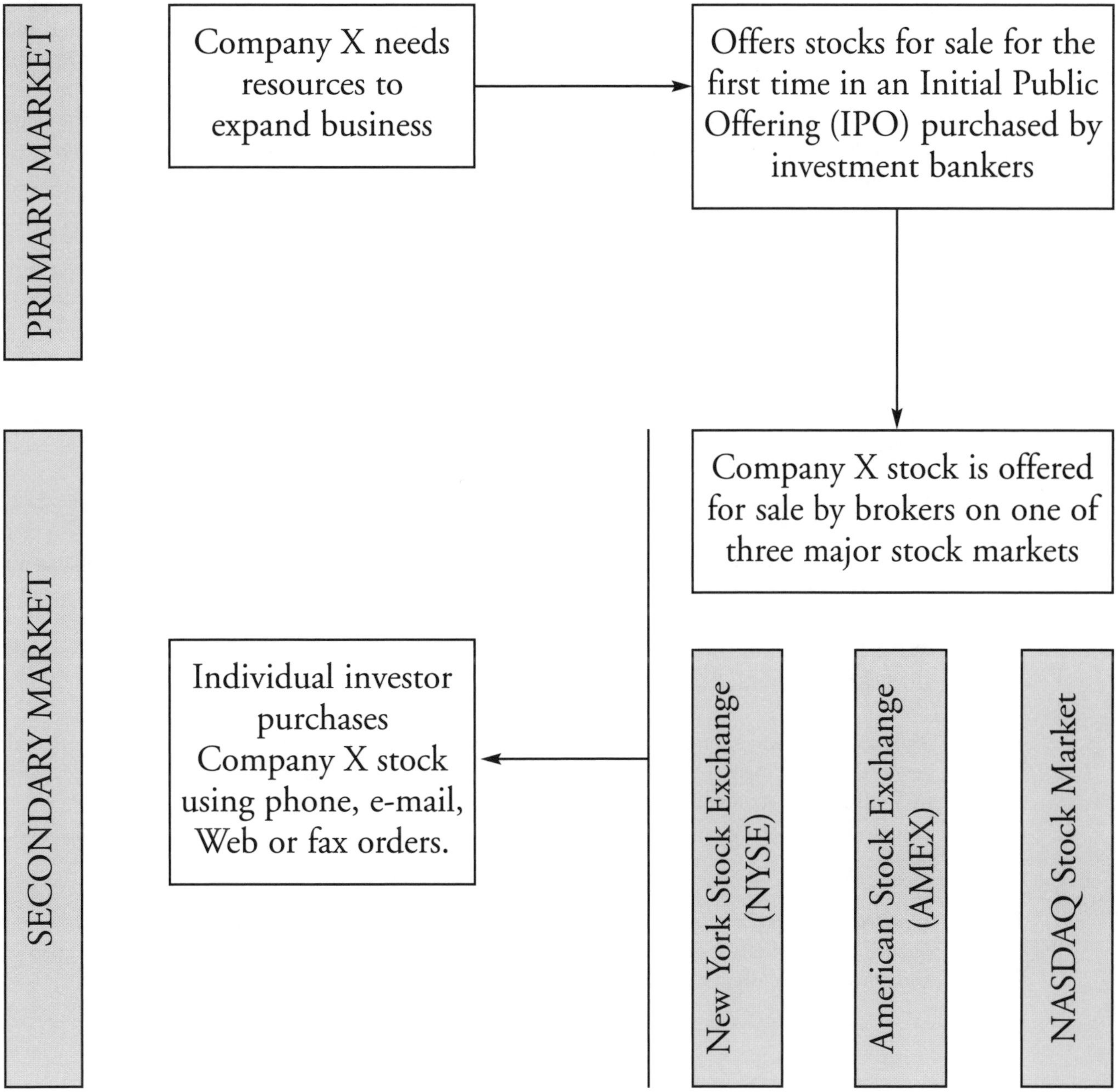
PRIMARY MARKET
Company X needs resources to expand business
Offers stocks for sale for the first time in an Initial Public Offering (IPO) purchased by investment bankers
SECONDARY MARKET
Company X stock is offered for sale by brokers on one of three major stock markets
Individual investor purchases Company X stock using phone, e-mail, Web or fax orders.
New York Stock Exchange (NYSE)
American Stock Exchange (AMEX)
NASDAQ Stock Market

Lesson 9 Activity 1

To Market, To Market…

The fundamental economic problem is that of scarcity, as illustrated by that famous London School of Economics student Mick Jagger, who once sang "you can't always get what you want." Throughout history societies have faced the fundamental economic questions of deciding what to produce and for whom to produce it in a world of scarce resources. In recent times, two very different economic systems evolved in response to these questions. *Command economies* are directed by a centralized government and characterized by limited choices on the part of buyers and sellers. *Market economies* are based on private enterprise and consumer and producer choice. Markets enable buyers and sellers to get together. In a market, a buyer agrees to give up money in return for a good, while a seller agrees to give up a good and gets money in return. Some additional features that distinguish a market economy from a command economy include the following.

Private Property. In a market economy, resources used to produce goods and services in the economy are largely owned by private individuals and private institutions rather than government. This private ownership means individuals can negotiate legally binding contracts to obtain and use resources as they choose, including selling the property they own to other individuals.

Competition. Buyers and sellers are free to enter or leave any market, and buyers and sellers act independently in the marketplace. Competition pressures firms to satisfy consumer demand or be forced from the market by firms that can.

Self-interest. According to Adam Smith, each individual's promotion of his or her own self-interest is the "invisible hand" that is the driving force in a market economy. Consumers try to get the most "bang for their buck," firms try to earn the highest profits, and workers want to earn the highest possible wages and salaries.

Profit Motive. Profits act as incentives for firms. Those firms that satisfy consumer desires and produce efficiently are rewarded with greater profits.

Voluntary Exchange. Individuals are free to obtain resources, use them in the production of goods and services, and sell them in markets of their choice. Consumers are free to buy the goods and services that best satisfy their economic wants. This freedom allows consumers and producers to focus on what they do best, and to freely trade surplus production or wealth. Because markets encourage trade, they also help create wealth.

Limited Government. Because a market economy is self-regulating, the government does not set prices or quantities. Government does play a role by maintaining the monetary system, enforcing property rights and correcting failures in the market.

LESSON 9 ACTIVITY 1 (CONTINUED)

Market or Not?

Use the characteristics of a market economy described on page 118 to determine whether the following scenarios represent a market or not. If you think that a scenario represents a market, place an M for market in the blank. If you think that this scenario does not represent a market, place a NM for not market in the blank. If you are not sure, place a U for uncertain in the blank.

____ 1. People are lined up outside a car dealership waiting for it to open. A special deal was advertised in today's paper, and many consumers have come early to try to get the best bargain they can.

____ 2. People are lined up outside Yellowstone National Park waiting to buy a ticket to enter the park. Visitors must purchase a day pass from park rangers in order to drive into the park.

____ 3. People are lined up outside the Department of Motor Vehicles office to buy license plates. A vehicle can be driven legally only if it has a license plate and is registered with the state.

____ 4. People swamp the Web site of a new long-distance phone company offering rates that are 50 percent less than the rates of the large, national long-distance carriers. Many who log on are hoping to switch to the new carrier.

____ 5. People are lined up outside a national doughnut chain store opening today for the first time; they want to be among the first to buy a dozen doughnuts.

____ 6. People are lined up outside a government building waiting to receive free cheese provided by a federal government program.

Lesson 9 Activity 2

The Pop Music Market

A very large market in the United States is the one for popular music. If you have purchased a CD, listened to the radio or downloaded MP3 files from the Internet, then you have participated in this market. Imagine that you have just heard about the latest CD released from that pop diva Britainia Arrows. You know that Britainia's last two CDs have topped the charts, so you know you'll have to rush right down to the CD Emporium if you hope to get a copy. On your way to the CD Emporium, take a moment to think about how your desire to purchase Britainia's CD and her record company's desire to sell the CD represent characteristics of a market economy. Use the data chart below to provide examples for each of the features of a market (not all cells will be full for both you and Straight-as–an-Arrow Records).

	You	**Straight-as-an-Arrow Records (Britainia Arrows' record company)**
Private property		
Competition		
Profit motive		
Self-interest		
Voluntary exchange		
Limited role of government		

LESSON 9 ACTIVITY 3

MEET THE STOCK MARKETS

The stock market is an institution enabling people who want to buy shares of stock to buy them from people who want to sell shares of stock. This market matches buyers and sellers and provides the means for mutual agreement on price. That is, the price of a share of stock is set at the moment when a buyer and seller agree to make a trade, and not before. The stock market is more than a physical location (and need not be a physical location at all); it is a set of arrangements, advertisements, online transactions, computer listings and personal relationships that make it possible for stocks to be traded.

Although often referred to as if it were a single entity, "the stock market" is actually a number of different markets. The three major stock markets in the United States are the New York Stock Exchange (NYSE), the American Stock Exchange (AMEX) and the NASDAQ Stock Market.

The New York Stock Exchange (NYSE)

The oldest of the three major stock markets, the NYSE was founded in 1792 when 24 brokers agreed to form the Exchange. About 2,800 public companies are listed on the NYSE, and these companies have a combined value of more than $15 trillion. Generally, small corporations' stocks are not listed on the NYSE. In order to be listed on the NYSE, a company must have outstanding share value (the value of all shares of stock not owned by the company itself) of at least $100,000,000 and must trade at a volume of at least 100,000 shares per day.

The NYSE is home to several important stock indexes. A stock index is a composite of the value of a large number of stocks used to measure the ups and downs of the overall market. The most famous stock index is the Dow Jones Industrial Average (DJIA), or "the Dow," which consists of 30 of the biggest companies in the United States including firms such as Walt Disney, ExxonMobil and Wal-Mart. Today, the Dow is the most widely followed measurement of the stock market. A second important index of stocks listed on the NYSE is the Standard and Poor's (S & P) 500. This index uses the stock prices of 500 companies listed on the NYSE including Boeing and 3M.

All stock trades at the NYSE take place in a single location on the NYSE's trading floor in New York City. Members of the NYSE — 1,366 brokers and specialists — carry out all trades. Members are said to have a "seat" on the NYSE, although they never actually sit down, and such seats routinely sell for $2 million. Investors purchase stocks by placing orders with brokers from around the United States and the world. These brokers then place floor orders at the NYSE, and those orders are filled by one of the 1,366 members.

American Stock Exchange (AMEX)

The precursor to the AMEX was founded during the Civil War when brokers would gather outside the NYSE trading floor (literally on the curb) to trade stocks that did not qualify to be listed on the NYSE. In fact, even when it moved inside in 1921, this precursor was known as the New York Curb Exchange and did not take the name American Stock Exchange until the 1940s.

Generally speaking, companies with shares traded on the AMEX are smaller than those listed on the New York Stock Exchange, although this is not always the case. Membership in the AMEX is limited to 807 regular members who conduct trades much like those on the NYSE. The AMEX is smaller than the NYSE, listing about 800 companies. Listing requirements vary, but companies must have between 500,000 and one million shares of outstanding stock, with average shares traded per day exceeding 1,000.

Lesson 9 Activity 3 (continued)

NASDAQ Stock Market

The NASDAQ Stock Market began trading in 1971, and in 1999 it surpassed the NYSE as the largest stock market (in volume of stock trades) in the United States. The NASDAQ Stock Market is unique because it does not reside in one physical location. Rather, trades are executed through the NASDAQ's sophisticated computer and telecommunication network. As the world's first electronic stock market, it is made up of the NASDAQ National Market and the NASDAQ Small Cap Market. The NASDAQ allows multiple market participants to trade through its electronic communication networks structure, thus increasing competition.

The NASDAQ Stock Market currently lists the stocks of more than 3,700 companies, with a combined value of $2.9 trillion dollars. The NASDAQ is widely known as the home of many of the largest technology-based companies, particularly computer software companies and other Internet businesses. More shares of stock are traded on the NASDAQ than on any other stock market, in part because membership in the NASDAQ is not limited to a fixed number of seats. Any firm or individual that meets certain requirements can join the NASDAQ. This policy allows more than 300 "market makers" (known as dealers to their customers) to operate like retail store owners, buying inventories of stock shares to sell to their customers.

Place the Stock

Listed below are brief descriptions of nine stocks that are listed on one of the three major stock markets described above. After reading these descriptions, and using what you know about each market, place each stock in the appropriate place on the grid that follows. Pay close attention to the information provided. For example, if the stock was listed before 1971, it cannot be part of the NASDAQ Stock Market (which opened in 1971).

1. **Atari**

   The group's principal activities are to develop, publish and distribute interactive entertainment software for leisure entertainment, gaming enthusiasts and children's markets for a variety of platforms. This stock was first listed in 1998, and shares traded often average more than 100,000 per day.

2. **Consolidated Edison (ConEd)**

   Con Edison of New York provides electric power in all of New York City (except part of Queens) and most of Westchester County. This stock was first listed in 1824. Shares traded per day often exceed one million.

3. **Eastman Kodak**

   Eastman Kodak Company is primarily engaged in developing, manufacturing and marketing traditional and digital imaging products, services and solutions for consumers, professionals, healthcare providers, the entertainment industry and other commercial customers. This stock was first listed in 1905 and was a member of the Dow Jones Industrial Average index for many years. Shares traded per day often exceed four million.

LESSON 9 ACTIVITY 3 (CONTINUED)

4. **Intel**

   The group's principal activities are to design, develop, manufacture and market computers, networking and communication products. Listed since 1998, this stock regularly averages over 10 million shares traded per day.

5. **McDonald's**

   McDonald's Corporation operates in the food-service industry, franchising quick-service restaurant businesses under the McDonald's brand. This stock was first listed in 1966 and is a part of the Dow Jones Industrial Average index. Shares traded often average near 10 million per day.

6. **Puradyn**

   Puradyn Filter Technologies, Inc. (PFT) manufactures, markets and distributes the Puradyn bypass oil filtration system (the Puradyn) worldwide for use with substantially all internal combustion engines and hydraulic equipment that uses lubricating oil. First listed in 2001, this stock averages less than 1,000 shares traded per day.

7. **The Rowe Companies**

   The Rowe Companies (ROW) operate in two segments of the home furnishings industry: the wholesale (manufacturing) home furnishings segment and the retail home furnishings segment. This stock was first listed in 2003 and averages less than 5,000 shares traded per day.

8. **Tag-It Pacific**

   Tag-It Pacific, Inc. (TAG) is an apparel company that specializes in the distribution of a full range of trim items to manufacturers of fashion apparel and licensed consumer products to specialty retailers and mass merchandisers. Share trades average under 1,000 per day.

9. **Telekom Austria**

   The group's principal activities are to provide fixed-line and wireless communication services in Austria and throughout Europe. Listed since 1998, this stock averages under 1,000 shares traded per day.

Market	Stocks		
New York Stock Exchange (NYSE)			
American Stock Exchange (AMEX)			
NASDAQ Stock Market			

Lesson 10 The Language of Financial Markets

Middle School

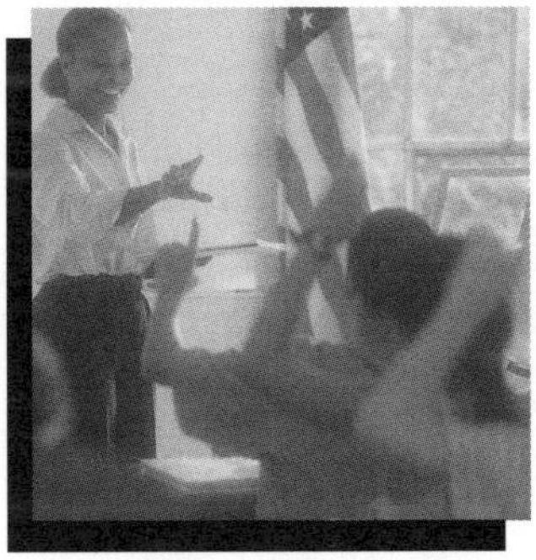

Lesson 10 The Language of Financial Markets

Lesson Description

The students work in small groups to make flash cards to display terms commonly used in financial markets. The terms are grouped in five categories: *Buying and Selling in the Market; Exchanges and Indexes; People in Financial Markets; Stocks, Bonds and Mutual Funds; Technical Terms.* Each group of students begins by learning the terms in one category. Then the students pass their flash cards from group to group until everyone has had an opportunity to learn all the terms. The lesson concludes with a Language of Financial Markets Bee.

Knowing these terms can improve the students' understanding of financial information reported in the daily business news and help them make better financial decisions.

Concepts

This lesson includes several concepts related to the vocabulary of financial markets. Some key concepts are:

- Bonds
- Mutual funds
- Securities indexes
- Stocks

Objectives

Students will:

1. Recognize the definitions of terms commonly used in financial markets.
2. Explain the meaning of financial terms as used in one or more business news articles.

Time Required

90 minutes

Materials

- A transparency of Visuals 1 and 2
- A copy of Visual 1 for each student
- A copy of Activity 1 for each student
- 5 note cards and one marker for each of 5 groups
- Optional: Small prizes for the Language of Financial Markets Bee
- Business news articles that use terms featured in this lesson

Procedure

1. Explain to the students that participation in the world of finance requires learning a new language. In order to participate effectively in financial markets, a person must know the appropriate terms.

2. **Distribute a copy of Activity 1** to each student and give the students a few moments to peruse the terms and definitions shown. Assure the students that they will be able to learn the terms and definitions in small portions — a few terms and definitions at a time.

3. **Display Visual 1** and distribute a copy of the visual to each student. This visual is a list of words that organizes the financial terms into five categories: *Buying and Selling in the Market; Exchanges and Indexes; People in Financial Markets; Stocks, Bonds and Mutual Funds; Technical Terms.*

4. Divide the class into five groups of equal size. Distribute note cards and markers for making flash cards. The five groups will make flash cards as follows: Group 1: *Buying and Selling in the Market;* Group 2: *Exchanges and Indexes;* Group 3: *People in Financial Markets;* Group 4: *Stocks, Bonds and Mutual Funds;* Group 5: *Technical Terms.*

5. Tell the students to write a term on one side of each flash card and the definition of the term on the other side. When the groups have prepared their flash cards, ask them to quiz one another within their group to practice learning the terms and the definitions.

6. When you think the time is right, ask the students to pass their cards to the next group. Group 1 should pass its cards on to Group 2, Group 2 should pass its cards on to Group 3, and so forth, so that students in each group can learn a new set of terms. Rotate each group's cards through the five groups until all the students have had an opportunity to learn the terms in the five categories.

7. Conduct the Language of Financial Markets Bee.

- Each of the five student groups will compete as a team in the Bee.
- Tell the students that they will quiz one another on all the terms on the flash cards.
- To get started, call on a student from Group 1 to select a term and challenge the students in Group 2 to define it. The students in Group 2 have up to 30 seconds to come up with the correct definition and present it to the class.
- The teacher (or perhaps a business volunteer) decides whether the definition is correct or not. If the term is correctly defined, enter the points to the team's score on

Visual 2 and go to the next team. If the term is not correctly defined, the term can be selected again by another group.

- Call on a student from Group 2 to select a definition and challenge the students in Group 3 to identify the term that matches the definition.
- Tell the students to continue the Bee in this manner, rotating the questioning and answering responsibility from group to group.
- Keep score on Visual 2. Award points 5 points for each complete/accurate answer; 0 points for each incorrect answer.
- Declare the group that earned the most points the winner. Optional: Award prizes to members of the winning team.

Closure

1. Review key terms in the lesson.

2. Bring to class several news articles that use one or more of the terms featured in the lesson. Read excerpts from the news articles out loud. Ask the students to explain these excerpts in their own words, using the terms or their definitions correctly in their explanations.

Assessment

Multiple-Choice Questions

1. Which of the following is a capital gain?

   a. A car owner sells her used car to a dealer for more than she expected to receive.

   b. A shipping clerk gets a raise from $10 an hour to $12 an hour.

   c. An investor buys Microsoft stock for $30 and sells it for $21.

   d. An investor buys Microsoft stock for $21 and sells it for $30.

2. Assume that the Dow Jones Industrial Average was at 10,000 at the beginning of a year. If it gains seven percent in the first quarter of the year, it becomes

   a. 17,000.

   b. 10,070.

   c. 10,700.

   d. 10,007.

3. If you purchased 87 shares of IBM stock, you purchased

   a. a round lot of shares.

   b. an odd lot of 78 shares.

   c. an odd lot of 87 shares.

   d. on the margin.

4. Which of the following is a stock exchange?

   a. AMEX

   b. DJIA

   c. IPO

   d. AAA

Essay Questions

1. Explain the difference between common stock and preferred stock.
Common stocks represent shares of ownership in a corporation. There is no guarantee that common stocks will hold their value or pay a dividend. Preferred stocks also represent shares of ownership. However, preferred stocks guarantee a dividend before a common-stock dividend is paid.

2. When people ask, "How did the market do today?" they usually have one indicator in mind. What is the indicator and why is it important?
When people wonder how the market is doing, they are wondering about what happened to the Dow Jones Industrial Average or the Dow. The DJIA is an index of 30 of the largest companies traded on the New York Stock Exchange. It is the most commonly known stock-market indicator.

LESSON 10 VISUAL 1

THE LANGUAGE OF FINANCIAL MARKETS

Buying and Selling in the Market
Buying on Margin
Commission
Odd Lot
Price
Round Lot
Selling Short

Exchanges and Indexes
AMEX
DJIA
NASDAQ
NYSE
Over-the-Counter Market

People in Financial Markets
Broker
Dealer
Institutional Investor
Investment Banker
Stockholder

Stocks, Bonds and Mutual Funds
Bond
Common Stock
Initial Public Offering (IPO)
Mutual Fund
Preferred Stock

Technical Terms
Capital Gain
Dividend
Growth Stock
Income Stock
Stock Split

LESSON 10 VISUAL 2

THE LANGUAGE OF FINANCIAL MARKETS BEE SCORE SHEET

Directions: Each team receives 5 points for each correct definition.

Team	*Score*
1	
2	
3	
4	
5	

Lesson 10 Activity 1

Terms from the World of Finance

In this activity, you will learn a new language — the language of financial markets. Before you participate in a stock market simulation or use your own funds to participate in a financial market, you need to learn the language.

AMEX Stands for American Stock Exchange. Located in New York City, this stock exchange sells memberships, or seats, so that brokers can trade stocks.

Broker A professional trader who buys or sells stocks for individuals and institutional customers.

Buying on Margin Buying stock by paying a percentage of the purchase price (typically 50 percent) and borrowing the balance from a broker. If the buyer can sell the stock at a higher price than she or he paid for it, the amount of the loan can be repaid (plus interest and commission) and the buyer can keep the profit. However, if the stock price falls, the buyer must repay the loan (plus interest and commission) and suffer a loss.

Capital Gain A profit realized from the sale of property, stocks or other investments.

Commission A percentage of a stock trade (a buy or a sell) paid to a stockbroker.

Common Stock An ownership share or shares of ownership in a corporation. A common stock offers no guarantee that it will hold its value or pay dividends.

Dealer Someone who buys and sells stocks from his or her own accounts or the accounts of the firm he or she works for. Some dealers also act as brokers.

Dividend A share of a company's net profits paid to shareholders.

Dow Jones Industrial Average (DJIA) Often referred to as the "Dow" or the "Dow Jones Average," it is the most commonly known stock-market indicator. The Dow Jones Average is an index of 30 industrial companies traded on the New York Stock Exchange, including ExxonMobil and General Motors. You may hear on the news that "the market was up 50 points today." This usually means that the Dow gained 50 index points.

Growth Stock A stock that often pays no dividend, but the stockholder gains if the price of the stock increases (grows).

Income Stock A stock that pays dividends regularly.

Institutional Investor An organization (an insurance company or pension fund, for example) that invests in the stock market.

Investment Banker A financial firm that agrees to underwrite a new issue of stocks or bonds and sell them to its best customers.

Mutual Fund A company that pools money from investors and uses it to buy stocks, bonds or money market instruments on the investors' behalf. Provides diversification and professional management for investors.

NASDAQ An electronic marketplace enabling buyers and sellers to get together via computers and hundreds of thousands of miles of high-speed data lines to trade stocks.

New York Stock Exchange (NYSE) The oldest stock exchange in the United States, founded in 1792. The exchange is located in New York City.

LESSON 10 ACTIVITY 1 (CONTINUED)

Odd Lot Stocks are usually purchased in multiples of 100 shares, called a round lot. A small investor may buy a single share of stock or some number of shares less than 100. Doing this means the investor has purchased an odd lot.

Over-the-Counter Market (OTC) The OTC market is a network of dealers connected by a computer system. There is no centralized trading floor. The stocks often represent new, start-up companies, and the stock prices are relatively low.

Preferred Stock An ownership share in a corporation with a guaranteed dividend that is paid before dividends paid on common stock.

Round Lot The purchase of stock in multiples of 100 shares.

Selling Short To sell short, the buyer borrows shares he or she does not own from a broker. The buyer orders the shares to be sold and takes the money from the sale. Then the buyer waits for the stock price to fall. If the stock price falls, the buyer buys the shares at the lower price, pays the broker's commission and any fees, and gains a profit. Selling short is risky; if the stock price increases, the buyer loses money.

S & P 500 Stock Index This is shorthand for the Standard and Poor's 500 Stock Index. The index includes 500 stocks and is important to large-stock investors.

Stock An ownership share or shares of ownership in a corporation.

Stock Certificate An official document certifying that a person is an owner of stock.

Stockholder A person who owns stock; sometimes called a shareholder.

Stock Split The division of the outstanding number of shares into a higher number of shares. A stock split often occurs when the price of a stock is considered too high by a corporation. The purpose is to lower the price of the stock to attract more stock buyers.

Lesson 11 Financial Institutions in the U.S. Economy

Middle School

11 Financial Institutions in the U.S. Economy

Lesson 11 Financial Institutions in the U.S. Economy

Lesson Description

The students participate in a brief trading activity to illustrate the role institutions play in bringing savers and borrowers together, thus channeling savings to investment. The students discuss financial institutions, such as banks and credit unions, and they participate in a simulation activity to help them understand primary and secondary stock markets and bond markets.

In a market economy, financial institutions channel savings into investments. The process of channeling funds from one group of people to others is important to the overall economy. Banks provide a place for individuals to keep checking and savings accounts, and borrowers go to banks to obtain loans. Some people use loans to start or expand businesses or to invest in new factories and machines. Some use loans to purchase homes and expensive durable goods. Other specialized financial institutions, such as stock and bond markets, also play an important role in promoting investment.

Concepts

- Debt financing
- Economic growth
- Economic investment
- Equity financing
- Financial institutions
- Financial investment
- Interest
- Primary markets
- Secondary markets

Objectives

Students will:

1. Define *financial institutions, interest, financial investment* and *economic investment.*
2. Explain the difference between primary and secondary markets.
3. Explain the difference between debt and equity financing.
4. Explain the role of financial institutions in channeling savings to investment.

Time Required

90 minutes

Materials

- Activity 1, duplicated and cut apart to provide a card for each student
- Activity 2, one copy that students will cut apart
- Activity 3, duplicated and cut apart to provide a card for each student
- Activity 4, cut apart to provide 26 payment cards
- 5 pairs of scissors

Procedure

1. Explain that the purpose of this lesson is to help the students understand the role that financial institutions such as banks and financial markets play in a market economy. Tell the students that they are going to participate in a brief trading activity. **Distribute a card from Activity 1** to each student. Tell the students that they should try to find someone who wants *exactly* what they have and has *exactly* what they want.

2. Allow about two minutes for the students to trade. Discuss the following:

- How many of you were able to find someone who had what you wanted?
  No one.
- How many of you were willing to lend money if you could earn interest?
  Five. There may be more than five if additional copies of Activity 1 were used.
- How many of you wanted to borrow money and pay interest on the loan?
  Five.
- Why didn't you borrow from and lend to one another?
  No one wanted to borrow the amount I had to lend.
  No one wanted to lend the amount I wanted to borrow.
- How many of you wanted to buy stock? *Four.*
- How many of you wanted to sell stock? *Four.*
- Why didn't you buy from and sell to one another?
  Each wanted to buy a different stock than the stock available for sale.
- How many of you wanted to buy bonds?
  Two.

- How many of you wanted to sell bonds?
  Two.
- Why didn't you buy from and sell to one another?
  Each wanted to buy a different bond than the bonds available for sale.

3. Explain that it is easy to imagine how people who wish to buy or sell stocks or bonds might have trouble finding partners with whom to make exchanges. People who want to borrow money may not know who has money to lend. People who want to lend money at certain interest rates may not know who wants to borrow at those rates. People who want to buy bonds or stocks may not know who is selling bonds or stocks. And those selling bonds or stocks may not know who wants to buy. In market economies, people develop *financial institutions*, such as banks and credit unions, to make it easier for these interactions to occur. Financial institutions are intermediaries that channel savings into economic investment. There are many examples of financial institutions, including life insurance companies investment companies, finance companies and pension funds. Financial institutions also provide a way for individuals and companies to invest.

4. Explain that economists distinguish between two types of investment: *economic investment* and *personal investment.* Economic investment is putting money into capital — into factories and machines, for example, or into other resources used to make goods and services.

5. Explain that people make *personal investments* when they decide where to put their savings — for example, by depositing it in a bank account or by purchasing stocks and bonds. Savings deposited in bank accounts earn *interest.* Banks and credit unions use money deposited in accounts to make loans to customers. Borrowers are charged interest. Interest is the price people pay for using someone else's money; it is also money people earn for letting others use their money.

6. Explain that there are other ways to earn money in the financial markets. Some savers earn money by purchasing *stocks* and *bonds.* A stock is a share of ownership or equity in a corporation. As a corporation's profits and revenues increase, its stock price often increases as well. When that happens, an investor who bought stock at a low price may choose to sell it later at a higher price. A saver who buys a bond makes a loan to the company or government issuing the bond; the issuer then is obligated to pay the bond holder back, with interest.

7. Explain that the students will participate in a simulation activity intended to help them understand how stocks are bought and sold in two different sorts of markets.

8. Assign the five major roles needed for the simulation activity and **give the students their materials:**

- A representative of the Great American Computer Company (GACC). Give this student a copy of Activity 2, the GACC name tag from Activity 3 and a pair of scissors.
- A representative of G. Mann, Inc. Give this student the G. Mann, Inc. name tag from Activity 3, a payment card from Activity 4 and a pair of scissors.
- Three Best Customers. Give each of these students a Best Customer name tag from Activity 3, a payment card from Activity 4 and a pair of scissors.
- **Give each of the remaining students a payment card from Activity 4.**

9. Write *Primary Market* on one section of the board and *Secondary Market* on another section. Tell the representative of GACC and the representative of G. Mann, Inc. to stand in front of the section labeled *Primary Market.*

10. Explain that the Great American Computer Company needs money to build a factory and buy equipment. The company decides to offer one million shares of its stock through G. Mann, Inc., an investment bank. Tell the GACC representative to cut out the stock rectangle along the solid lines and give it to the G. Mann, Inc. representative in exchange for the payment card. Explain that G. Mann, Inc. now has the new GACC stock and GACC has the money it needs for economic investment; that is, investment in new physical capital — the factory and equipment.

11. Explain that this is part of the primary market where new securities are offered for sale for the first time. The primary stock market channels savings to economic investment because the corporation issuing the stock gets money to spend on capital goods.

12. Explain that G. Mann, Inc. provides an initial public offering or IPO of shares of GACC to its best customers. Tell the G. Mann, Inc. representative to cut the stock apart on the two dashed vertical lines. Have the students representing Best Customers come forward and buy shares of stock by exchanging their payment cards for shares of stock. These customers have bought their shares on the primary market.

13. Explain that these best customers can now sell their shares of GACC stock to others through secondary markets. Have them move to the section of the board labeled *Secondary Market.* Have these students cut their shares of stock apart on the six horizontal dashed lines. Tell the remaining students to come forward and buy shares of

GACC stock by giving a Best Customer their payment cards.

14. Explain that most people have heard of secondary stock markets, such as the New York Stock Exchange (NYSE), the American Stock Exchange (AMEX) and the NASDAQ Stock Market. These are secondary markets because they are not directly linked to the companies issuing the stock in question. Instead, these are markets in which stocks can be bought and sold after the initial public offering.

15. Ask all the students to return to their seats. Discuss the following.

- What are stocks?
  Shares of ownership in a corporation.
- Why do companies issue stocks?
  To raise money for economic investment and to operate the company.
- What is an IPO?
  An initial public offering.
- Who buys stock at an initial public offering?
  Investment bankers and their best customers.
- Is this the primary or secondary market? *Primary.*
  Why? *It is the first time the stock is offered. It is the sale for which the corporation actually receives money.*
- What do the investment bankers do with the stock?
  They sell it to their best customers.
- Once the best customers have purchased the stock, what can they do with it?
  Keep it or sell it in secondary stock markets.
- What are some familiar names of secondary stock markets?
  NYSE, AMEX, NASDAQ.

16. Remind the students that corporations issue stock to obtain money they need. When people buy stocks they acquire equity or ownership in the corporation. Stocks are referred to as a means of *equity financing* because those who purchase the stock gain ownership shares in the corporation.

17. Explain that people can also purchase bonds with their savings. Bond purchases are referred to as *debt financing.* When people buy bonds, they are lending money to the bond issuer in return for a promise that they will be paid the amount borrowed plus interest — usually at a fixed rate. The bond issuer — a corporation or government — also promises to repay the debt on time and in full. Corporations and governments issue bonds to obtain money they need. Corporations often use the money for economic investment in new buildings, plants and equipment. Governments may use the money for economic investment in schools, buildings, equipment, roads, bridges and other infrastructure items.

18. Explain that most corporate bonds are initially sold through investment bankers (often called underwriters). This is the primary sale of the bond. The underwriters sell these bonds to their best customers. The best customers in turn sell the bonds in secondary markets, such as the New York Bond Market.

19. Remind the students that when individuals buy stocks and bonds in the secondary market, they do not provide additional funds for investment in capital goods, such as factories and machines. When stocks and bonds are sold in primary markets, funds are provided that the corporation or government may use for investment in capital goods. When stocks or bonds are sold in secondary markets, such as stock exchanges, money does not go to the government or corporation that issued the stocks or bonds; it goes to the seller of the stock or bond.

20. Explain that the capacity of financial institutions to efficiently channel savings into economic investments affects a nation's rate of *economic growth,* since investments increase a nation's capacity to produce goods and services in the future. Economic growth is a sustained rise in a nation's production of goods and services. Historically, economic growth has been the primary means by which market economies reduce poverty and raise standards of living.

Closure

Review the important points of the lesson:

1. What is a financial institution?
An intermediary that helps channel savings into economic investments.

2. Give an example of a financial institution.
Bank, credit union, investment company, pension fund, life insurance company.

3. What is personal investment?
Putting money someplace with the intention of making a financial gain. Financial investment options include stocks, bonds, mutual funds.

4. What is interest?
The price people pay for using someone else's money; also, the money people earn by lending money to others.

5. What is economic investment?
The purchase of physical capital.

6. What are stocks?
Shares of ownership or equity in a corporation.

7. What are bonds?
Certificates of indebtedness. When an investor buys a bond, he or she makes a loan to the bond issuer. The bond specifies the borrowers' obligation to repay the lender, with interest and at a specified time.

8. What is the primary market for stocks or bonds?
The market in which securities are offered for sale for the first time. Investment banks buy shares of stock or bonds from the corporations and sell them to their best customers.

9. What is the secondary market for stocks or bonds?
The market in which stocks and bonds are bought and sold by the public. The New York Stock Exchange is an example.

10. When corporations issue stocks, why is it called equity financing?
Because stockholders own equity in or shares of the corporation.

11. When corporations issue bonds, why is it called debt financing?
Because the corporation owes a debt to the people who bought bonds. These people lent the corporation money in exchange for the corporation's promise to repay the amount of the bond in full, on time, and with interest.

Assessment

Multiple-Choice Questions

1. Stocks are
   a. an example of debt financing.
   b. shares of ownership in a corporation.
   c. agreements to repay money borrowed with no interest.
   d. agreements to repay money borrowed along with a fixed rate of interest.

2. Bonds are
   a. an example of equity financing.
   b. shares of ownership in a corporation.
   c. agreements to repay money borrowed with no interest.
   d. certificates of indebtedness, obligating borrowers to repay borrowed money and pay interest.

3. Economic investment includes
   a. building new factories.
   b. putting money in a savings account at a bank.
   c. purchasing corporate bonds in the New York Bond Market.
   d. buying shares of stock through the New York Stock Exchange.

4. Personal investment includes
   a. building new factories.
   b. buying new equipment for an office.
   c. providing training and education for employees.
   d. purchasing corporate bonds in the New York Bond Market.

Essay Questions

1. What is the difference between equity financing (a corporation issuing stock) and debt financing (a corporation issuing bonds)?
Equity financing refers to ownership. Stocks represent shares of ownership in the corporation. Debt financing refers to debt. Bonds represent the corporation's promise to repay the bond holder and to pay interest.

2. How do banks and other financial institutions channel savings to economic investment?
By accepting money from savers and lending it to corporations, governments and individuals.

3. What is the difference between the primary and secondary markets?
The first or initial sale of stocks and bonds occurs in primary markets. When these transactions occur, the corporations that issued the stocks or the corporations or governments that issued the bonds receive money. Secondary sales take place in stock and bond exchanges, which are secondary markets. These transactions do not provide money for the corporations or government that issued the stocks or bonds.

Lesson 11 Activity 1

Save, Lend, Buy, Sell Cards

You have saved $10,000. You are willing to lend the money if the borrower will pay interest.	You want to borrow $17,000 to buy a new car. You are willing to pay interest on the loan.
You have saved $3,000. You are willing to lend the money if the borrower will pay interest.	You want to sell MSTrans Incorporated stock to expand your business.
You have saved $20,000. You want to buy stock in Aerostar Corporation.	You need money to send your daughter to college. You are willing to sell your Burger Barn stock.
You have saved $15,000. You are willing to lend the money if the borrower will pay interest.	You want to borrow $5,000 to go on vacation. You are willing to pay interest on the loan.
You have saved $6,000 and want to buy StarPics stock.	You want to build a factory. You want to sell DelMouse corporate bonds to raise the money to build the factory.
You have saved $15,000. You want to buy Automotors corporate bonds.	You are the state government. You want to borrow $500,000 to repair roads. You want to sell bonds to do this.
You have saved $50,000. You want to buy NewsAmerica stock.	You want to borrow $10,000 to put an addition on your home. You are willing to pay interest on the loan.
You have saved $7,000. You are willing to lend the money if the borrower will pay interest.	You want to borrow $800 to buy a new refrigerator. You are willing to pay interest on the loan.
You want to sell your Electroworks stock and use the money to make a down payment on a house.	You want to buy 500 shares of Medicine Makers stock.
You have saved $20,000 and you want to buy LV Power and Light corporate bonds.	You want to sell your shares of Invest Up stock.
You have saved $2,000. You are willing to lend the money if the borrower will pay interest.	You want to borrow $9,000 to buy a used car. You are willing to pay interest on the loan.

LESSON 11 ACTIVITY 2

INITIAL PUBLIC OFFERING

GACC Stock Certificate	**GACC Stock Certificate**	**GACC Stock Certificate**
GACC Stock Certificate	**GACC Stock Certificate**	**GACC Stock Certificate**
GACC Stock Certificate	**GACC Stock Certificate**	**GACC Stock Certificate**
GACC Stock Certificate	**GACC Stock Certificate**	**GACC Stock Certificate**
GACC Stock Certificate	**GACC Stock Certificate**	**GACC Stock Certificate**
GACC Stock Certificate	**GACC Stock Certificate**	**GACC Stock Certificate**
GACC Stock Certificate	**GACC Stock Certificate**	**GACC Stock Certificate**

LESSON 11 ACTIVITY 3

NAME TAGS

Representative of the Great American Computer Company	**Representative of G. Mann, Inc. Investment Bank**
Best Customer	**Best Customer**
Best Customer	

Lesson 11 Activity 4

Payment Cards

Payment for shares	Payment for shares
Payment for shares	Payment for shares
Payment for shares	Payment for shares
Payment for shares	Payment for shares
Payment for shares	Payment for shares
Payment for shares	Payment for shares
Payment for shares	Payment for shares

Lesson 12 Building Wealth Over the Long Term

Middle School

Lesson 12 Building Wealth Over the Long Term

Lesson Description

The students are introduced to the case of Charlayne, a woman who becomes, accidentally, a millionaire. Charlayne's success, the students learn, was unexpected, but not a miracle. It can be explained by three widely understood rules for building wealth over the long term: saving early, buying and holding, and diversifying. The lesson uses Charlayne's decisions to illustrate each of these rules. It also addresses the risks and rewards associated with different forms of saving and investing.

Making use of compound interest, holding for the long term and diversification are widely regarded as successful strategies for building wealth. Albert Einstein once called compounding "the greatest mathematical discovery of all time." Time is the critical factor for compounding to work best. Starting to save early allows savings to earn interest on the interest earned previously. Literally, your money works for you. Allowing savings to grow over many years is also an important strategy for success. This means that to build wealth over time, you have to hold on to your long-term savings. You can't be dipping into them frequently, or they won't compound over time in the same way. Finally, don't put all your eggs in one basket. To diversify means to hold a variety of financial assets rather than just one. To diversify is to take on many small risks rather than one large risk.

Concepts

- Compound interest
- Diversification
- Forms of saving and investing
- Reward
- Risk

Objectives

Students will:

1. Explain why an early start in saving and investing increases a household's capacity to build wealth.
2. Compare the strategy of buying and holding financial assets as opposed to trading assets frequently.
3. Explain the benefits of diversification.
4. Identify different forms of saving and investing; discuss the costs and benefits of each.

Time Required

90 minutes

Materials

- A transparency of Visuals 1 to 13
- A copy of Activities 1, 2 and 3 for each student
- Duplicated copies of Floor Markers 1 through 5 listing alternative assets: Savings Accounts, Certificates of Deposit, Bonds, Stocks, Real Estate

Procedure

1. Tell the students that the purpose of this lesson is to explain how individuals can build wealth over the long term. **Display Visual 1**; introduce, briefly, the three rules of saving and investing to be emphasized in the lesson:

- Start early
- Buy and hold
- Diversify

2. Explain that it is possible to become a millionaire by saving regularly. The lesson will show how an ordinary wage earner named Charlayne did just that. **Display the first line of Visual 2.** Mask the other lines on the transparency. Explain that savings of $20 per week, matched by an employer's contribution of $20 per week, comes to $2,080 per year. Show how that sum of money can grow to $2,168.40 at the end of the year. **Then reveal the next line of Visual 2** and indicate that the second-year total would be $4,521.11. Note that because all her earnings stay in her account, Charlayne is now receiving earnings on earnings.

3. Move down to year 9 of Visual 2 and show that Charlayne's account at that point was worth $32,168.43. Point out that in this year, Charlayne continued to save. And because she had started early and kept at it, she did amazingly well. **Display Visual 3** to show that by the time Charlayne reached retirement age, the value of her account had grown to more than $1 million.

4. **Display Visual 4.** Explain that when you leave money in an account to earn a return for a long time, it's not just your original money that's working for you. Instead, you earn interest on interest, or earnings on earnings.

5. **Display Visual 5.** Explain that Charlayne's co-worker

Marcus had the same opportunity that Charlayne had. But Marcus didn't get an early start. He tried to make up for his later start by saving diligently for 36 years. **Display Visual 6.** Note that while Marcus accumulated an impressive $400,000 plus, he never caught up with Charlayne.

6. **Display Visual 7.** Explain that in addition to starting early, individuals also can help themselves to be financially successful if they buy and hold for the long run. To buy and hold for the long run, people should do the following:

- Spend less than they receive.
- Become connected to financial institutions.
- Manage credit responsibly.

7. Develop the idea of buying and holding stocks, bonds and mutual funds for the long run. **Display Visual 8.** Explain that Charlayne held on to her investments over the years as financial markets went up and down. Emphasize these points:

- It's easy to get pessimistic when financial assets go down, but that's a bad time to sell.
- It's easy to get optimistic when financial assets go up, but that's a bad time to buy.
- Historically, the stock-market roller coaster ends up higher than it started out. Over long periods of time, people have done well by leaving their money in.

8. Introduce the topic of diversification. **Display Visual 9.** Explain that people have long known it is unwise to concentrate risk. For investors, reducing risk involves holding various assets instead of concentrating wealth on a single asset. Diversifying is taking on many small risks rather than one large risk.

9. **Distribute a copy of Activity 1** to each student. Explain that Activity 1 reviews the saving experiences of Charlayne and Marcus and explains the other two rules for building wealth over the long term. Ask the students to read Activity 1 and complete the Questions for Discussion. ***Ask:***

A. What are the three rules of wealth building?
Start early, buy and hold, and diversify.

B. Explain how Charlayne, the accidental millionaire, followed all three rules.
Charlayne began saving regularly when she started her first job. She left her savings alone even when she encountered financial difficulties. Her savings therefore grew, enhanced by compound interest. Her savings plan provided for diversification; she was able to own many different financial assets at the same time.

10. **Distribute a copy of Activity 2** to each student; ask the students to read the Activity and then follow along as you explain several of its key points. **Display Visual 10** and discuss the advantages and disadvantages of different forms of saving and investing.

11. Place Floor Markers 1 through 5 on the floor at the edges of the room. Tell the students that each of them has $5,000 to invest. Ask them to show where they would put their money. For example, those who prefer stocks will walk over to the floor marker that says *Stocks*.

12. When all the students have chosen a position, ask them to explain their decisions. Then have them sit down again. In their explanations, the students usually mention both risk and return. Some will insist they need more information to make a decision.

13. **Display Visual 11.** Explain that the students may be able to make better decisions if they learn more about the situation. The first item on Visual 11 is the $5,000 generic decision the students just made. Read the second item and ask the students to stand up and show where they would put their money. Some students will return to the same floor marker as before, but some will make different decisions. Go through the other items on Visual 11, showing how the students' movements correspond to "movements" by investors — making different decisions, depending on the circumstances.

14. **Display Visual 12.** Explain that the preceding activity has illustrated something about the trade-off between risk and return. If you want a safe investment, you have to settle for a low return (at the bottom of the pyramid). If you want the prospect of higher returns, you have to take risk (move toward the top of the pyramid).

15. **Display Visual 13.** Explain that a mutual fund pools investors' money and puts it into the markets on their behalf. Tell the students that mutual funds allow people in effect to own small amounts of many different assets. Thus mutual funds provide one means by which investors can easily diversify.

16. Ask the students to complete the Question for Discussion on Activity 2. ***Ask:***

What are the advantages and disadvantages of alternative forms of saving and investing?

- Savings accounts: They provide a small but steady return, and they involve virtually no risk.
- Certificates of deposit (CDs): They are safe, too, but they pay little more in interest than regular savings accounts.

- Bonds: Buying bonds is in effect lending money to a corporation or government. The return on bonds is higher than the return on savings accounts and CDs, but bonds also involve more risk.
- Stocks: When investors buy stock, they acquire ownership shares in a company. Stocks are a higher-risk investment option than bonds and savings accounts; stocks also offer the potential of higher returns.
- Real estate: People who invest in real estate face the risks and potential benefits of being a landlord. (Note that here we're talking about owning real estate as an investment — not owning our own homes.)

Closure

1. Summarize the lesson briefly by stating that, over time, it is possible for ordinary people to become well off. ***Ask:*** What are the three rules for building wealth? *Start early, buy and hold, diversify.*

2. Stress the importance of diversification. Explain that it is very difficult to know in advance how stocks, bonds or mutual funds are likely to perform in the future. **Distribute a copy of Activity 3** to each student. Explain that the Callan Periodic Table of Investment Returns illustrates how investment returns change from year to year by sector. For example, point out that U.S. bonds, including U.S. corporate and mortgage-backed bonds with maturities up to 30 years, earned a return of 10.25 percent in 2002 — the best performer for 2002. In 2003, however, U.S. bonds were listed at the bottom with a 4.10 percent return. In 2002, small-cap growth stocks were the worst performer with a return of -30.26 percent. In 2003, small-cap growth stocks were the best performer earning a 48.54 percent return. It pays to diversify!

Assessment

Multiple-Choice Questions

1. What are the three rules for building wealth over the long term?
   a. Start early, buy and hold, and diversify.
   b. Seek liquidity, loans and limits.
   c. Trade early, trade often, trade confidently.
   d. Short buy, short cover and buy on margin.

2. Trying to "time the market" by frequent buying and selling violates which rule of long-term savings?
   a. Start early
   b. Buy and hold
   c. Seize and desist
   d. Diversify

3. Which of the following would be considered the savings alternative with the highest risk and the highest reward?
   a. Bonds
   b. Real estate
   c. Certificate of deposit
   d. Stocks

4. Which of the following would be considered the savings alternative with the lowest risk and the lowest reward?
   a. Bonds
   b. Real estate
   c. Certificate of deposit
   d. Stocks

Essay Questions

1. Roosevelt is 25 years old and has just started his job as an elementary-school teacher. He had never thought much about becoming financially independent until he attended a seminar called Three Rules to Help Teachers Become Millionaires. Based on Charlayne's experience, explain the three rules that Roosevelt learned to consider.
Roosevelt learned about the importance of starting to save at a young age. He also learned that it is important to buy and hold. This would allow his savings to grow from compound interest. Finally, he learned that the savings plan he chooses should provide for diversification. By investing in a mutual fund, for example, he would be able to own many different financial assets at the same time.

2. Will has saved $3,000. He intends to use it to make a down payment on a car. But he wants to buy the car in six months, not right now. He is thinking about using the $3,000 in the meantime to buy stock in a company he has been studying. Use the concepts of *risk* and *reward* to explain why this may not be his best alternative. Suggest a better alternative for him to consider.
All investment decisions involve at least an implicit decision about risk and reward. Buying stock usually involves more risk than putting money into a savings account or a certificate of

deposit. Investing over time and spreading the risk over several alternatives (that is, diversifying) helps to reduce the risks associated with holding stocks. Will is planning to use his $3,000 relatively soon. If he buys stock now in one company, he gets none of the benefits that come with diversification. A better idea would be to place the $3,000 in a savings account or a certificate of deposit. The rewards would be less, but the risks would be near zero. Will could count on having his $3,000, plus a bit more, in six months.

LESSON 12 VISUAL 1

THREE RULES FOR BUILDING WEALTH

1. Start early.
   - Give money time to grow.

2. Buy and hold.
   - Keep your money invested.

3. Diversify.
   - Don't put all your eggs in one basket.

Lesson 12 Visual 2

Charlayne Becomes a Millionaire — Accidentally

Year	Beginning Balance	Addition to Principal	Return	Ending Balance
0	$0.00	$2,080.00	$88.40	$2,168.40
1	$2,168.40	$2,080.00	$272.71	$4,521.11
2	$4,521.11	$2,080.00	$472.69	$7,073.81
3	$7,073.81	$2,080.00	$689.67	$9,843.48
4	$9,843.48	$2,080.00	$925.10	$12,848.58
5	$12,848.58	$2,080.00	$1,180.53	$16,109.11
6	$16,109.11	$2,080.00	$1,457.67	$19,646.78
7	$19,646.78	$2,080.00	$1,758.38	$23,485.16
8	$23,485.16	$2,080.00	$2,084.64	$27,649.80
9	$27,649.80	$2,080.00	$2,438.63	$32,168.43
10	$32,168.43	$2,080.00	$2,822.72	$37,071.15
11	$37,071.15	$2,080.00	$3,239.45	$42,390.59
12	$42,390.59	$2,080.00	$3,691.60	$48,162.19
13	$48,162.19	$2,080.00	$4,182.19	$54,424.38
14	$54,424.38	$2,080.00	$4,714.47	$61,218.85
15	$61,218.85	$2,080.00	$5,292.00	$68,590.85
16	$68,590.85	$2,080.00	$5,918.62	$76,589.48
17	$76,589.48	$2,080.00	$6,598.51	$85,267.98
18	$85,267.98	$2,080.00	$7,336.18	$94,684.16
19	$94,684.16	$2,080.00	$8,136.55	$104,900.72
20	$104,900.72	$2,080.00	$9,004.96	$115,985.68
21	$115,985.68	$2,080.00	$9,947.18	$128,012.86
22	$128,012.86	$2,080.00	$10,969.49	$141,062.35
23	$141,062.35	$2,080.00	$12,078.70	$155,221.05
24	$155,221.05	$2,080.00	$13,282.19	$170,583.24
25	$170,583.24	$2,080.00	$14,587.98	$187,251.22

Lesson 12 Visual 3

Charlayne Becomes a Millionaire — Accidentally (continued)

Year	Beginning Balance	Addition to Principal	Return	Ending Balance
26	$187,251.22	$2,080.00	$16,004.75	$205,335.97
27	$205,335.97	$2,080.00	$17,541.96	$224,957.93
28	$224,957.93	$2,080.00	19,209.82	$246,247.75
29	$246,247.75	$2,080.00	$21,019.46	$269,347.21
30	$269,347.21	$2,080.00	$22,982.91	$294,410.12
31	$294,410.12	$2,080.00	$25,113.26	$321,603.38
32	$321,603.38	$2,080.00	$27,424.69	$351,108.07
33	$351,108.07	$2,080.00	$29,932.59	$383,120.66
34	$383,120.66	$2,080.00	$32,653.66	$417,854.31
35	$417,854.31	$2,080.00	$35,606.02	$455,540.33
36	$455,540.33	$2,080.00	$38,809.33	$496,429.66
37	$496,429.66	$2,080.00	$42,284.92	$540,794.58
38	$540,794.58	$2,080.00	$46,055.94	$588,930.52
39	$588,930.52	$2,080.00	$50,147.49	$641,158.01
40	$641,158.01	$2,080.00	$54,586.83	$697,824.84
41	$697,824.84	$2,080.00	$59,403.51	$759,308.35
42	$759,308.35	$2,080.00	$64,629.61	$826,017.96
43	$826,017.96	$2,080.00	$70,299.93	$898,397.89
44	$898,397.89	$2,080.00	$76,452.22	$976,930.11
45	$976,930.11	$2,080.00	$83,127.46	$1,062,137.57

Lesson 12 Visual 4

The Magic of Compounding

- When you save, you earn interest.
- When you take the interest out and spend it, it stops growing.
- But if you leave the interest in your account so it can grow, you start to earn interest on the interest you earned previously.
- Interest on interest is money you didn't work for. It is money your money makes for you!
- Over time, interest on interest can increase your total savings greatly.

Lesson 12 Visual 5

Marcus's Mistake

Year	Beginning Balance	Addition to Principal	Return	Ending Balance
0	$0		$0	$0
1	$0		$0	$0
2	$0		$0	$0
3	$0		$0	$0
4	$0		$0	$0
5	$0		$0	$0
6	$0		$0	$0
7	$0		$0	$0
8	$0		$0	$0
9	$0		$0	$0
10	$0.00	$2,080.00	$88.40	$2,168.40
11	$2,168.40	$2,080.00	$272.71	$4,521.11
12	$4,521.11	$2,080.00	$472.69	$7,073.81
13	$7,073.81	$2,080.00	$689.67	$9,843.48
14	$9,843.48	$2,080.00	$925.10	$12,848.58
15	$12,848.58	$2,080.00	$1,180.53	$16,109.11
16	$16,109.11	$2,080.00	$1,457.67	$19,646.78
17	$19,646.78	$2,080.00	$1,758.38	$23,485.16
18	$23,485.16	$2,080.00	$2,084.64	$27,649.80
19	$27,649.80	$2,080.00	$2,438.63	$32,168.43
20	$32,168.43	$2,080.00	$2,822.72	$37,071.15
21	$37,071.15	$2,080.00	$3,239.45	$42,390.59
22	$42,390.59	$2,080.00	$3,691.60	$48,162.19
23	$48,162.19	$2,080.00	$4,182.19	$54,424.38
24	$54,424.38	$2,080.00	$4,714.47	$61,218.85
25	$61,218.85	$2,080.00	$5,292.00	$68,590.85

LESSON 12 VISUAL 6

MARCUS'S MISTAKE (CONTINUED)

Year	Beginning Balance	Addition to Principal	Return	Ending Balance
26	$68,590.85	$2,080.00	$5,918.62	$76,589.48
27	$76,589.48	$2,080.00	$6,598.51	$85,267.98
28	$85,267.98	$2,080.00	$7,336.18	$94,684.16
29	$94,684.16	$2,080.00	$8,136.55	$104,900.72
30	$104,900.72	$2,080.00	$9,004.96	$115,985.68
31	$115,985.68	$2,080.00	$9,947.18	$128,012.86
32	$128,012.86	$2,080.00	$10,969.49	$141,062.35
33	$141,062.35	$2,080.00	$12,078.70	$155,221.05
34	$155,221.05	$2,080.00	$13,282.19	$170,583.24
35	$170,583.24	$2,080.00	$14,587.98	$187,251.22
36	$187,251.22	$2,080.00	$16,004.75	$205,335.97
37	$205,335.97	$2,080.00	$17,541.96	$224,957.93
38	$224,957.93	$2,080.00	$19,209.82	$246,247.75
39	$246,247.75	$2,080.00	$21,019.46	$269,347.21
40	$269,347.21	$2,080.00	$22,982.91	$294,410.12
41	$294,410.12	$2,080.00	$25,113.26	$321,603.38
42	$321,603.38	$2,080.00	$27,424.69	$351,108.07
43	$351,108.07	$2,080.00	$29,932.59	$383,120.66
44	$383,120.66	$2,080.00	$32,653.66	$417,854.31
45	$417,854.31	$2,080.00	$35,606.02	$455,540.33

Lesson 12 Visual 7

Buy and Hold

In order to leave money in savings or investments, you have to do these things:

- Spend less than you receive. How?
  Perhaps you could…

  Earn more by improving your formal education or job skills.

  Spend less by using a budget to keep track of where your money is going.

- Become connected to financial institutions. How?

  Open and maintain accounts at mainstream financial institutions — banks, credit unions and brokerages.

- Manage your credit responsibly. How?

  Limit the number of credit cards you have.

  Limit your purchases to what you can pay off each month.

  Apply for loans when you are confident that your current income (in the case of college loans, future income) will allow you to repay the loan.

LESSON 12 VISUAL 8

THE STOCK-MARKET ROLLER COASTER

If you buy and sell on the ups and downs, you may lose money.

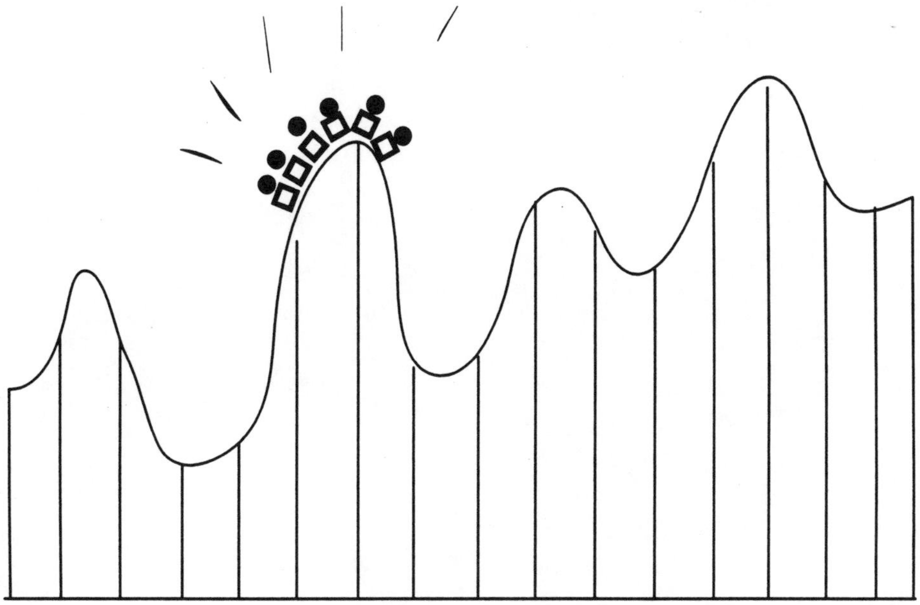

But if you hold on for the long term, the ups are greater than the downs.

Lesson 12 Visual 9

Don't Put All Your Eggs in One Basket

If you put all your money in one stock, a disaster befalling that stock will hit you hard — as if you had put all your eggs in one basket and then dropped the basket. With your money spread out across a variety of assets (stocks, bonds and cash, for example), you're not hurt as badly when any one asset does poorly.

LESSON 12 VISUAL 10

FORMS OF SAVING AND INVESTING: SOME BENEFITS AND COSTS

- ***Savings accounts:*** provide a small but steady return.
- ***Certificates of deposit:*** very safe, but instant access carries a penalty.
- ***Bonds:*** lending money to a corporation or government, with a promise of higher returns than those offered by bank savings accounts and CDs.
- ***Stocks:*** part ownership in a company, offering higher risks and, potentially, higher returns than some other investments.
- ***Real estate:*** the risks and benefits of being a landlord.

Lesson 12 Visual 11

Investment Situations

1. You have $5,000 to invest. No other information is available.

2. You have $4,000 that you'll need six months from now.

3. You inherited $10,000 from your great-aunt; she has suggested that you save it for use in your old age.

4. You are just starting a career and can save $50 per month for retirement.

5. A new baby arrives, and Mom and Dad plan to save $100 a month for the child's college education.

Lesson 12 Visual 12

The Pyramid of Risks and Reward

Highest Risk — Highest Potential Return or Loss

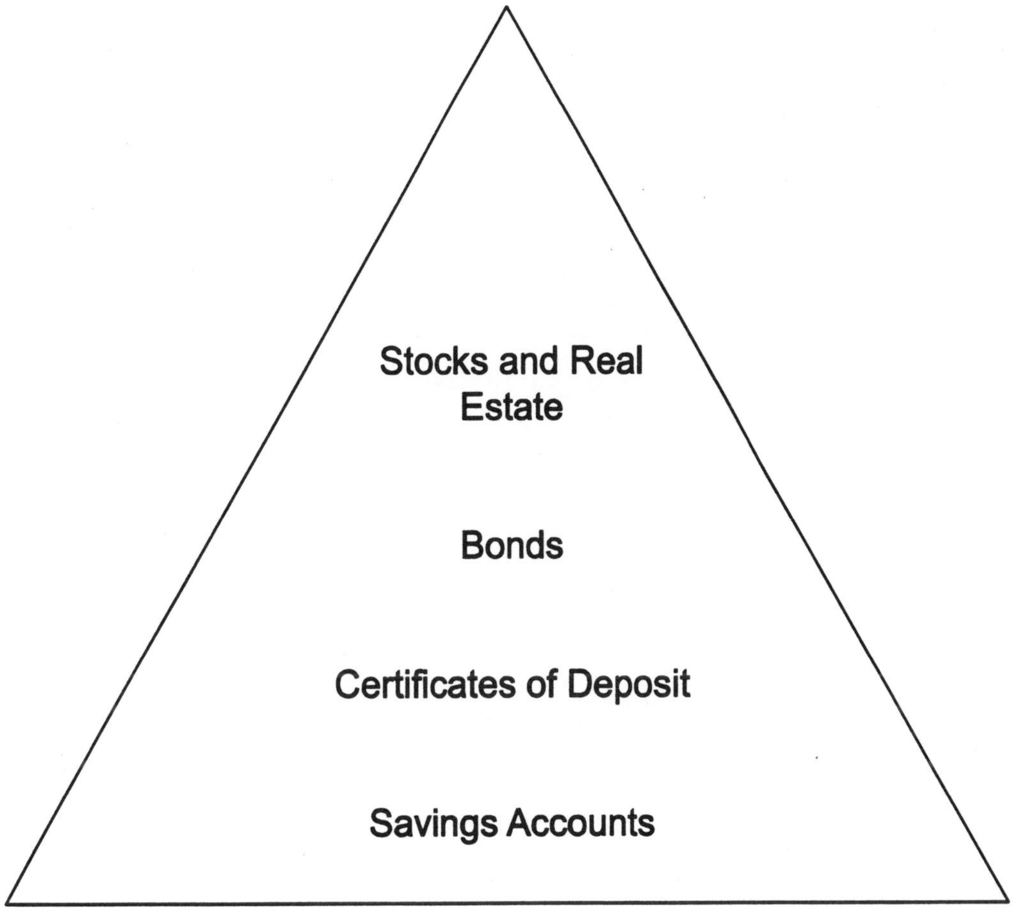

Lowest Risk — Lowest Potential Return or Loss

Lesson 12 Visual 13

Mutual Funds

- A mutual fund pools investors' money.
- The fund puts its investors' money into the markets on their behalf.
- In effect, investors own small amounts of many different assets.
- Mutual funds enable investors to avoid the risk that comes from owning any one asset. In other words, mutual funds make it easy to diversify.

FLOOR MARKER 1

SAVINGS
ACCOUNT

FLOOR MARKER 2

CERTIFICATE
OF DEPOSIT

Floor Marker 3

BONDS

Floor Marker 4

STOCKS

Floor Marker 5

Real Estate

LESSON 12 ACTIVITY 1

STRATEGIES FOR WEALTH BUILDING

For many people who are struggling from month to month financially, even the term "wealth building" seems alien. Yet when people spend less than they receive and make good decisions, they can, slowly over time, build up the value of what they own.

Wealth building is good for individuals, families and society because it improves people's quality of life. Whatever goods and services you would like for yourself, your family or nation — better housing, higher-quality medical care or anything else — they can be more nearly within reach if you engage effectively in wealth building.

The Three Rules

Many people act as if wealth building were very complex. In fact, an effective approach to wealth building can be summarized in three rules:

1. Start early.
2. Buy and hold.
3. Diversify.

Case Study: Charlayne, the Accidental Millionaire

When Charlayne was getting started in her first job, she didn't use any of her pay to play the lottery or head for the casino along with all her friends. "Come on," they said. "It's the only way you'll ever be a millionaire." She took note of the "Who Wants to Be a Millionaire?" show on television. But she was pretty sure she would never become a millionaire by hitting the lottery or answering game-show questions.

Yet Charlayne became a millionaire. How?

Charlayne made an important decision when she began to work. With advice from the company's benefits manager, she decided to have $20 withheld from each weekly paycheck and put into a mutual fund account. That wasn't easy to do. Charlayne had many possible uses for an extra $20 each week. But the benefits manager persuaded her that putting $20 aside each week would be the best thing to do for her future.

Charlayne's company matched the $20 deposit she made each week. This meant an immediate doubling of Charlayne's weekly savings.

Over time, Charlayne didn't exactly forget about her account, but she didn't always monitor it closely. As printed statements arrived in the mail, generally showing that the value of her account was increasing, Charlayne became increasingly comfortable about her retirement plan.

There were times when Charlayne really would have liked to have the money she was saving. But she never considered trying to take her money out of the retirement account. Somehow she found a way to scrape through when there was a financial crisis.

When Charlayne retired, it became clear that her sustained program of investment had served her well. She had become a millionaire. Her retirement account was worth more than a million dollars. Steady payments from that account enabled Charlayne to travel and visit her grandchildren, go to movies or concerts when she wanted to, and live in comfort. She was even able to help with college expenses for next-generation members of her family.

Most people are skeptical when they're told that matched weekly contributions of $20 could make them

Lesson 12 Activity 1 (continued)

millionaires — but the math works. Figure 1 shows how the money kept growing, in this case, until Charlayne became a millionaire.

Figure 1 assumes an average return of 8.5 percent each year, calculated on the average yearly balance and compounded once per year.

Figure 1: Charlayne Becomes a Millionaire — Accidentally

Year	Beginning Balance	Addition to Principal	Return	Ending Balance
0	$0.00	$2,080.00	$88.40	$2,168.40
1	$2,168.40	$2,080.00	$272.71	$4,521.11
2	$4,521.11	$2,080.00	$472.69	$7,073.81
3	$7,073.81	$2,080.00	$689.67	$9,843.48
4	$9,843.48	$2,080.00	$925.10	$12,848.58
5	$12,848.58	$2,080.00	$1,180.53	$16,109.11
6	$16,109.11	$2,080.00	$1,457.67	$19,646.78
7	$19,646.78	$2,080.00	$1,758.38	$23,485.16
8	$23,485.16	$2,080.00	$2,084.64	$27,649.80
9	$27,649.80	$2,080.00	$2,438.63	$32,168.43
10	$32,168.43	$2,080.00	$2,822.72	$37,071.15
11	$37,071.15	$2,080.00	$3,239.45	$42,390.59
12	$42,390.59	$2,080.00	$3,691.60	$48,162.19
13	$48,162.19	$2,080.00	$4,182.19	$54,424.38
14	$54,424.38	$2,080.00	$4,714.47	$61,218.85
15	$61,218.85	$2,080.00	$5,292.00	$68,590.85
16	$68,590.85	$2,080.00	$5,918.62	$76,589.48
17	$76,589.48	$2,080.00	$6,598.51	$85,267.98
18	$85,267.98	$2,080.00	$7,336.18	$94,684.16
19	$94,684.16	$2,080.00	$8,136.55	$104,900.72
20	$104,900.72	$2,080.00	$9,004.96	$115,985.68
21	$115,985.68	$2,080.00	$9,947.18	$128,012.86
22	$128,012.86	$2,080.00	$10,969.49	$141,062.35
23	$141,062.35	$2,080.00	$12,078.70	$155,221.05
24	$155,221.05	$2,080.00	$13,282.19	$170,583.24
25	$170,583.24	$2,080.00	$14,587.98	$187,251.22

Lesson 12 Activity 1 (continued)

Year	Beginning Balance	Addition to Principal	Return	Ending Balance
26	$187,251.22	$2,080.00	$16,004.75	$205,335.97
27	$205,335.97	$2,080.00	$17,541.96	$224,957.93
28	$224,957.93	$2,080.00	19,209.82	$246,247.75
29	$246,247.75	$2,080.00	$21,019.46	$269,347.21
30	$269,347.21	$2,080.00	$22,982.91	$294,410.12
31	$294,410.12	$2,080.00	$25,113.26	$321,603.38
32	$321,603.38	$2,080.00	$27,424.69	$351,108.07
33	$351,108.07	$2,080.00	$29,932.59	$383,120.66
34	$383,120.66	$2,080.00	$32,653.66	$417,854.31
35	$417,854.31	$2,080.00	$35,606.02	$455,540.33
36	$455,540.33	$2,080.00	$38,809.33	$496,429.66
37	$496,429.66	$2,080.00	$42,284.92	$540,794.58
38	$540,794.58	$2,080.00	$46,055.94	$588,930.52
39	$588,930.52	$2,080.00	$50,147.49	$641,158.01
40	$641,158.01	$2,080.00	$54,586.83	$697,824.84
41	$697,824.84	$2,080.00	$59,403.51	$759,308.35
42	$759,308.35	$2,080.00	$64,629.61	$826,017.96
43	$826,017.96	$2,080.00	$70,299.93	$898,397.89
44	$898,397.89	$2,080.00	$76,452.22	$976,930.11
45	$976,930.11	$2,080.00	$83,127.46	$1,062,137.57

Call Charlayne lucky if you want to, but most people could do what she did. In getting her lifetime net wealth to $1 million by age 65, she followed the three rules:

1. **Start early.** Charlayne began saving when she turned 20, so she had 45 years in which her savings could grow.
2. **Buy and hold.** Charlayne bought a tiny bit more in financial assets each payday with the small amount withheld from her pay. She never touched that account as it grew over the years. Most importantly, she did not withdraw her money and spend it even when times were tough.
3. **Diversify.** Charlayne's retirement account was invested in a broad variety of financial assets. It wasn't put into any one asset.

And that is how Charlayne became a millionaire. Let's look at the three rules she followed in more detail.

LESSON 12 ACTIVITY 1 (CONTINUED)

Rule 1: The Importance of an Early Start

Rule 1 says "Start early." Money that's saved early so that it can work for a long time has a great deal of importance in overall wealth building.

An early start works well because of the magic of compounding. When you save money, you receive a return. In the case of bank accounts, that return is called interest. If you leave the interest in the account, that money also earns interest. In other words, you earn interest on interest. The longer this process goes on, the more it works for you.

Here is a different example that also shows the importance of an early start: Charlayne had a co-worker who didn't start early. Instead of starting to save at the beginning of his career, Marcus held off for 10 years. Then, like Charlayne, he saved $20 per week, and his company matched these deposits for the next 35 years. Marcus accumulated more than $400,000 by saving as he did. (See Figure 2.)

That's a lot of money. But because Charlayne started early, she became a millionaire and Marcus did not.

This example shows how you need to get an early start in order to build significant wealth in a lifetime. But even if you don't get an early start, then (like Marcus) you can still take big steps toward wealth building. You just have to save more (or settle for less) than if you had gotten off to an early start.

Figure 2: Marcus's Mistake: Waiting to Start Saving

Year	Beginning Balance	Addition to Principal	Return	Ending Balance
0	$0		$0	$0
1	$0		$0	$0
2	$0		$0	$0
3	$0		$0	$0
4	$0		$0	$0
5	$0		$0	$0
6	$0		$0	$0
7	$0		$0	$0
8	$0		$0	$0
9	$0		$0	$0
10	$0.00	$2,080.00	$88.40	$2,168.40
11	$2,168.40	$2,080.00	$272.71	$4,521.11
12	$4,521.11	$2,080.00	$472.69	$7,073.81
13	$7,073.81	$2,080.00	$689.67	$9,843.48
14	$9,843.48	$2,080.00	$925.10	$12,848.58
15	$12,848.58	$2,080.00	$1,180.53	$16,109.11

Lesson 12 Activity 1 (continued)

Year	Beginning Balance	Addition to Principal	Return	Ending Balance
16	$16,109.11	$2,080.00	$1,457.67	$19,646.78
17	$19,646.78	$2,080.00	$1,758.38	$23,485.16
18	$23,485.16	$2,080.00	$2,084.64	$27,649.80
19	$27,649.80	$2,080.00	$2,438.63	$32,168.43
20	$32,168.43	$2,080.00	$2,822.72	$37,071.15
21	$37,071.15	$2,080.00	$3,239.45	$42,390.59
22	$42,390.59	$2,080.00	$3,691.60	$48,162.19
23	$48,162.19	$2,080.00	$4,182.19	$54,424.38
24	$54,424.38	$2,080.00	$4,714.47	$61,218.85
25	$61,218.85	$2,080.00	$5,292.00	$68,590.85
26	$68,590.85	$2,080.00	$5,918.62	$76,589.48
27	$76,589.48	$2,080.00	$6,598.51	$85,267.98
28	$85,267.98	$2,080.00	$7,336.18	$94,684.16
29	$94,684.16	$2,080.00	$8,136.55	$104,900.72
30	$104,900.72	$2,080.00	$9,004.96	$115,985.68
31	$115,985.68	$2,080.00	$9,947.18	$128,012.86
32	$128,012.86	$2,080.00	$10,969.49	$141,062.35
33	$141,062.35	$2,080.00	$12,078.70	$155,221.05
34	$155,221.05	$2,080.00	$13,282.19	$170,583.24
35	$170,583.24	$2,080.00	$14,587.98	$187,251.22
36	$187,251.22	$2,080.00	$16,004.75	$205,335.97
37	$205,335.97	$2,080.00	$17,541.96	$224,957.93
38	$224,957.93	$2,080.00	$19,209.82	$246,247.75
39	$246,247.75	$2,080.00	$21,019.46	$269,347.21
40	$269,347.21	$2,080.00	$22,982.91	$294,410.12
41	$294,410.12	$2,080.00	$25,113.26	$321,603.38
42	$321,603.38	$2,080.00	$27,424.69	$351,108.07
43	$351,108.07	$2,080.00	$29,932.59	$383,120.66
44	$383,120.66	$2,080.00	$32,653.66	$417,854.31
45	$417,854.31	$2,080.00	$35,606.02	$455,540.33

Lesson 12 Activity 1 (continued)

Rule 2: Buy and Hold

The second rule is "Buy and hold." This means that to build wealth over time, you have to hold on to your long-term savings. You can't be dipping into them frequently, or they won't compound over time in the same way.

To buy and hold, you have to have your finances in order. Here are three steps to consider:

- Spend less than you receive. You do this either by earning more or spending less. You can help yourself to spend less by keeping track of where your money is going; then you cut back in places where you can save small amounts. You take the small amounts you're saving and get them out of sight so you won't be tempted to spend what's there.
- Make intelligent choices about financial institutions. Here the goal is to open and maintain accounts at mainstream financial institutions such as banks, credit unions and brokerages. Then you can accomplish savings and budgeting goals that simply wouldn't be possible if you were still operating on a cash basis.
- Manage your credit properly. When you're managing your credit properly, you're limiting the number of credit cards you have. You're limiting your purchases to what you can pay off each month, without leaving a balance to accumulate interest that you'll also have to pay. As time goes by, your credit score goes up, making it possible for you to borrow when you have a good reason to borrow.

If you're doing all this, you can buy and hold with confidence. Remember the case of Charlayne, the accidental millionaire? Surprisingly, one of the smartest things she did with her retirement account was to neglect it. She just kept having money taken out of her paycheck and put into financial assets, no matter what.

That meant that when her financial assets declined in value because of the normal ups and downs of the market, she didn't change her strategy. Financial assets were then, at down-market times, relatively cheap, and her regular contributions bought more than they bought when financial assets were more expensive.

When financial markets went up, those inexpensively-bought financial assets became worth a whole lot more. Charlayne saw televised accounts of people who became rich overnight playing the stock market because the values of their financial assets had become so high. But she didn't think she could play that game, so she just left her retirement fund alone. She held onto it and kept most of the gains, though she was aware that markets were always going up and down.

Over time, Charlayne came out better than many people who worked much harder trying to make more. They tried to jump in and out of the markets with their retirement money. They tried to "buy low" and "sell high," but in the end didn't do as well as people like Charlayne who stuck with the dull rule, "buy and hold."

Lesson 12 Activity 1 (continued)

Rule 3: Diversify

Somebody probably once told you, "Don't put all your eggs in one basket." This saying hearkens back to the time when knocking over a single basket might wipe out a week's supply of eggs from the henhouse — if you had put all the eggs in one basket (see Figure 3).

Figure 3: Don't Put All Your Eggs in One Basket

To diversify is to take on many small risks rather than one large risk. If you put all of your savings into a new start-up toy company, you could get rich if the company succeeded. Or you could lose all your money if the company failed. That's like having all your eggs in one basket. The same point would apply if you were approached by someone proposing that you invest in a business opportunity. If you put all your savings there, you would again be putting your money at risk.

Any time you take one large risk with your money, you're not diversifying. That's dangerous. It's far safer to spread risks out. This means holding a variety of financial assets rather than just one.

Questions for Discussion

1. What are the three rules of wealth building?

2. Explain how Charlayne, the accidental millionaire, followed all three rules.

LESSON 12 ACTIVITY 2

FORMS OF SAVING AND INVESTING

Below are some of the assets you can choose when you're thinking about where to put your money. We'll start with the safest kinds and then proceed down the list to some riskier ones.

- **Savings Accounts.** These accounts are kept at banks. They are insured by the federal government, and no one has ever lost even a penny of federally-insured individual savings deposits. Your money will be safe in a savings account. There are two other things to know about savings accounts, however. The first is that the money won't be as easy to spend as cash or money in a checking account. You'll have to make a separate transaction to withdraw the money from a savings account before you can spend it. The second is that the money will not earn a high return. The interest paid on savings is small but steady.
- **Certificates of Deposit.** Just like savings accounts, certificates of deposit (often called CDs) are made available by banks and are federally insured. When you buy a certificate of deposit, you're tying your money up for a specified period — from one month to a number of years. That means it's harder to spend than money from a checking or savings account. Before spending it, you have to wait until the term is up — or be assessed interest penalties for an early withdrawal. In return for giving the bank greater use of your money, you earn interest at rates somewhat higher than the rates paid on a savings account.
- **Bonds.** When you buy a bond, in effect you're making a loan. You're lending your money to the organization that issued the bond. The bond will specify under what terms you get your money repaid and what the interest will be. Some bonds are very safe, such as those issued by the federal government. Some bonds have medium safety, such as those issued by major corporations. Almost certainly, you'll get your money back with interest, but there's a chance that a major corporation could fail. Finally, some bonds are known as "junk bonds." Junk bonds are high-risk investments. There is a real probability that the companies issuing them may not be able to pay investors back.
- **Stocks.** When you buy a stock, you're actually becoming a part-owner of a corporation. Ownership is easy to see when four people contribute equally to a new corporation and each owns a fourth of the venture. All four would share in the profits of the business and all four would have a fourth of the decision-making authority. Ownership is harder to see in today's corporations. But while modern corporations issue millions of shares, the principle is the same. If a corporation issues 200 million shares of stock, then buying a share makes you a 1 200-millionth owner of the corporation. You have a claim on 1 200-millionth of the worth of the corporation, and you have 1 200-millionth of the decision-making authority in the corporation. More importantly for investors, some corporations make payments to shareholders called dividends. You can earn money with stocks by getting dividends, and also by the increase in the value of the stock over time, if the company does well. Of all the assets mentioned so far, stocks carry the highest risk. A company could have great success, making its shareholders rich. Or it could go down the tubes, making its shareholders lose whatever they invested.
- **Real Estate.** When you own your own home, it's a relatively safe investment. You pay on the home and you get a place to live. Over time, its value will likely go up and you'll pay down the amount of the loan. But it's also possible to invest in real estate as a landlord. You might buy half of a duplex and rent it out, for example. Being a landlord can be rewarding, but you should know that there are risks that come with investing in real estate (other than your own home). You are responsible for the upkeep on a rental property you own, and also for finding renters who will pay their rent on time. If something breaks, you have to fix it or hire someone to fix it. If a renter is late with a monthly payment, that doesn't excuse you from making payments to the bank on any loans you used to buy the property.

Lesson 12 Activity 2 (continued)

Risk and Return

You may have noticed a relationship in reading about different forms of investing. Safe investments don't offer a big return. If you choose the safety of a bank account for your money, you won't earn a lot of money on that.

The other side of the coin is that riskier investments offer the possibility of a larger return. If they didn't, nobody would invest in them. As we move from bank assets to bonds to stocks and real estate, we're moving toward assets with many possibilities for things to go wrong — and for things to go right. A company whose stock you buy may succeed wildly or go bankrupt, or anything in between. You take that risk when you own a single company's stock.

Look at the pyramid in Figure 1. Notes toward the bottom of the pyramid identify safe places to keep money. They offer lower returns than the riskier investments noted toward the top. In investing, you should build the bottom of the pyramid with safe investments like bank accounts and CDs first. Later you can venture into riskier stocks and bonds, closer to the top of the pyramid.

Figure 1 : The Risk-Return Pyramid

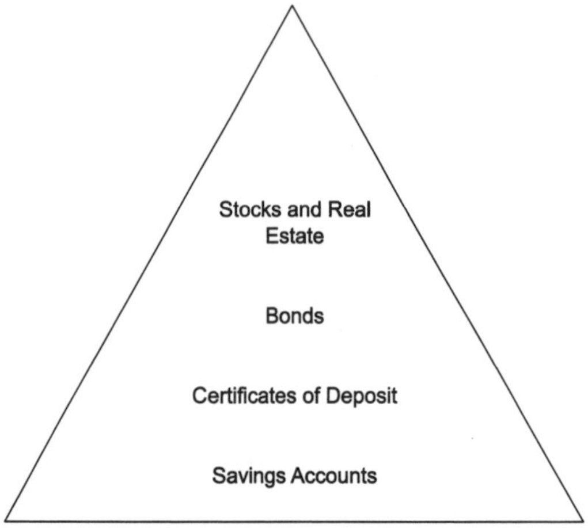

Mutual Funds

How do we get a high return while managing the risk? The answer lies in diversifying. When we diversify, we take a lot of small risks rather than a single large risk. The small risks don't add up to much, and they get smaller and smaller over time for an investor who buys and holds onto a variety of financial assets.

We might think of diversifying as a matter of buying small amounts of a lot of different stocks or bonds. But because it costs something to buy each asset, that approach would quickly get to be expensive. Fortunately, there are mutual funds that act to buy financial assets on behalf of individual investors.

A mutual fund gets a pool of money by accepting funds from thousands of individual investors. It invests its pool of money in a collection of assets. As that collection generates income, the mutual fund sends that income back to its investors in proportion to how much money they have put in. Because of its large size, a mutual fund can efficiently buy large numbers of different stocks and bonds.

Lesson 12 Activity 2 (continued)

Charlayne, the accidental millionaire, owes much of her success to mutual funds. The money in her retirement fund — as is true for most retirement funds — was invested in diversified mutual funds. Charlayne indirectly owned stock in a wide variety of companies. Thus when technology stocks boomed in the 1990s, some of her money was in technology stocks. Also, when automotive company stocks lost value, she didn't lose nearly as much as she would have, had she owned only auto stocks.

Mutual funds are nowhere near as safe as bank deposits. When markets go down, mutual funds follow them down, depending on which stocks and bonds the funds are holding. Over time, however, mutual funds have been an excellent investment, far surpassing bank accounts and bonds in their long-term returns. Many ordinary people have become millionaires by starting early, buying and holding, and using mutual funds to diversify.

Question for Discussion

What are the advantages and disadvantages of alternative forms of saving and investing?

- Saving Accounts
- Certificates of Deposit
- Bonds
- Stocks
- Real Estate

Lesson 12 Activity 3

Diversification

UBS Global Asset Management

The Callan Periodic Table of Investment Returns[1]

Annual Returns for Key Indices (1982–2003*) Ranked in order of performance (Best to Worst)

1982	1983	1984	1985	1986	1987	1988	1989	1990	1991	1992	1993	1994	1995	1996	1997	1998	1999	2000	2001	2002	2003
US Bonds 32.65%	Small Cap Value 38.63%	US Bonds 15.15%	Int'l Stocks 56.14%	Int'l Stocks 69.46%	Int'l Stocks 24.64%	Small Cap Value 29.47%	Large Cap Growth 36.40%	US Bonds 8.96%	Small Cap Growth 51.18%	Small Cap Value 29.15%	Int'l Stocks 32.57%	Int'l Stocks 7.78%	Large Cap Growth 38.13%	Large Cap Growth 23.97%	Large Cap Growth 36.52%	Large Cap Growth 42.16%	Small Cap Growth 43.09%	Small Cap Value 22.83%	Small Cap Value 14.03%	US Bonds 10.25%	Small Cap Growth 48.54%
Small Cap Value 28.52%	Small Cap Stocks 29.13%	Large Cap Value 10.52%	Large Cap Growth 33.31%	Large Cap Value 21.67%	Large Cap Growth 6.50%	Int'l Stocks 28.26%	Large Cap Stocks 31.69%	Large Cap Growth 0.20%	Small Cap Stocks 46.05%	Small Cap Stocks 18.42%	Small Cap Value 23.86%	Large Cap Growth 3.14%	Large Cap Stocks 37.58%	Large Cap Stocks 22.96%	Large Cap Stocks 33.36%	Large Cap Stocks 28.58%	Large Cap Growth 28.25%	US Bonds 11.63%	US Bonds 8.44%	Small Cap Value -11.43%	Small Cap Stocks 47.25%
Small Cap Stocks 24.95%	Large Cap Value 28.89%	Int'l Stocks 7.41%	Large Cap Stocks 31.73%	Large Cap Stocks 18.67%	Large Cap Stocks 5.25%	Small Cap Stocks 24.89%	Large Cap Value 26.13%	Large Cap Stocks -3.11%	Small Cap Value 41.70%	Large Cap Value 10.52%	Small Cap Stocks 18.89%	Large Cap Stocks 1.32%	Large Cap Value 36.99%	Large Cap Value 22.00%	Small Cap Value 31.78%	Int'l Stocks 20.00%	Int'l Stocks 26.96%	Large Cap Value 6.08%	Small Cap Stocks 2.49%	Int'l Stocks -15.66%	Small Cap Value 46.03%
Large Cap Growth 22.03%	Int'l Stocks 23.69%	Large Cap Stocks 6.27%	Small Cap Stocks 31.04%	US Bonds 15.30%	Large Cap Value 3.68%	Large Cap Value 21.67%	Small Cap Growth 20.16%	Large Cap Value -6.85%	Large Cap Growth 38.37%	Small Cap Growth 7.77%	Large Cap Value 18.61%	Large Cap Value -0.64%	Small Cap Growth 31.04%	Small Cap Value 21.37%	Large Cap Value 29.98%	Large Cap Value 14.69%	Small Cap Stocks 21.26%	Small Cap Stocks -3.02%	Small Cap Growth -9.23%	Small Cap Stocks -20.48%	Int'l Stocks 38.59%
Large Cap Stocks 21.55%	Large Cap Stocks 22.56%	Large Cap Growth 2.33%	Small Cap Value 31.01%	Large Cap Growth 14.50%	US Bonds 2.75%	Small Cap Growth 20.38%	Small Cap Stocks 16.25%	Small Cap Growth -17.42%	Large Cap Stocks 30.47%	Large Cap Stocks 7.62%	Small Cap Growth 13.37%	Small Cap Value -1.55%	Small Cap Stocks 28.44%	Small Cap Stocks 16.53%	Small Cap Stocks 22.36%	US Bonds 8.70%	Large Cap Stocks 21.04%	Large Cap Stocks -9.10%	Large Cap Value -11.71%	Large Cap Value -20.85%	Large Cap Value 31.79%
Large Cap Value 21.04%	Small Cap Growth 20.14%	Small Cap Value 2.27%	Small Cap Growth 30.97%	Small Cap Value 7.41%	Small Cap Value -7.12%	Large Cap Stocks 16.61%	US Bonds 14.53%	Small Cap Stocks -19.50%	Large Cap Value 22.56%	US Bonds 7.40%	Large Cap Stocks 10.08%	Small Cap Stocks -1.81%	Small Cap Value 25.75%	Small Cap Growth 11.32%	Small Cap Growth 12.93%	Small Cap Growth 1.23%	Large Cap Value 12.72%	Int'l Stocks -14.17%	Large Cap Stocks -11.88%	Large Cap Stocks -22.10%	Large Cap Stocks 28.68%
Small Cap Growth 20.99%	Large Cap Growth 16.24%	Small Cap Stocks -7.13%	Large Cap Value 29.68%	Small Cap Stocks 5.69%	Small Cap Stocks -8.76%	Large Cap Growth 11.95%	Small Cap Value 12.43%	Small Cap Value -21.77%	US Bonds 16.00%	Large Cap Growth 5.06%	US Bonds 9.75%	Small Cap Growth -2.44%	US Bonds 18.46%	Int'l Stocks 6.05%	US Bonds 9.64%	Small Cap Stocks -2.55%	US Bonds -0.82%	Large Cap Growth -22.07%	Large Cap Growth -12.73%	Large Cap Growth -23.59%	Large Cap Growth 25.66%
Int'l Stocks -1.86%	US Bonds 8.19%	Small Cap Growth -15.84%	US Bonds 22.13%	Small Cap Growth 3.59%	Small Cap Growth -10.48%	US Bonds 7.89%	Int'l Stocks 10.53%	Int'l Stocks -23.45%	Int'l Stocks 12.14%	Int'l Stocks -12.18%	Large Cap Growth 1.68%	US Bonds -2.92%	Int'l Stocks 11.21%	US Bonds 3.64%	Int'l Stocks 1.78%	Small Cap Value -6.46%	Small Cap Value -1.48%	Small Cap Growth -22.43%	Int'l Stocks -21.44%	Small Cap Growth -30.26%	US Bonds 4.10%

Small Cap Value, represented by the Russell 2000 Value Index, contains those Russell 2000 securities with a less-than-average growth orientation. Securities in this index generally have lower price-to-book and price-to-earnings ratios than those in the Russell 2000 Growth Index.

Small Cap Growth, represented by the Russell 2000 Growth Index, contains those Russell 2000 securities with a greater-than-average growth orientation. Securities in this index generally have higher price-to-book and price-to-earnings ratios than those in the Russell 2000 Value Index.

Large Cap Stocks, represented by the S&P 500 Index, is a market-value-weighted index of 500 stocks that are traded on the NYSE, AMEX and NASDAQ. The weightings make each company's influence on the performance of this index directly proportional to that company's market value.

Large Cap Growth and Large Cap Value, represented by the S&P Growth and the S&P Value Indexes, are constructed by dividing the stocks in the S&P 500 Index according to price-to-book ratios. The Growth Index contains stocks with higher price-to-book ratios. The Value Index contains stocks with lower price-to-book ratios. The indexes are market-capitalization weighted, and their holdings are mutually exclusive.

International Stocks, represented by the MSCI EAFE Index, is a Morgan Stanley Capital International Index that is designed to measure the performance of the developed stock markets of Europe, Australasia and the Far East.

US Bonds, represented by the Lehman Brothers Aggregate Bond Index, includes US government, corporate and mortgage-backed securities with maturities up to 30 years.

Small Cap Stocks, represented by the Russell 2000 Index, is a market-value-weighted index of the 2000 smallest stocks in the broad-market Russell 3000 Index. These securities are traded on the NYSE, AMEX and NASDAQ.

Past performance is no guarantee of future results. For illustration purposes only. Indices are unmanaged and unavailable for direct investment.

*Annual Returns in 1981 were: Small Cap Value +14.85%; US Bonds +6.26%; Small Cap Stocks 2.03%; Large Cap Value +0.02%; Int'l Stocks -2.27%; Large Cap Stocks -4.92%; Small Cap Growth -9.23%; Large Cap Growth -9.81%.

Source: Data from the Callan Periodic Table. Callan Associates, Inc., 2004. Used with permission.

[1] Used with permission of UBS.

Lesson 13 Researching Companies

Middle School

13 Researching Companies

Lesson 13 Researching Companies

Lesson Description

The students apply an economic way of thinking to gathering information regarding securities. They learn that the cost of acquiring information must be compared to the anticipated benefit the information will provide. The students discuss the example of LeBron James and recognize that there is intense competition to find information about companies. They select companies to research by participating in a classroom drawing and by listing companies they know. They gather fundamental information about each of the companies they select.

In the search for information about investments, individual investors are not alone. Banks, brokerage firms and mutual funds employ specialists to find and interpret information, and in their research activities they compete intensively with one another as they try to win customers. Because these specialists compete to produce detailed information for all sectors of the economy, the field is heavily tracked over. It is therefore difficult for individuals to find surprises — to find companies likely to produce unexpected high returns. Acknowledging these difficulties, this lesson surveys certain practices often used to research investment prospects. This lesson focuses on the fundamental analysis of company performance.

Concepts

- Alternatives
- Choice
- Fundamental analysis
- Opportunity cost
- Scarcity

Objectives

Students will:

1. Develop criteria to use in choosing stocks.
2. Use criteria to choose among stock investment possibilities.
3. Identify the cost of seeking more information.
4. Recognize the basic features of fundamental analysis.

Time Required

90 minutes

Materials

- A copy of the financial pages from a newspaper
- Access to the Internet
- Several copies of mutual fund prospectuses
- A transparency of Visuals 1, 2, 3, 4 and 5
- A copy of Activity 1 for each student
- Activity 2, cut up to use in a drawing

Procedure

1. Tell the students that this lesson focuses on research investors might carry out in order to increase chances for success in making investment decisions. Show the students some stock pages from a newspaper. Turn the pages slowly and note the many stocks, bonds and mutual funds that are available for investors to buy.

2. Explain that about 2,800 firms are listed on the New York Stock Exchange. Thousands more are listed on the American Stock Exchange (AMEX) and the NASDAQ, and still more are listed on stock exchanges based in other countries. Out of all these companies, how does one pick the stocks most likely to increase in price?

3. **Display Visual 1** and discuss the guidelines for applying economic reasoning to researching stocks. Stress the point that there is a great deal of investment information available. The important idea here is to not get overwhelmed. Investors engaged in research face a classic scarcity problem: an investor's time is limited, while the available information is vast.

4. **Display Visual 2.** Note that there is intense competition among financial institutions to find information about companies. Specialists doing research for these institutions are not looking merely for good companies. It is easy to identify good companies, and good companies don't necessarily provide high returns on investments. That is because good companies typically attract many investors, and high demand pushes stock prices up for those companies, decreasing investors' chances to make big gains. Instead of searching merely for good companies, institutional researchers look for companies that might generate surprises: unexpected high returns. Paradoxically, surprises are hard to find precisely because so many people are trying to find them. In a field that gets examined so carefully, it is difficult for individuals to get in early, ahead of others, on the purchase of stocks that are underpriced and likely to produce unexpectedly high returns.

5. **Display Visual 3.** Explain that the value of Nike shares increased after Nike became associated with LeBron James. James is an exciting young basketball player who jumped straight from high school to a starting role in the National Basketball Association. James had surprising success as an NBA rookie, and he signed with Nike to endorse Nike products early in his professional career. ***Ask:*** Could you make big money today by purchasing Nike stock, thinking that its value might be enhanced by the LeBron James connection?

No, probably not today. But you might have done well if you had gotten in early — if you had bought Nike stock just before James became a star and signed with Nike.

6. **Distribute a copy of Activity 1** to each student. Explain that this handout provides a useful tool to summarize important characteristics regarding various companies. We will explain the sections of the handout shortly, but first we need to decide which companies to study.

7. Explain that many economists believe it is not possible to predict stocks that will outperform others. Stocks picked at random sometimes perform as well as stocks picked by experts. Conduct a brief demonstration to illustrate picking stocks by random — a low-cost approach. Place the cards you have cut out from Activity 2 in a container in front of the room for a drawing. Explain that the names of 30 well-known companies and their stock symbols are marked on cards in the container. Walk around the room to each student's desk; ask each student to draw the name of one company from the container. Tell the students to enter the names of their companies into the first place for a Company Name in Activity 1. Now that each student has one company to study, let's examine some other approaches.

8. Explain that another easy method to select stocks is by focusing on companies one knows. If you have noticed companies that seem popular — their stores are crowded or your friends make favorable comments about a product or service — perhaps you should look further into the company. Ask the students to identify companies whose products they buy, stores they shop in or games they play. Tell the students to add the names of three of these companies to Activity 1.

9. A more time-consuming method of choosing stocks involves researching a company's financial information. **Display Visual 4.** This visual introduces an approach for analyzing stocks called fundamental analysis. Fundamental analysts use basic information about a company — information about sales, earnings and stock prices — to make decisions.

10. Now that the students have identified some companies to study, they need to obtain some information on these companies. Explain that information is abundant and may be obtained from many different sources. Activity 1 suggests that students visit the Web sites of www.quicken.com or www.smartmoney.com. Students may also use http://lei.ncee.net — the Web site that accompanies this curriculum. *Value Line* publications are also good sources, providing information in print and electronically on stocks, mutual funds and other products. *Value Line Ratings & Reports*, for example, contain one-page reports on approximately 1,700 companies and more than 90 industries. *Value Line Ratings & Reports* are often available in libraries or from brokerage firms.

11. To elaborate on the fundamental analysis approach, **display Visual 5**. Explain the terms introduced on the visual that correspond with the terms in Activity 1:

- **Share Price:** Most often, students hope to select a stock whose share price increases after they purchase it. Most sources display charts reflecting the changes in the share price over the past month, one year, two years and so forth.
- **Price/Earnings Ratio:** The price/earnings or P/E ratio is the recent stock price divided by 12 months of earnings per share. It is a measure of how much the investor will pay for a dollar of earnings or profits. A high P/E within an industry could indicate a young, fast-growing company. A low P/E within an industry indicates a less risky, more stable company. Companies with low P/E ratios are more likely to pay dividends. A start-up company may have no earnings yet, and thus no P/E ratio.
- **Annual Revenue or Sales:** Sales over the past three to five years point to how well a company is doing in its industry. Rising sales suggests that a company is producing goods or services that are popular with its customers.
- **Earnings per Share:** Companies that are profitable over the long term tend to have rising share prices. Earnings per share is a measure of how a company's profits compare to the number of shares. Rising earnings per share suggest that a company is well managed.

12. Explain that a final method for selecting stocks is to let other people do research for you so that you can follow the recommendations of experts in the field. This method is called following expert advice. Stock analysts are professionals who study stocks for a living. Their recommendations to buy, sell or hold stocks can be found at many different Web sites, such as www.quicken.com.

13. Ask the students to complete Activity 1 by using the suggested sources of information. They should analyze this information with their classmates and decide which companies they think they would like to own for the long term. They may wish to add new companies to study during the semester.

Closure

1. Summarize the key generalizations emphasized in this lesson:

- The number of stocks listed on stock exchanges is great. Investors could never master all relevant information about all these stocks; therefore investors will always make choices based on less-than-complete information.
- Many economists believe that it is impossible to predict stocks that will be surprises, yielding unexpected high returns.
- People can make investment decisions by random selection or by personal preferences. Neither of these approaches involves much cost of acquiring information.
- Fundamental analysis is another research method. This approach establishes criteria which may indicate future increases in stock prices. Fundamental analysts stress the importance of basic information about companies, such as sales and profits.
- It is costly in time and effort to acquire information about individual stocks. Investors should seek to acquire such information if the anticipated benefits of the research outweigh the anticipated costs.
- Sources of stock information include Web sites such as www.quicken.com and the *Value Line Ratings & Reports*.
- No matter how carefully one makes financial choices, the choices may turn out to involve surprising results. No one can foresee the future.

Assessment

Multiple-Choice Questions

1. Which of the following is used by fundamental analysts to research a stock?
   a. The P/E ratio
   b. Resistance level
   c. Support level
   d. The S/E ratio

2. There are thousands of stocks, but investors have limited time and resources to use in researching stocks. The economic concept that refers to this problem is
   a. inflation.
   b. multiple propensity to consume.
   c. scarcity.
   d. density.

3. Random selection of stocks is the easiest and least costly method of selecting stocks for investment. Why don't people use this method more often?
   a. It is too easy to make money this way. People would feel guilty.
   b. Companies do not allow investors to choose stocks in this manner.
   c. Governmental regulation does not permit investors to select stocks in this manner.
   d. Investors think the benefits of doing more research outweigh the costs of the research.

Essay Questions

1. Respond to the following statement, commenting on potential advantages and disadvantages of selecting stocks at random:

> "People waste their time researching stocks. Just pick one! If the market goes up, the stock will go up."

Advantage: Competition to acquire information about stocks is intense. It is almost impossible to know in advance whether a stock will yield an unexpectedly high return. It might be wiser to simply select stocks at random. Disadvantage: Not all stocks move as the market average moves. The market could move up while one particular stock does not. Also, the cost of researching stocks may be worth paying if the research helps the investor find stocks that become more valuable than randomly picked stocks.

2. Respond to the following statement.

> "Investing in individual stocks is a good way to gain financial wealth, but only if you are willing to do the work. Investors must learn everything about the stocks they own. They should read every financial article, every annual report, and every newspaper article as well as *Value Line Reports*. If you can't do this homework, you should not invest in individual stocks."

No one can read everything about all the stocks on the market. Investors should focus on the information that is most important to them and become familiar with that information. Even if one could read everything about a stock, it still would not guarantee big gains. No information predicts the future perfectly.

Lesson 13 Visual 1

Thinking Economically about Researching Stocks

- Recognize that you cannot know it all.
- Select a few companies to research. Then follow their progress closely.
- Find a few good places to get stock information.
- Stop looking for new information when you think the benefits received from more information are less than the costs of additional research.

LESSON 13 VISUAL 2

SURPRISES ARE RARE IN THE SECURITIES MARKETS

- Many individuals spend a great deal of time and effort trying to find companies whose stock prices might increase faster than average for the market.

- Many financial institutions — brokerage companies, banks, life insurance companies — spend even more time and effort trying to identify companies whose stock price might increase faster than average for the market.

- It is very difficult to earn unusual gains in the stock market because most of the information about most companies is already known.

- People who earn above-average returns from their stock are usually surprised. But it is hard even for experienced investors to find surprises in the market.

Lesson 13 Visual 3

LeBron James

LeBron James joined the National Basketball Association (NBA) out of high school. He is known for his ability to jump, pass, involve teammates and score.

Some regard LeBron James as the Michael Jordan of the future.

Could you earn an unexpectedly high return by buying Nike stock today, thinking that its value would be enhanced by the LeBron James connection?

LESSON 13 VISUAL 4

FUNDAMENTAL ANALYSIS

Fundamental stock analysts examine the basic performance of a company and use results to make investment decisions.

They pay special attention to these factors:

- Changes in sales
- Changes in earnings
- Demand for goods and services produced

Lesson 13 Visual 5

Stock-Selection Criteria Used by Fundamental Stock Analysts

- Share Price
- Price/Earnings Ratio
- Annual Revenue or Sales
- Earnings per Share

LESSON 13 ACTIVITY 1

INFORMATION ON MY STOCK PICKS

Directions: Choose the companies that you wish to study. List their names below. Visit Web sites such as www.quicken.com or www.smartmoney.com to find and record the information requested in each section. *Value Line Ratings & Reports* are another good source of information on many companies. Write the information in the spaces provided.

Company Name (Selected in the classroom drawing)	**Symbol**	**Exchange**	**Date**
Share Price	**P/E Ratio**	**Annual Revenue or Sales**	**Earnings per Share**

Company Name (Company I know)	**Symbol**	**Exchange**	**Date**
Share Price	**P/E Ratio**	**Annual Revenue or Sales**	**Earnings per Share**

Company Name (Company I know)	**Symbol**	**Exchange**	**Date**
Share Price	**P/E Ratio**	**Annual Revenue or Sales**	**Earnings per Share**

Company Name (Company I know)	**Symbol**	**Exchange**	**Date**
Share Price	**P/E Ratio**	**Annual Revenue or Sales**	**Earnings per Share**

Lesson 13 Activity 2

Company Names for Class Drawing

Allstate Insurance Co. ALL	American Eagle Outfitters AEOS	American Express Company AXP	AOL Time Warner AOL	Apple Computer Inc. AAPL
Applebees International Inc. APPB	AutoZone Inc. AZO	Bank of America BAC	Bemis Company BMS	Best Buy Company, Inc. BBY
Campbell Soup Co. CPB	Cisco Systems Inc. CSCO	Coca-Cola Co. KO	Dell Computer DELL	Disney Company DIS
ExxonMobile Corp. XOM	FedEx Corp. FDX	Ford Motor Company F	Gillette Company G	Harley Davidson HDI
Home Depot Inc. HD	Johnson & Johnson JNJ	Krispy Kreme Doughnuts Inc. KKD	Liz Claiborne Inc. LIZ	McDonald's Corp. MCD
Metro-Goldwyn Mayer Inc. MGM	Nokia Corp. NOK	Southwest Airlines Co. LUV	Starbucks Corp. SBUX	Target Corp. TGT
The Limited Inc. LTD	Toyota Motor Corp. TM	Toys R Us Inc. TOY	United Parcel Services Inc. UPS	Yahoo Inc. YHOO

Lesson 14 Credit: Your Best Friend or Your Worst Enemy?

Middle School

14 Credit: Your Best Friend or Your Worst Enemy?

Lesson 14 Credit: Your Best Friend or Your Worst Enemy?

Lesson Description

The students do an exercise that shows how credit can be their worst enemy. They learn how quickly credit-card balances can grow and how long it can take to pay off a credit-card debt. They also learn that credit can be their best friend. Working in small groups, they consider seven scenarios and decide in each case whether it would be wise for the people involved to use credit. They discuss their conclusions and develop a list of criteria suitable for use in making decisions about credit.

Unwise use of credit can lead people to spend more money than they can afford to pay back, reducing their ability to make purchases or save money in the future. Many borrowers fall behind in their credit payments, jeopardizing their capacity to borrow in the future, and some wind up declaring bankruptcy. When it is well used, however, credit can provide many benefits. People can use credit to deal with emergency situations or to purchase valuable assets such as an automobile, a home or an education. It is in the students' interest, therefore, to learn to analyze the costs and benefits of using credit.

Concepts

- Choice
- Costs and benefits
- Credit
- Debt
- Interest
- Revolving credit

Objectives

Students will:

1. Calculate interest payments, minimum balances and the cost of credit.
2. Develop and apply criteria for determining when the use of credit is appropriate.

Time Required

45 minutes

Materials

- A transparency of Visual 1
- A copy of Activities 1, 2 and 3 for each student

Procedure

1. Tell the students that in this lesson they will look at the good and the bad sides of credit. They will learn how to decide when it is and is not a good idea to use credit.
To get started, ask the students to define *credit*.
Credit is the ability to obtain goods or services before paying for them, based on a promise to pay later. Thus, each time a person uses credit, he or she is in effect borrowing money.

2. Tell the students that one particular variety of credit is called *revolving credit*. Ask them if they know what revolving credit is.
It is credit that is available up to a limit and automatically renewed as debts are paid off or paid down. People who use revolving credit often make partial payments on their unpaid balances at regular intervals. For example, credit-card accounts offer revolving credit to credit-card users, many of whom make partial payment on their balance each month.

3. **Distribute a copy of Activity 1 and Activity 2** (the accompanying worksheet) to each student. Tell the students to read Activity 1 and then complete Activity 2; also tell them to use their answers on the worksheet to fill in the blanks of Activity 1. (Students may calculate their answers individually or in groups. With younger students, you may want to make a transparency of Activity 1 and handle the worksheet as a whole-class activity. Note: Many credit cards now charge considerably less than 18 percent interest; but as Justin is quite young and this is his first credit card, 18 percent is not an unrealistic figure in his case.)

4. **Display Visual 1** and review the answers to Activity 2.
Answers to Activity 2: January Purchases $235.00, Minimum Payment $11.75, Unpaid Balance $223.25; February Purchases $157.00, Previous Balance $223.25, Finance Charge $3.35, Total Owed $383.60, Minimum Payment $19.18, Unpaid Balance $364.42; March Purchases $270.00, Previous Balance $364.42, Finance Charge $5.47, Total Owed $639.89, Minimum Payment $31.99, Unpaid Balance $607.90; April Purchases $490.00, Previous Balance $607.90, Finance Charge $9.12, Total Owed $1,107.02, Minimum Payment $55.35, Unpaid Balance $1,051.67. Answers to Activity 1: $235, $11.75, $223.25; $383.60, $19.18; $639.89, $31.99; $1,107.02. The answer to the last question ("How long do you think it would take him to pay what he owes?") is given in Procedure 5.

5. Write the following terms on the board at widely spaced intervals: *6 months, 12 months, 18 months, 24 months, 30 months*. Tell the students to go to the board and stand next to the term that they believe best approximates the amount of time it would take Justin to pay off his credit-card balance if he did not make any more charges and paid the minimum balance each month. When the students have lined up, tell them that it would take 23 months for Justin to pay off his credit-card balance if he paid $55 each month. Remind them that interest is charged each month on the unpaid balance — even if no further purchases are made using the card. Tell the students that the total amount Justin will have to pay back is $1,226.88. Justin made total purchases of $1,051.67. The remaining $175.21 is the cost of credit.

6. Explain that credit can cause problems. People with high monthly payments often find that they cannot afford to buy things that they want to buy now, and cannot afford to save any money, because so much of their income is going to pay for past purchases. Sometimes people fall behind and fail to make monthly payments on their unpaid balances; this leads to financial penalties that add to their debt. Some people accumulate so many debts that they declare bankruptcy, which severely limits their capacity to borrow in the future. Still, when it is wisely used, credit can be a good friend.

7. Ask the students to consider this situation: "It is midnight and your car breaks down on [some local highway]. You are far from home. You use your cell phone to call an emergency auto-repair service. The service representative tells you that a service visit will cost $50, plus the cost of any parts and labor that are necessary to get you driving again. You have $7.57 in your pocket. Should you use a credit card?" Most students will probably agree that this would be a wise use of credit.

8. Divide the class into groups of three or four students and **hand out a copy of Activity 3** to each student. Give the groups 15 minutes to discuss the scenarios and decide whether the use of credit is a good idea in each case.

- *Ana should take out the student loan. The additional training will increase her income and allow her to repay the loan.*
- *For Dave Larson, using credit to buy the stamp now may be a good idea, since the stamp may become more valuable in the future. On the other hand, Dave can't be certain how much the stamp will gain in value. The decision here could go either way.*
- *Caroline Potter should use credit to buy a more dependable car. She might lose her income completely if she cannot get to work regularly and on time. Her current repair bills are large.*
- *Jake Purdy might increase his income by buying the new car — if it actually is true that the new car would impress his customers. That is uncertain. But it is certain that payments on the new car would be high, and Jake's salary is not high. Jake should keep his old car and explore other, less costly ways to please his customers — by providing better service, for example.*
- *Felicia Washington should buy the cheaper dress and pay cash rather than borrow.*
- *Mike Chiang is paying only the minimum balance on each of his credit-card accounts, and he has to work a part-time job to make those payments. How will he be able to make the higher payments that will result from his trip? This is an easy call: don't do it, Mike!*
- *Bill Baker's case for using credit is clear. If Bill puts the mattress and box spring on his credit card and pays $50 each month, and if his credit-card account charges 18 percent annual interest, Bill will pay off the charge in six months, and his total cost of credit will be $12.24 — much less than the additional $100 he would wind up paying if he waited until he had enough money saved to pay cash. His back will feel better, too. And by borrowing and paying back his loan promptly, Bill will improve his credit score — perhaps enabling him to qualify for a credit card with a lower interest rate.*

Closure

Ask the class to develop criteria for determining when it is appropriate to use credit. List their criteria on the board. *Possibilities include using credit to make an investment in your future, as Ana Rodriguez and Caroline Potter did; to meet an emergency situation, such as the car breakdown in the example; to buy something that will cost more later, as long as the cost of credit does not exceed the savings on the item you purchase; or to acquire something of great value that you may not be able to obtain at a later date.*

Assessment

Multiple-Choice Questions

1. A disadvantage of a revolving credit account is that
   a. it is illegal.
   b. it is very difficult for borrowers to qualify for such an account.
   c. the balance must be paid off every month.
   d. balances can rise quickly if only the minimum payment is made each month.

2. Making purchases on credit
   a. is never a good idea.
   b. is a good idea if the benefits to the purchaser are greater than the costs.
   c. decreases the cost of the purchase to the borrower.
   d. is a good idea if the purchaser has so many credit payments that he or she is unable to live comfortably.

3. If you have a credit card charging 12 percent annual interest, the total amount you owe each month is
   a. the unpaid balance on your credit card plus 1 percent interest on the previous balance.
   b. the unpaid balance on your credit card plus 12 percent interest on the previous balance.
   c. 1 percent interest on the unpaid balance.
   d. 12 percent interest on the unpaid balance.

4. Which of the following is the best use of credit?
   a. You can't buy everything you want on your current income.
   b. You can take advantage of a sale price that is lower than the normal cost of the item plus your cost of credit.
   c. You have a credit card with a low interest rate.
   d. You want to purchase something now instead of having to wait to use it.

Essay Questions

1. What are the advantages and disadvantages of using credit?
Advantages: *Credit is useful in an emergency, can be used to acquire valuable assets and allows consumers to take advantage of opportunities such as sales.*

Disadvantages: *Credit increases the cost of purchases, reduces the capacity of borrowers to make future purchases and may cause individuals to borrow more than they can afford to pay back — perhaps leading to personal bankruptcy.*

2. Define *revolving credit* and discuss its advantages and disadvantages.
Revolving credit is credit that is available up to a limit and automatically renewed as debts are paid off or paid down by partial payments. Revolving credit enables consumers to pay for their purchases over a period of time rather than immediately. But interest continues to accrue on unpaid balances; and, since many people make only the minimum payment each month, revolving credit may come at a high cost.

Lesson 14 Visual 1

Answers to Worksheet for Justin Jabowski

January	Purchases	$235.00
	Minimum payment	11.75
	Unpaid balance	223.25
February	Purchases	157.00
	Previous balance	223.25
	+ Finance charge	3.35
	Total owed	383.60
	- Minimum payment	19.18
	Unpaid balance	364.42
March	Purchases	270.00
	Previous balance	364.42
	+ Finance charge	5.47
	Total owed	639.89
	- Minimum payment	31.99
	Unpaid balance	607.90
April	Purchases	490.00
	Previous balance	607.90
	+ Finance charge	9.12
	Total owed	1,107.02
	- Minimum payment	55.35
	Unpaid balance	1051.67

Lesson 14 Activity 1

Justin Jabowski and His Magical Money Machine

Justin Jabowski is a high school junior with a part-time job. In January he acquired his first credit card. His credit-card account charges an annual interest rate of 18 percent. This means that every month Justin pays a finance charge of 1.5 percent (that's 18 percent ÷ 12 months) on his unpaid balance. And every month Justin must make a minimum payment of 5 percent of the unpaid balance.

In January Justin used his credit card to buy two shirts and a pair of pants, at a total price of $160. He also charged a new pair of shoes on his card, at a price of $75. When his first credit-card bill arrived in February, Justin owed ______. Since his account provides for a 30-day grace period, Justin did not owe any finance charges immediately. Justin has heard that it is a good idea to pay the entire bill each month and thus avoid finance charges; but he was a little short of cash in February, so he mailed in only the minimum payment of ___________. His unpaid balance on the card was ________.

In February Justin treated himself and his girlfriend to an evening out at a rock concert. He charged two concert tickets for $50 each, plus a handling fee of $3 per ticket. He enjoyed the performing group's music so much that he bought three of their CDs at $17 each, using his credit card. When his bill for March arrived, Justin owed ____________ for the new charges, his previous balance and the finance charge on the previous balance. He was a little short of cash at the time, so he made only the minimum payment of _________.

In March, Justin had a great opportunity to go skiing with his friend Travis. Travis's parents had rented a ski condo. They planned to make the trip by driving; by joining them, Justin was able to get free lodging, transportation and breakfasts. But lunches and dinners for the three-day outing cost him $150 (he treated Travis and his parents to lunch one day), and ski-lift tickets for three days came to $120. Justin's total credit-card bill at the beginning of April was _________ for the new charges, the previous balance and the finance charge on the previous balance. By then Justin had become alarmed at the size of his credit-card bill; but he was still a little short on cash, so he made only the minimum payment of ___________.

After he mailed off his April payment, Justin resolved firmly to stop charging things on his card until he could get his entire balance paid off. Unfortunately, his car broke down the next day, and the repair bill came to $490. He needed the car to get to work and to school, so he charged the repairs. His total credit-card balance in May was ____________.

Taken aback by his growing balance, Justin swore not charge another dime until he paid it off entirely. He decided to pay $55 a month for as long as it would take to pay it off.

If Justin held to his resolution and made payments of $55 each month, how long do you think it would take him to pay what he owes?

LESSON 14 ACTIVITY 2

WORKSHEET FOR JUSTIN JABOWSKI

January	Purchases	________
	- Minimum payment	________
	Unpaid balance	________
February	Purchases	________
	Previous balance	________
	+ Finance charge	________
	Total owed	________
	- Minimum payment	________
	Unpaid balance	________
March	Purchases	________
	Previous balance	________
	+ Finance charge	________
	Total owed	________
	- Minimum payment	________
	Unpaid balance	________
April	Purchases	________
	Previous balance	________
	+ Finance charge	________
	Total owed	________
	- Minimum payment	________
	Unpaid balance	________

Lesson 14 Activity 3

Should You Borrow?

Ana Rodriguez graduated from high school last year with a good grade-point average. She works as a receptionist at a physical-therapy clinic, making $8.50 an hour. She would like to become a physical therapist. The work appeals to her, and salaries for physical therapists are excellent. Within a few years of finishing her training, she could earn more than $50,000 a year. But Ana's parents cannot afford to pay for the training Ana would need to complete. Ana has investigated student loans, but she knows she would have to pay back anything she might borrow over a 10-year period. Should Ana take out a student loan?

Dave Larson is an avid stamp collector. For a long time he has wanted to own a Bolivian Double Eagle stamp. This stamp is very hard to find, and Dave believes it will gain value in the future. Dave learns that his favorite stamp store has a Bolivian Double Eagle for sale, priced at $200. Dave doesn't have that much money in savings, but he is afraid that if he doesn't buy the stamp now, someone else will. Should he use his credit card to buy the stamp?

Caroline Potter is a single mother with two small children. She commutes 15 miles to work five days a week, driving an old car that has developed several problems. Caroline has been late to work twice in the last month because of car problems, and each of the problems has saddled her with a large repair bill. Should Caroline buy a better used car, even though she will have to borrow money and take on monthly car payments?

Jake Purdy just got a great job working as a salesman. His salary isn't high, but he can earn excellent commissions if he makes a lot of sales. Jake has a reliable car, but he has his eye on an expensive new model that would make a better impression on his customers (and also on his dates), he thinks. Car payments for the new model would be high, but Jake feels that he can make enough in sales commissions to cover the cost. Should he take out a loan and buy the new car?

Felicia Washington is the homecoming queen at her high school. She is going to the homecoming dance with the best-looking guy in the senior class. She goes shopping for a new dress to wear to the dance. She finds one nice dress for $79—an amount she could pay in cash. However, she also finds a spectacular dress priced at $169. She could buy this dress with her credit card. Sure, it's a lot of money, Felicia thinks, but she owes it to her public and her date to look dazzling for the big event. Should Felicia put the spectacular dress on her credit card?

Mike Chiang is a community-college student. He has three credit cards, all charged close to the limit. Mike manages to make the minimum payments each month, thanks to his part-time job at Pizzas-R-Us. Mike really, really wants to go with his friends on a spring-break trip to Padre Island, Texas, but he doesn't see how he can afford to do it. Then he receives a friendly letter from one of his credit-card companies. "Dear Mr. Chiang," it begins, "Since you are one of our most valued customers and always make your payments on time, we are raising your credit limit by $2,000." Mike is thrilled! Now he can go to Padre Island with his friends. Should he do it, charging his expenses to his card?

Bill Baker needs a new mattress and box spring. He's still sleeping on the same set he used as a kid, and his back is killing him. He has started putting away $50 a month for a new mattress and box-spring set that costs $400. Then the set he wants goes on sale, for a limited time only. The sale price is $300. Should Bill put the mattress and box-spring set on his credit card now, or should he wait until he can save $400 to buy it?

LESSON 15 WHY DON'T PEOPLE SAVE?

MIDDLE SCHOOL

LESSON 15 WHY DON'T PEOPLE SAVE?

Lesson Description

The students examine risk-oriented behavior, considering why people often engage in behavior that is dangerous or unhealthy. They are introduced to the concept of *cost/benefit analysis* and asked to apply what they learn to questions about saving. They generate lists of savings goals and categorize those goals as short-term, medium-term and long-term. They learn why long-term goals are more difficult to achieve than short-term goals.

It is a basic principle of economics that people strive to make decisions that will serve their interests. Saving money early and often would serve most people well, helping them to achieve their goals. Yet many people are poor savers, saving too little or not at all. Why? The explanation has to do with a particular complication involved in the weighing of costs and benefits. The costs of some decisions are immediate and certain, while the benefits sought may occur only in the future and may therefore seem uncertain to the people involved.

Concepts

- Benefits
- Costs
- Goals
- Incentives
- Interest
- Long-term goal
- Medium-term goal
- Opportunity cost
- Saving
- Short-term goal

Objectives

Students will:

1. Define *costs, benefits, incentives, interest, saving* and *opportunity cost.*
2. Analyze the costs and benefits of saving.
3. Give examples of opportunity cost.
4. Identify short-, medium- and long-term savings goals.
5. Explain why a savings goal might be short-term for one person and medium- or long-term for another.
6. Explain why long-term savings goals are more difficult to achieve than short-term savings goals.

Time Required

90 minutes

Materials

- A transparency of Visuals 1 and 2
- Sticky notes and a pencil for each group of 3-4 students
- 1/2 sheet each of red, blue and yellow construction paper for each group
- 1/2 sheet of poster board for each group
- A ruler, pencil, two pairs of scissors, a marker and a container of glue for each group
- One copy of Activities 1 and 6 for each group
- One copy of Activities 2, 3, 4 and 5 (on appropriately-colored paper; see procedure 1) for each group
- One die for each group
- One coin, milk-bottle lid, bingo chip, paper clip or other small item (to be used as a game piece) for each student

Procedure

1. Before class, make a copy of Activity 2 on green paper for each group of three or four students. Make a copy of Activity 3 on blue paper for each group. Make a copy of Activity 4 on red paper for each group. Make a copy of Activity 5 on yellow paper for each group.

2. Introduce the mystery underlying this lesson: People usually know what is good for them, but they often act as if they don't know. Some people, for example, drive too fast on icy roads, or they fail to take medications prescribed by a doctor, or they never get around to checking the oil in their cars. Such behavior seems odd. Why would people do things that don't seem to be in their interest? Invite the students to suggest explanations; discuss their ideas briefly. Then tell them that in this lesson they will use principles of economic reasoning to analyze one particular form of puzzling behavior: the failure of many people to save money.

3. **Display Visual 1.** Explain that the points shown on the visual will allow the class to continue the line of thought you have introduced at the lesson's beginning. Reveal one question from the visual at a time and have the students raise their hands in response to each question. Next to each question, record the number of students who respond positively.

Discuss the following in relation to the new examples:

A. If people know that certain behaviors are risky or unhealthy, why do they engage in those behaviors?
Answers will vary.

B. If people know that something is good for them, why do they fail to engage in that activity or behavior?
Answers will vary.

4. Explain that it might help to understand these puzzling events if we approach them with certain principles of economics in mind. Economic analysis involves comparing the *costs* and the *benefits* of the alternatives in any situation that requires a decision. *Costs* are all the things that have to be given up when a choice is made. *Benefits* are any gains or favorable outcomes that make people more satisfied when a choice is made. Costs are negative; benefits are positive. However, people don't get benefits unless they pay some costs.

5. Pursue the analysis by reference to diet and exercise. Most people know that eating a healthful diet and participating in regular exercise are important. Discuss the following:

A. What are the benefits of eating a healthful diet and exercising regularly?
Feel better, look better, reduce your risk of heart disease, reduce your risk of cancer, boost your life expectancy.

B. Do these benefits of diet and exercise occur now or in the future?
Although people may start to feel better right away, most of the benefits occur in the future.

C. If people choose a healthful diet and exercise regularly, are they guaranteed these benefits? Can they count on them for sure?
No. Some people may still get heart disease or cancer, no matter what they eat or how well they exercise. Also, a person engaged in a diet-and-exercise program could die prematurely from any number of causes other than heart disease or cancer.

D. What are the costs of choosing a healthful diet and exercising regularly?
Possibilities include giving up food that tastes really good, paying dues for membership at a fitness club, spending time on exercise that you could spend in other ways — napping, reading, gardening, watching television, playing video games.

6. Emphasize the point that the costs of choosing a healthful diet and exercising regularly occur right now, and they are certain. However, most of the benefits of choosing a healthful diet and exercising regularly occur in the future, and they are uncertain. Many people will choose to avoid immediate, certain costs if the alternative choice offers only remote, uncertain benefits. A similar analysis applies in the case of decisions about saving.

7. Explain that the term *saving* refers to income not spent on consumption or taxes. Most people know that starting to save money at an early age and saving regularly are good habits that lead to financial well being. Yet many people in the United States fail to save early and regularly. Discuss the following:

A. What are the benefits of saving?
Ability to attain your goals for the future, a feeling of security and satisfaction.

B. What are the costs of saving?
Things you could obtain now if you weren't saving.

C. When do the benefits of saving occur?
In the future.

D. When do the costs of saving occur?
In the present.

8. Emphasize the point that the costs of saving are immediate and certain. If people choose to save part of their income, they give up the things they could buy with their income now. The benefits of saving occur in the future, and they are uncertain. Events can conspire to prevent people from reaping the benefits of saving; one might save money to build a comfortable retirement home, for example, and then get killed in an automobile crash prior to retirement.

9. Explain that when we use cost-benefit analysis, it is important to consider the broad idea of *opportunity cost*, not just dollars spent. An opportunity cost is the next-best alternative a person gives up in making a choice. For example, the choice to exercise for an hour each day means giving up the next-best alternative use of that hour — perhaps watching television or reading or spending time with a child. In the case of budgeting, saving money for the future means giving up the opportunity to spend money in the present.

10. Explain that setting *goals* is an important factor related to saving money. Goals are aims or desired results that act as *incentives*. Incentives are rewards or advantages that encourage people to do something. People usually save with goals in mind, such as vacations, gifts, video games, continuing education and retirement. Such goals act as incentives — as things to shoot for — thus motivating people to develop savings habits. Another incentive for saving is *interest*. Interest is a payment made to savers by financial institutions for their use of the savers' money.

11. Tell the students that they are going to identify some of their savings goals. Divide the class into groups of three or four students. Give each group sticky notes and pencils. Explain that each group will have five minutes to identify things for which students in the group would like to save. Group members should write the name of one savings goal on each sticky note.

12. While the students are working, draw three columns on the board. Label the first column *Short-term savings goals.* Label the second column *Medium-term savings goals.* Label the third column *Long-term savings goals.* Beneath the heading in column one, write "can be achieved in one year or less." Beneath the heading in column two, write "may take from one to five years to achieve." Beneath the heading in column three, write "requires over five years to achieve."

13. After the students have had time to work, point out the column labels and explain the following.

- People who save usually have savings goals. These are aims or desired results that people hope to achieve.
- Short-term savings goals are those that can be achieved in one year or less. For example, the goal of saving to buy a new CD might be a short-term goal.
- Medium-term savings goals are those that can be achieved in one to five years. For example, the goal of saving to pay for a vacation might be a medium-term goal.
- Long-term savings goals require over five years to achieve. For example, the goal of saving enough money for a college education would be a long-term goal.

14. Tell the students to decide whether the items listed on their sticky notes represent short-, medium- or long-term goals and to come up and post their sticky notes in the appropriate columns on the board. When the students have posted their sticky notes, review the items in each column. Discuss the following.

A. Are there any items in the short-term column that you think should be in the medium-term column?
Answers will vary. Why? *It would take longer than one year for me to reach this goal.*

B. Are there any items in the medium-term column that you think should be in the short-term column?
Answers will vary. Why? *I could achieve this goal in less than one year.*

C. Are there any items in the medium-term column that you think should be in the long-term column?
Answers will vary. Why? *It would take longer than one to five years for me to reach this goal.*

D. Are there any items in the long-term column that you think should be in the medium-term column?
Answers will vary. Why? *It would not take longer than one to five years for me to reach this goal.*

E. Why might a short-term goal for one saver be a long-term goal for another saver? *One person might have more income than another, and/or fewer expenses.*

15. Explain that the amounts people can save in any time period vary depending upon their income, earnings and expenses. Long-term goals are usually more difficult to meet than short-term goals. When people strive to save for more than five years, there is ample time for emergencies or attractive opportunities to present themselves before the long-term savings goal is met. If an emergency or an opportunity that seems more compelling than the long-term savings goal does arise, the saver may give up on the savings goal in order to obtain something that looks important in the present. As economists would put it, the opportunity cost of saving may seem greater than the opportunity cost of the emergency or the attractive opportunity.

Closure

1. Tell the students that they will play a game to help them review the things they have learned about saving, savings goals, opportunity cost and costs and benefits.

2. Divide the class into groups of three or four students. **Distribute a copy of Activities 1, 2, 3, 4 and 5** to each group. Also distribute to each group 1/2 sheet of red, blue and yellow construction paper; 1/2 sheet of poster board; a ruler, two pairs of scissors, a pencil and glue. Review Activity 1 to clarify the instructions for creating the game board.

3. Allow time for groups to create their game boards.

4. **Distribute a copy of Activity 6**, game pieces, and a die to each group. Review the instructions for playing the game. Make sure the students in each group have pencils and paper as needed for answering the mathematics questions.

5. When all the students in each group have drawn their green, long-term goal cards and have had time to answer the question on the card, **display Visual 2**.

6. Allow time for the groups to play the game.

7. Review the following.

- What does it mean to save?
  To set aside money for future use. Money saved is money not spent to buy things now, or to pay taxes.
- Suppose that you wanted to convince your parents to purchase a new computer. What are some benefits of owning the computer that you could use to make your argument?
  Possibilities include ability to do school work better and faster, entire family can use the computer, you and your sisters/brothers can play educational games, all family members can enjoy e-mail access to keep in contact with friends and relatives.
- Your parents will probably point out that there are costs associated with buying a new computer. What are some of these costs?
  The amount paid for the computer; time spent playing games on the computer could be spent doing other things; additional expense of Internet connection and trouble shooting; individuals absorbed in computer activity may spend less time with the family.
- What is opportunity cost?
  The next-best alternative given up when a choice is made.
- Next year, you can choose an elective class. The options are woodworking, a family and consumer science class or an introduction to business class. You choose woodworking. What is your opportunity cost?
  Either the family and consumer science class or the introduction to business class — whichever one you would have identified as your next-best choice.
- What is the opportunity cost of buying things today?
  Things you could buy in the future, or future savings.
- What is a short-term savings goal?
  One that can be achieved in one year or less.
- What is a medium-term savings goal?
  One that can be achieved in one to five years.
- What is a long-term savings goal?
  One that takes more than five years to achieve.
- Why might a long-term goal for one person be a medium-term goal for another?
  Because one person may be able to save more each week or month, thus reaching the goal sooner than a person who saves less.
- Why are long-term savings goals more difficult to achieve than short-term goals?
  For long-term goals there is more time for emergencies or consumer-purchase opportunities to arise — possibly displacing long-term goals. Often an emergency or consumer-purchase opportunity will seem more important or more desirable than the long-term goal. The saver then gives up saving for the long-term goal in favor of spending for the emergency or the consumer purchase.
- Give an example from the game of an emergency or consumer purchase that interfered with achieving your long-term goal.
  Students should give examples from the Chance cards that caused them to move back spaces.

Assessment

Multiple-Choice Questions

1. A short-term goal is one that
   a. must be achieved.
   b. can be achieved in less than one year.
   c. can be achieved in one to five years.
   d. can be achieved in over five years.

2. A long-term goal is one that
   a. must be achieved.
   b. can be achieved in less than one year.
   c. can be achieved in over five years.
   d. can be achieved in one to five years.

3. Mark has decided to bring a bag lunch from home to school each day and to give up playing arcade games in order to save money so that he will have plenty of spending money for a family trip that is coming up before long. Buying lunch at school and playing arcade games are examples of
   a. goals that Mark wants to achieve.
   b. incentives that encourage Mark to save.
   c. opportunity costs related to Mark's decision to save.
   d. opportunity benefits related to Mark's decision to save.

4. Which of the following is an incentive that encourages people to save money?
   a. The marginal cost of saving
   b. The opportunity cost of saving
   c. Giving up things that could be purchased now
   d. Earning interest on money saved

Essay Questions

1. You want your parents to buy you a new bike. They ask you to prepare an argument that will convince them they should buy the bike. Write a paragraph in which you describe the costs and benefits associated with buying the bike.
Although answers will vary, students should identify costs that include the amount to be paid for the bike, expenses to maintain the bike, any expenses for safety equipment and the cost of time spent riding the bike. Students should also identify benefits such as exercise, ability to be with friends, transportation and fresh air.

2. Your friend Alex is trying to save money to buy a leather jacket. This is a long-term goal for Alex, and he is having a lot of trouble saving toward the goal. Explain to Alex why long-term goals are more difficult to achieve than short-term goals.
With a long-term goal, there is more time in which emergencies or other occasions for spending might arise, interfering with saving. If the brakes fail on the family car, for example, spending money on new brakes might seem more important than saving for the long-term goal.

Lesson 15 Visual 1

Why Don't People Do What They Should Do?

Question	Number of Yes Responses
How many of you know that smoking is unhealthy?	
How many of you know people — even people your age — who smoke?	
How many of you know that eating foods that are high in transfats, such as packaged cookies, margarine and peanut butter, isn't healthy?	
How many of you know people who eat foods that are high in transfats?	
How many of you know that regular exercise provides many health benefits?	
How many of you know people who don't exercise regularly?	

Lesson 15 Visual 2

Answers for Long-Term Goal Cards

Long-term goal	Number of months
New stereo system: $1,500	75 months
Family vacation: $2,500	63 months
One year of premium payments for car insurance: $1,400	70 months
Guitar and one year of lessons: $1,600	64 months
New computer system: $2,000	67 months
Big-screen TV with DVD player and surround sound: $2,200	63 months

LESSON 15 ACTIVITY 1

MAKING YOUR GAME BOARD

1. Using a ruler, make one-inch marks along each side of the red, blue and yellow construction paper. Connect the marks to create a grid of one-inch squares. Cut out 20 squares of each color.

2. In the lower-left corner of the poster board, draw a three-inch by two-inch rectangle. Write "Start" inside the rectangle with a marker. In the upper-right corner of the poster board, draw a three-inch by two-inch rectangle. Write "Finish" inside the rectangle with a marker.

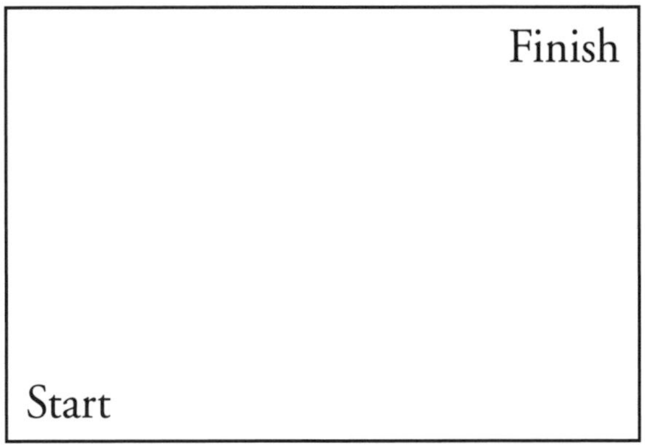

3. Use the one-inch squares of red, blue and yellow construction paper to form a path that begins at "Start" and ends at "Finish." Any pattern may be used for the path. After the layout of the game board has been designed, glue the squares down.

4. Cut apart the red, yellow, blue and green game cards. Keep the colored decks in separate stacks. Shuffle them within each stack. Place the stacks on or near your game board.

Lesson 15 Activity 2

Long-Term Goal Cards (Green Game Cards)

Directions to the teacher: Make one copy of these cards on green paper for each group of 3-4 students.

Long-Term Goal New stereo system $1,500 If you save $20 a month, how long will it take you to reach your goal?	Long-Term Goal Family vacation $2,500 If you save $40 a month, how long will it take you to reach your goal?
Long-Term Goal One year of premium payments for car insurance for a 16-year-old $1,400 If you save $20 a month, how long will it take you to reach your goal?	Long-Term Goal Guitar and a year's worth of lessons $1,600 If you save $25 a month, how long will it take you to reach your goal?
Long-Term Goal New computer system $2,000 If you save $30 a month, how long will it take you to reach your goal?	Long-Term Goal Big-screen TV with DVD player and surround sound for the family room. $2,200 If you save $35 a month, how long will it take you to reach your goal?

LESSON 15 ACTIVITY 3

PERSONAL FINANCE QUESTIONS (BLUE GAME CARDS)

Directions to the teacher: Make one copy of these cards on blue paper for each group of 3-4 students.

Personal Finance Questions Tia wants to buy a birthday gift for her mother. Tia thinks that she can save the $30 she needs in six months. Is this a short-term, medium-term or long-term goal for Tia? *Answer: short-term goal*	**Personal Finance Questions** Martin earned $325 at Burger Barn. He had to pay $100 in taxes, and he spent $100. He put the remaining $125 in the bank. What do we call the $125 not spent or used to pay taxes? *Answer: saving*
Personal Finance Questions Harry is saving to buy a mountain bike. He can save $25 a week. It will take him a little more than one year to save the money he needs. Is the mountain bike a short-term, medium-term or long-term goal for Harry? *Answer: medium-term goal*	**Personal Finance Questions** Incentives are rewards or advantages that encourage people to do something. True or False? *Answer: true*
Personal Finance Questions After school, Natasha can spend time with her friend playing chess or go to the mall with another friend. If Natasha chooses to play chess, what is her opportunity cost? *Answer: going to the mall*	**Personal Finance Questions** Opportunity cost is everything else that is given up when a choice is made. True or False? *Answer: false*
Personal Finance Questions If you are saving to buy a new video game and you can achieve that goal in six weeks, is the video game a short-term, medium-term or long-term goal? *Answer: short-term goal*	**Personal Finance Questions** Andrew wants a dog. He tells his parents that the dog would be a companion, that caring for a dog teaches responsibility and that running with the dog will improve his fitness. Has Andrew given examples of the costs of owning a dog or the benefits of owning a dog? *Answer: benefits*

LESSON 15 ACTIVITY 3

PERSONAL FINANCE QUESTIONS (BLUE GAME CARDS CONTINUED)

Directions to the teacher: Make one copy of these cards on blue paper for each group of 3-4 students.

Personal Finance Questions Interest is a payment financial institutions make to savers for their use of the savers' money. True or False? *Answer: true*	**Personal Finance Questions** Tadashi wants to buy a new stereo system. He says that it will take him four years to save enough to reach this goal. Is this a short-term, medium-term or long-term goal for Tadashi? Why? *Answer: It is a medium-term goal because it will take one to five years for him to achieve it.*
Personal Finance Questions Opportunity cost is the next-best alternative that is given up when a choice is made. True or False? *Answer: true*	**Personal Finance Questions** The only cost of owning a pet is the amount paid for the pet. True or False? *Answer: false*
Personal Finance Questions Costs are what people give up or sacrifice when they make choices. True or False? *Answer: true*	**Personal Finance Questions** Benefits are any gains or favorable outcomes that make people more satisfied when a choice is made. True or False? *Answer: true*
Personal Finance Questions Taylor works at a movie theater. She gets paid \$75 each week, after taxes. Taylor uses \$50 each week to buy things for school and entertainment. She puts \$25 in the bank. The \$25 is saving. True or False? *Answer: true*	**Personal Finance Questions** Maria saved \$30 to buy a Father's Day gift in four weeks. Was the gift a short-term, medium-term or long-term goal for Maria? *Answer: short-term goal*

Lesson 15 Activity 4

Mathematics Questions (Red Game Cards)

Directions to the teacher: Make one copy of these cards on red paper for each group of 3-4 students.

Mathematics Questions Mark's long-term goal is to buy a stereo system for $1,500. If he saves $20 per month, how many years will it take him to reach his goal (not considering interest earned)? *Answer: 75 months (more than 5 years)*	**Mathematics Questions** Miyoko saved $10 a month for 10 months to reach her savings goal. How much did she save? *Answer: $100*
Mathematics Questions Juan saves 10 percent of his allowance each week. His allowance is $5 a week. How much does he save each week? *Answer: 50 cents*	**Mathematics Questions** Henrik has saved $150. He did this by depositing the same amount of money into his savings account each week for 15 weeks. How much did he save each week? *Answer: $10*
Mathematics Questions Roseanne wants to buy a DVD that is on sale for 20 percent off. The regular price is $15. How much less will the DVD cost on sale? *Answer: $3*	**Mathematics Questions** If Ron saves $2 each week, how long will it take him to save $40? *Answer: 20 weeks*
Mathematics Questions If a $400 mountain bike is on sale for 25 percent off, what is the sale price? *Answer: $300*	**Mathematics Questions** If the price of a CD is $15 and you have a coupon for $3 off, how much must you pay for the CD? *Answer: $12*

Lesson 15 Activity 4

Mathematics Questions (Red Game Cards continued)

Directions to the teacher: Make one copy of these cards on red paper for each group of 3-4 students.

Mathematics Questions Tom wants to buy a leather jacket that costs $500. Uncle Mort agrees to pay one-half of the $500. How much will Uncle Mort pay? *Answer: $250*	**Mathematics Questions** Bonnie and Sara want to buy their friend Mary a gift for $54. They agree that each of them will pay half of the cost. How much will Bonnie and Sara each pay? *Answer: $27*
Mathematics Questions You have a regular babysitting job for the summer and earn $35 a week. You want to save 40 percent of your money each week so you can buy some new things for school. How much will you have left to spend each week? *Answer: $21*	**Mathematics Questions** If you save $3 each week, how long will it take you to save $15? *Answer: 5 weeks*
Mathematics Questions You want to rent a new video game for three days from Video Buster. Rental is $2 per day. How much will you spend to rent the game for three days? *Answer: $6*	**Mathematics Questions** The new snowboard that you want is on sale for 15 percent off. The regular price is $200. What is the sale price? *Answer: $170*
Mathematics Questions A new pair of jeans from Gapper and Finch is priced at $65. If your mom agrees to give you $30 for new jeans, how much more will you need to buy the jeans from Gapper and Finch? *Answer: $35*	**Mathematics Questions** Your class is taking an overnight trip to the state capital. You want to take $75 along with you on the trip. Your parents have said they will contribute $25. How much will you have to save? *Answer: $50*

LESSON 15 ACTIVITY 5

CHANCE QUESTIONS (YELLOW GAME CARDS)

Directions to the teacher: Make one copy of these cards on yellow paper for each group of 3-4 students.

Chance Questions You are invited to a friend's birthday party. You spend $15 on a gift and can't save as much for your long-term goal. *Go back three spaces.*	**Chance Questions** Your brother asks to borrow $20. You decide to lend it to him. You can't save for your long-term goal. *Go back four spaces.*
Chance Questions You and your friends have half-price tickets to an amusement park. You don't save toward your long-term goal this month. *Go back two spaces.*	**Chance Questions** There's a class trip coming up and you want to have some spending money. For the next two months you save for the class trip. You can't save for your long-term goal. The short-term goal is more important right now. *Go back four spaces.*
Chance Questions A tornado has struck a neighboring community. You donate to help the victims of the tornado. You save only half as much as you normally save toward your long-term goal. *Go back two spaces.*	**Chance Questions** You and you friends decide to go to get pizza and rent movies on Friday night. You have to use some of the money you were saving for your mom's birthday gift. *Go back three spaces.*
Chance Questions Your grandparents are celebrating their 45th wedding anniversary. You and your brother decide to buy them a special gift. You can't save as much toward your long-term goal. *Go back three spaces.*	**Chance Questions** Your friend invites you to go on a weekend trip with his/her family. You really want to go. Your parents tell you that you must provide your own spending money. You decide to use money from your savings account. *Go back three spaces.*

LESSON 15 ACTIVITY 5

CHANCE QUESTIONS (YELLOW GAME CARDS CONTINUED)

Directions to the teacher: Make one copy of these cards on yellow paper for each group of 3-4 students.

Chance Questions You decide you want to buy an expensive pair of basketball shoes. Your parents will pay only $50 for shoes. You have to pay the rest. You can't save as much toward your long-term goal. *Go back three spaces.*	**Chance Questions** Your school collects money to help pay medical expenses for a child who is sick. You decide to contribute $25. You can't save as much toward your long-term goal. *Go back two spaces.*
Chance Questions Your sister wins an award for her science project. The award will be given at a special dinner, and she wants to buy a new outfit for the dinner. She needs an extra $25. You lend her the money. *Go back two spaces.*	**Chance Questions** Your grandparents give you $25 for your birthday. You decide to save the $25. This will help you reach your goal faster. *Go forward three spaces.*
Chance Questions Your sister can't babysit for the neighbors on Friday night. She gives you the job. You earn $20. You decide to add $10 to your savings. This will help you reach your goal faster. *Go forward two spaces.*	**Chance Questions** You win $50 in an essay contest. You decide to add $25 to your savings. This will help you reach your goal faster. *Go forward three spaces.*
Chance Questions Your bank pays you $5 in interest on your savings. This brings you closer to your savings goal. *Go forward three spaces.*	**Chance Questions** Your mom tells your Uncle Mort that you are saving for a long-term goal. He is very proud of you for saving and gives you an extra $10 for your birthday. You add the $10 to your savings account. *Go forward two spaces.*

LESSON 15 ACTIVITY 6

GAME DIRECTIONS

Your object in this game is to achieve your long-term goal by reaching the Finish box on the game board.

Set-up

Place the red, blue, yellow and green cards face-down in a blank area on the board or on the side of the game board.

To Start

Each player places a game piece in the Start position and draws a green card. The player reads the card and writes down the answer to the question on the card. Players stop and wait for the teacher to display answers. Players check their answers. Those with correct answers should move ahead two spaces.

Players roll the die to see who starts. The player with the highest number on the die begins.

To Play

Players roll the die and move ahead by the number showing on the die. Then they follow the directions below.

- If you land on a RED or BLUE square, take a card of the same color. DO NOT LOOK AT THE CARD; give it to the player on your left. The red cards are mathematics questions. You may use a paper and pencil to help answer these questions. The blue cards are personal finance questions.
- The player on your left reads the question and you answer it. If your answer is correct, take another turn. If your answer is incorrect, your turn is finished. After you answer, the card is returned to the bottom of the card pile. Play moves to the player on your left.
- If you land on a yellow square, take a yellow Chance card, read it, follow the directions and place the card on the bottom of the card pile. Your turn is finished. Play moves to the player on your left.
- Continue playing until someone reaches Finish or the teacher says "stop."

LESSON 16 WHAT WE'VE LEARNED

MIDDLE SCHOOL

Lesson 16 What We've Learned

Lesson Description

This lesson features a game in which the students review key vocabulary words and concepts presented in earlier lessons. The game is called Flyswatter Review. The teacher divides the class into two teams. Using transparencies, the teacher projects financial terms from the visuals onto a screen or wall. The teams compete to select the correct definition.

Concepts

This lesson refers to several concepts introduced in earlier lessons.

Objectives

Students will:

- Recognize and apply definitions introduced in earlier lessons.

Time Required

45 minutes

Materials

- Two fly swatters, one marked "S," the other "B"
- A transparency of Visuals 1, 2, 3, 4, 5 and 6
- Teacher Answers to Accompany Visuals 1, 2, 3, 4, 5 and 6
- Optional: Small prizes
- Note that the overhead projector should be placed to project an image on a large screen or classroom wall to allow students to "swat" the correct word in the Flyswatter game.

Procedure

1. Announce that the purpose of this lesson is to review key financial terms. The class is going to play a game called Flyswatter Review.

2. Provide an overview of the game. The teacher will project terms from a visual onto a very large screen or a classroom wall. (The image must be large enough so that students can "swat" the correct word in such a way that their selection is obvious but not so large that both teams can swat it at the same time.) Then the teacher will read a definition of one of the terms. The students will be divided into two lines. The students at the front of each line will be asked to respond to the definition by "swatting" the correct word. Points will be awarded for correct answers.

3. Select two students to serve as referees and a third student to be the scorekeeper. Divide the remainder of the class into two teams. Have the students count off: "Stock," "Bond," "Stock," "Bond" to form one stock team and one bond team.

4. Have the teams form two lines facing the front of the room. Hand one swatter marked "S" to the first person in line in the stock team and the other swatter marked "B" to the first person in line for the bond team. The "S" or "B" marked on each swatter will help the referees determine who has won each point.

5. Select any one of the six visuals and project it to the front of the class. Using the *Answers for the Teacher* sheets (see Activities 1-6), read the definition of one of the terms displayed. The students at the front of the lines (and everyone else) should listen. At any time while you are reading the definition, the students in the front of the lines may move quickly to the board and "swat" the term that has been defined. (Because some swats might miss their marks, swatters should call out the terms they are aiming at while they swat.) Give students 30 seconds to swat the correct word. The student who first swats the correct term earns one point for his or her team. Only one swat is allowed per student. Team members are not allowed to call out answers; if they do, their team loses the point. If the students fail to get the correct answer, the word may be passed to the pair of students next in line. If no one gets the answer after two tries, read the correct answer to the class.

6. After a turn, students at the front of the line should go to the back, and the students who then move into position at the front will get their get their turns to swat. The referees will declare the winner for each term. The scorekeeper will keep track of the scores.

7. Continue until all the terms you wish to review have been mentioned or until all the students have had an opportunity to participate. Change back and forth among Visuals 1 to 6 during the game so that students will not be able to memorize locations for any of the terms. Acknowledge the winning team; congratulate all the students. Optional: Give small prizes to members of the winning team.

Closure

Remind the students that learning about saving and investing has been an investment in their own human capital. Knowing and using this information in the future may help them to achieve financial independence.

Assessment

Multiple-Choice Questions

1. Ryan is afraid that he won't be able to sleep at night if his investments involve high risks. Which one of the following is his safest investment option?

   a. Stocks

   b. A savings account

   c. Bonds

   d. Mutual funds

2. Stocks are different from bonds in that

   a. stocks have ratings while bonds do not.

   b. stocks mature and bonds do not.

   c. stocks represent ownership while bonds represent loans.

   d. stocks guarantee a certain rate of return while bonds do not.

3. Mutual funds

   a. are insured by the FDIC.

   b. have standardized fees.

   c. are pools of assets.

   d. offer a guaranteed rate of return.

4. You would want to sell a stock short only if you expect

   a. a bull market.

   b. interest rates to fall.

   c. the price of that stock to rise.

   d. the price of that stock to fall.

Essay Questions

1. Imagine that you are 30 years old and have a family. Explain how you might invest your money in these real-world circumstances — as opposed to the approach you might take if you were a student participating in a stock-investment simulation.
Answers should refer to the amount of risk each investor would feel comfortable with. The student engaged in a simulation activity probably will try riskier investments. The time horizon will also be a factor. The student will have a shorter period of time in which investments may rise in value — only until the end of the semester, perhaps. Because of time and risk factors, a student might be more likely to choose individual stocks, while the 30-year-old might choose mutual funds and an otherwise more diversified portfolio.

2. Write a letter to a grandparent or another relative and tell what you have learned about investing.
Answers will vary, but should include some or all of the following: reasons why it is important to save, benefits of starting to save early, investment options, the importance of human capital, sources of financial information, descriptions of stocks, bonds, and mutual funds, financial planning, company research, credit, the history and importance of U.S. financial institutions.

Lesson 16 Visual 1

Flyswatter Review

Specialists	**Liquidity**	**Secondary Market**
Brokerage Fee	**New York Stock Exchange**	**Wall Street**
Dow Jones Industrial Average	**Primary Market**	**Certificate of Deposit (CD)**
American Stock Exchange	**Bulls**	**NASDAQ**

LESSON 16 VISUAL 2

FLYSWATTER REVIEW

Mutual Fund	**Stock Split**	**Price/Earnings Ratio**
Net Asset Value	**Rule of 72**	**Stock Symbol**
Capital Gain	**Trading Volume**	**Bond**
Market Economy	**Common Stock**	**Sell Short**

Lesson 16 Visual 3

Flyswatter Review

IPO	**Compound Interest**	**Savings Account**
Round Lot	**Credit Card**	**Dividend**
Three Rules of Building Wealth	**Fundamental Analysis**	**Price**
U.S. Savings Bonds	**FDIC**	**Economic Investment**

Lesson 16 Visual 4

Flyswatter Review

Maturity	**Coupon Bond**	**Short-term Bonds**
Bond Ratings	**Treasury Bonds**	**Face Value**
Zero-coupon Bond	**Debt**	**Junk Bonds**
Coupon	**Aaa**	**Long-term Bonds**

Lesson 16 Visual 5

Flyswatter Review

Earnings per Share	Portfolio	Bankruptcy
Market Order	Buy on Margin	Discount Brokers
Credit	Yield	Limit Order
Diversification	Full-service Broker	Closing Price

Lesson 16 Visual 6

Flyswatter Review

Bear Market	**Index Funds**	**Save**
Scarcity	**Human Capital**	**Long-term Savings Goal**
Corporation	**Risk-return Relationship**	**Money Market Fund**
Principal	**Loads**	**Capitalization**

Lesson 16 Activity 1

Flyswatter Review: Answers for the Teacher (to Accompany Visual 1)

Specialists These individuals work on the floor of a stock exchange. They make a market in a particular stock. The location where they work is called a post.	**Liquidity** The ease with which an asset may be converted to cash. This is an important criterion for some investors, especially those who might need cash right away.	**Secondary Market** A market in which stocks can be bought and sold once they are approved for public sale. The New York Stock Exchange is an example. Here stocks are exchanged among buyers and sellers without the involvement of the issuing company.
Brokerage Fee When stocks are bought or sold, this is the payment that goes to the firms that handle the transactions.	**New York Stock Exchange** Stocks are sold in this market on Wall Street in New York City. Brokers and specialists make transactions on the floor in a live auction market. This is the oldest stock exchange in the United States.	**Wall Street** A very famous street in New York, thought of worldwide as the center of financial activity in the United States.
Dow Jones Industrial Average An indicator of how the shares of the largest U.S. companies are doing. It includes 30 of the most actively traded blue-chip stocks, most of which are industrial.	**Primary Market** The market where new securities are offered for sale for the first time. When companies need funds to expand, they can sell stock or bonds in this market.	**Certificate of Deposit (CD)** A certificate issued by a bank to a person depositing money in an account for a specified period of time, such as six months or one year. A penalty is charged for early withdrawal.
American Stock Exchange Stocks are sold in this market. Brokers and specialists make transactions on the floor. This market is similar to the New York Stock Exchange, but generally lists smaller companies.	**Bulls** Investors who buy stocks because they believe that the stock market is going up are called by this name. Investors with the opposite view are called bears.	**NASDAQ** An electronic marketplace enabling buyers and sellers to get together via computer and hundreds of thousands of miles of high-speed data lines to trade stocks.

LESSON 16 ACTIVITY 2

FLYSWATTER REVIEW DESCRIPTIONS: ANSWERS FOR THE TEACHER (TO ACCOMPANY VISUAL 2)

Mutual Fund A pool of money used by a company to purchase a variety of stocks, bonds or money market instruments. It provides diversification and professional management for investors.	**Stock Split** Companies sometimes decide to give each shareholder two or three shares for each share they currently hold.	**Price/Earnings Ratio** Often referred to as P/E, it is the price of one share of stock divided by the earnings reported by the company over the past four quarters.
Net Asset Value A measure of the market value of a share in a mutual fund. Usually, it is calculated by taking the value of all securities minus liabilities and then dividing the result by the total number of shares.	**Rule of 72** A mathematical rule for determining the number of years it will take for an investment to double in value.	**Stock Symbol** A one-, two-, three- or four-letter description that stands for the name of a company traded on a stock exchange.
Capital Gain What a buyer obtains when he or she is able to sell a share of stock for more than he or she paid for it.	**Trading Volume** The number of shares of a stock traded on a trading day.	**Bond** A certificate of indebtedness issued by a government or a corporation. It is a promise to repay borrowed money to the lender at a fixed rate of interest and at a specified time.
Market Economy This type of economy has certain features such as private ownership of property, self-interest, competition, the profit motive, voluntary exchange and a limited role for government.	**Common Stock** A person who owns this owns a share of a company. The owner is entitled to a share of any dividends distributed and to vote in the election of directors.	**Sell Short** An investor who believes that a stock price is going to fall may ask a broker to lend the investor stocks which are then sold at the current price. Later, if the stock price falls, the investor can buy the stock back, return it to the broker and make a profit. If the stock price goes up instead, the investor loses money when the stock is returned.

Lesson 16 Activity 3

Flyswatter Review Descriptions: Answers for the Teacher (to Accompany Visual 3)

IPO A company's first sale of stock to the public. When a company "goes public," it sells blocks of stock shares to an investment firm that specializes in initial offerings of stocks and resells them to the public.	**Compound Interest** A payment based on the principal and on interest earned previously. It is interest paid on interest.	**Savings Account** An interest-bearing account at a financial institution. An insured, low-risk form of saving.
Round Lot The purchase of stocks in multiples of 100.	**Credit Card** A small, specially coded plastic card issued by a bank, business or another financial institution to enable consumers to purchase goods or services on credit.	**Dividend** The share of profits paid to shareholders.
Three Rules of Building Wealth 1. Start early to gain the advantages of compounding. 2. Buy and hold for the long term. 3. Diversify to spread risk over several forms of investment.	**Fundamental Analysis** This form of stock analysis examines changes in sales, earnings and demand for goods and services produced.	**Price** The amount people pay when buying a good, a service or a stock.
U.S. Savings Bonds Securities issued by the United States in relatively small denominations for individual investors. These securities represent loans to the U.S. government. They are low-risk investments.	**FDIC** A federal agency that provides insurance on bank accounts.	**Economic Investment** The purchase of capital goods such as machinery to increase production of goods and services.

Lesson 16 Activity 4

Flyswatter Review Descriptions: Answers for the Teacher (to Accompany Visual 4)

Maturity The time at which the bond holder is repaid, with interest, for money he or she lent to the bond issuer.	**Coupon Bond** A bond that pays out interest at fixed intervals over the time the bond is held by the investor.	**Short-term Bonds** These bonds mature in 1-5 years.
Bond Ratings In order to help bond buyers evaluate the risk associated with a particular bond, companies such as Moody's research the company or agency issuing the bond and give it a grade between C and Aaa.	**Treasury Bonds** These bonds, issued by the U.S. Treasury, usually offer low rates. They are low-risk investments because they are backed by the full faith and credit of the U.S. government.	**Face Value** The price an investor pays for a bond. Also called par value.
Zero-coupon Bond A bond whose purchase price is below the face value. One final payment that includes the principal plus interest is made at maturity.	**Debt** Money owed to someone else. It is also the state or condition of owing money.	**Junk Bonds** These instruments are high-yield bonds. The potential return is high because the risk is high. These bonds have poor credit ratings.
Coupon The interest on a bond.	**Aaa** Bond issuers are assigned a credit rating by companies such as Moody's. The lowest rating is C. This is the highest rating.	**Long-term Bonds** These bonds mature in more than 10 years.

Lesson 16 Activity 5

Flyswatter Review Descriptions: Answers for the Teacher (to Accompany Visual 5)

Earnings per share A measure calculated by dividing a company's profits by the number of shares. When this measure is rising, it suggests that a company is well managed.	**Portfolio** An investor's collection of assets. Investors try to reduce risk by diversifying the assets in their collection of holdings.	**Bankruptcy** A legal determination sometimes sought by people or corporations unable to pay their debts. In these proceedings, courts settle outstanding debts with creditors.
Market Order A customer order for immediate execution (of a stock purchase or sale) at the best price available when the order reaches the marketplace.	**Buying on Margin** Investors who own stock can often buy more stock even if they don't have more cash. They can borrow against the stock they already own.	**Discount Brokers** Brokerage firms that offer fewer services and charge lower fees.
Credit The ability of a customer to obtain goods or services before payment, based on an agreement to pay later.	**Yield** One measure of a stock's performance. It is the relationship between the dividend and the closing price of the day.	**Limit Order** A customer order to execute a transaction (for purchase or sale of a stock) only at a specified price (the limit) or better.
Diversification Owning different types of securities in different companies in unrelated industries. Investors follow this practice in order to reduce risk.	**Full-service Broker** This type of broker offers more services and charges higher fees.	**Closing Price** The last price at which a security traded during a trading session; the price reported in financial media.

Lesson 16 Activity 6

Flyswatter Review Descriptions: Answers for the Teacher (to Accompany Visual 6)

Bear Market An extended period of price declines in an individual security or in the securities market as a whole.	**Index Funds** A type of mutual fund that keeps a portfolio of securities designed to match the performance of the market as a whole, as represented by a market index such as the S&P 500.	**Save** To set money aside for future use. To divert money from current spending to a savings account or another form of investment.
Scarcity This is the condition that exists because human wants exceed the capacity of available resources to satisfy those wants.	**Human Capital** The knowledge, skills, values and health of workers.	**Long-term Savings Goal** A goal that will require five years of saving or more.
Corporation A business that has been granted a state charter, recognizing it as a separate legal entity having its own rights and liabilities, distinct from those of the individuals within it. Most large firms, especially in manufacturing, are organized as this type of business.	**Risk-return Relationship** The trade-off made by investors as they decide how to use their savings. Some investors favor safer investments, such as savings accounts, while others favor riskier investments, such as stocks.	**Money Market Fund** A fund restricted by law to investing in the short-term money market. It is a mutual fund that sells shares of ownership and uses proceeds to buy short-term, high-quality securities. Income earned by shareholders is received in the form of additional shares of stock (usually priced at $1 each).
Principal The original amount of money invested, deposited or borrowed.	**Load** The sales fee a buyer pays to acquire an asset. Many mutual funds charge these fees. As a result of this fee, only a portion of the investor's funds go into the investment itself.	**Capitalization** This statistic is calculated by multiplying a company's outstanding stock shares by the stock price.

Learning, Earning and Investing

Glossary

This glossary provides definitions for words and terms as they are used in financial markets. Some of the words and terms have other meanings in everyday usage (**load, principal** *or* **speculation,** *for example). The glossary does not address these other meanings.***

Alternative: One of two or more choices or courses of action in a given situation.

American Stock Exchange (AMEX): A stock exchange in New York City; provides facilities for trading securities of national interest; often trades in securities of younger and smaller firms.

Asset: Something of monetary value owned by an individual or an organization.

Bankruptcy: The financial status of a firm or an individual legally judged to have debts that exceed assets and thus unable to pay its bills. Formal bankruptcy may result in reorganization of the firm or it may require liquidation and distribution of proceeds to creditors. Stock transaction tables indicate that a company is in bankruptcy proceedings by appending a vi or q immediately before the name of the stock.

Bear/bear market: A bear is an investor who believes that a security's price or security prices in general will go down. A bear market is an extended period of price decline for a security or the securities market in general. (Compare **Bull/bull market.**)

Benefit: Monetary or non-monetary gain. (See also **Cost, Cost/benefit analysis**.)

Blue chip stock: A high-quality, low-risk stock. Usually refers to stock in nationally known companies that have been profitable for a long time.

Bond: A certificate of indebtedness issued by a governmental unit or a corporation, promising to repay borrowed money to the lender at a fixed rate of interest and at a specified time.

Bond fund: An investment company that invests in long-term debt securities; may specialize in certain bond categories, such as corporate or municipal.

Bond rating: The grading of a bond by reference to the bond issuer's ability to make interest and principal payments as specified in the terms of the bond. The three major rating services — Fitch, Moody's and Standard & Poor's — use AAA as their highest rating and grade down through Bs and Cs.

Broker: A professional trader who buys or sells stocks for individuals and institutional customers. (See also **Dealer, Discount broker and Full-service broker**.)

Bull/bull market: A bull is an investor or analyst who believes that the price of a security or security prices in general will rise. A bull market is an extended period of rising prices for a security or the securities market in general. (Compare **Bear/bear market.**)

Business cycle: Ups and downs in economic activity over time, often described in terms of expansion, peak, contraction and trough. (See also **Expansion, Peak, Contraction, Trough**.)

Buying on margin: Buying securities by paying only a percentage (a margin) of the purchase price and borrowing the remainder. The loan is usually arranged by the investor's broker. (See also **Margin requirement**.)

Capital gain: A profit realized from the sale of property, stocks or other investments.

Capitalization: A measure of the value of a corporation. It is calculated by multiplying the number of the company's outstanding shares by the stock price. Corporations are often referred to by their level of capitalization such as large cap, medium cap or small cap.

Capital goods: Goods that people use in their work to make other goods. Buildings, tools, machines and other equipment are capital goods.

Certificate of deposit (CD): A receipt issued by a bank to a person depositing money in an account (a CD account) for a specified period of time — often six months, one year or two years. CD accounts pay interest at specified, fixed rates; banks ordinarily impose penalties for early withdrawals from CD accounts.

Choice: A decision made or a course of action taken when faced with two or more alternatives. (See also **Scarcity**.)

Circuit breaker: The automatic response (usually a halt or slowdown) in activity at a securities exchange in response to certain occurrences in trading. Designed to reduce market volatility, circuit breakers were instituted following sharp market downturns in October 1987 and October 1989.

Closing price: The price of a stock reported at the end (close) of a trading day.

Command economy: An economy in which government makes most of the decisions about what goods and services will be produced, how they will be produced and how they will be distributed. (Compare **Market economy**.)

Commission: A percentage of a stock trade (a buy or sell) paid by a customer to a broker.

Common stock: An ownership share or shares of ownership in a corporation. A common stock offers no guarantee that it will hold its value or pay dividends. (Compare **Preferred stock**.)

Competition: The effort of two or more individuals or organizations to get the business of others by offering the best deal. Consumers compete with other consumers for goods and services. Producers compete with other producers for sales to consumers.

Compound interest: Interest paid on the principal (see **Principal**) and on interest earned previously. (Compare **Simple interest**.)

Contraction: A time of declining activity in the business cycle, marked by decreases in GDP, income, employment, investment and consumption. (See also **Business cycle**.)

Corporate bond: A bond issued by a corporation. (See also **Bond, Municipal bond, U.S. savings bond**.)

Corporation: A company authorized to act as a single entity (legally, as a person), having rights, privileges and responsibilities distinct from those of the individuals within the entity. A corporation has four major characteristics: limited liability, easy transfer of ownership through the sale of stock, continuity of existence and centralized management. Most large firms today are organized as corporations. (Compare **Partnership, Sole proprietorship**.)

Cost: An amount that must be paid to obtain something. (See also **Opportunity cost**.)

Cost/benefit analysis: A process of examining the advantages (benefits) and disadvantages (costs) of each alternative in arriving at a decision.

Coupon: The annual interest paid on a bond, usually stated in terms of the rate paid on a bond's face value. For example, a nine percent coupon, $1,000 bond would pay its owner $90 in interest annually up to maturity. (See also **Coupon bond, Coupon rate of return**.)

Coupon bond: A bond that pays interest at regular intervals with a final payment that includes the original principal when the bond matures. (See also **Zero-coupon bond**.)

Coupon rate of return: See **Coupon**.

Credit: The ability of a customer to obtain goods or services before payment, based on an agreement to pay later.

Credit card: A small, specially coded plastic card issued by a bank or other organization, authorizing the cardholder to purchase goods or services on credit.

Credit rating: An evaluation of a borrower's ability to meet financial obligations. (See also **Bond rating**.)

Currency markets: Foreign exchange markets in which the currency of one nation (such as the United States) can be used to purchase the currency of another nation (such as Mexico). (See also **Exchange rate**.)

Debt: Money owed to somebody else — as in *I'm $900 in debt.* Also the state or condition of owing money — as in *Jones is always in debt.*

Dealer: Someone who buys and sells stocks from his or her own accounts or the accounts of the firm he or she represents. Some dealers also act as brokers. (See also **Broker**.)

Debt financing: Obtaining funds by issuing bonds. (Compare **Equity financing**.)

Demand: The quantity of a good or service that customers are willing and able to buy at all possible prices during a period of time.

Depression: A severe, prolonged contraction in economic activity. The most famous example is the Great Depression of the 1930s. (See also **Great Depression, Recession.**)

Discount broker: An individual or firm that discounts commissions for individuals to trade securities. Discount brokers typically offer limited advice to investors. (See also **Full-service broker.**)

Disposable income: The money a person has left to spend or save after taxes and other required deductions have been taken out of his or her gross pay.

Diversification: Spreading investment funds out over various investment options (stocks, bonds, mutual funds and money market accounts, for example) in an effort to reduce risk.

Dividend: A share of a company's net profits paid to stockholders.

Dividend reinvestment plan (DRIP): A plan that allows stockholders to automatically reinvest dividends in additional shares of the company's stock.

Dow Jones Industrial Average (DJIA): One of the oldest and most widely quoted measures of stock market performance; also called *the Dow*. The average is calculated by reference to the share prices of 30 large, seasoned industrial firms.

Economic forecasting: Predicting what will happen to the economy in the future, often by reference to leading economic indicators. Forecasts may focus on GDP, prices, interest rates, employment and other variables. (See also **Leading economic indicators.**)

Economic investing: Purchasing capital goods — computers, delivery trucks or office buildings, for example — to be used in producing goods and services in the future.

Equilibrium price: A price at which the quantity demanded by buyers equals the quantity supplied by sellers; also called the *market-clearing price*.

Equities: Stocks, both common and preferred — as in *I prefer to invest in equities rather than bonds.*

Equity financing: Obtaining funds by issuing stock. (Compare **Debt financing.**)

Exchange rate: The price of one nation's currency in terms of another nation's currency.

Expansion: A time of growth in the business cycle, marked by increases in GDP, income, employment, investment and consumption. (See also **Business cycle.**)

Face value: For a bond, the dollar amount on which interest is calculated and the amount paid to the bondholder at maturity.

Federal Deposit Insurance Corporation (FDIC): The federal agency that insures deposits at commercial banks, savings banks and savings associations in the United States.

Federal funds rate: The interest rate banks pay when they borrow federal funds from other banks.

Federal Reserve: The central bank of the United States. Also called *the Fed*. Its main function is controlling the money supply through monetary policy. (See also **Monetary policy.**)

Finance charge: The cost of credit, including interest and transaction fees.

Financial institutions: Banks, credit unions, pension funds, insurance companies, mutual fund companies and other organizations that act as intermediaries, enabling savers and borrowers to engage in transactions.

Financial markets: Markets for the exchange of financial capital and credit. Most often, these are markets in which investors buy and sell stocks and bonds.

Full-service broker: An individual or firm that provides a wide range of services to investors, including research and advice. (Compare **Discount broker.**)

Fundamental analysis: Analysis of security values by reference to basic factors such as earnings, balance sheet variables and management quality. (Compare **Technical analysis.**)

Goal: Something a person or organization plans to achieve in the future; an aim or desired result. Financial planners often classify goals according to the time it would take individuals to save the money needed to attain them:

- Short-term goals: Goals that might be attained within two months.
- Medium-term goals: Goals that might be attained in two months to one year.
- Long-term goals: Goals that require three years or more to attain.

reat Depression: A time of deep, prolonged recession in the United States (and elsewhere) during the 1930s. Output fell drastically; unemployment soared; banks failed; and many individuals experienced deprivation and hardship. (See also **Depression, Recession**.)

ross domestic product (GDP): The market value of all goods and services produced in a nation in a calendar year. (Compare **Gross domestic product, real**.)

ross domestic product (GDP), real: Real GDP is GDP adjusted for inflation. (Compare **GDP**.)

rowth fund: An investment company whose major objective is long-term capital growth. (Compare **Income fund**.)

rowth stock: The stock of a firm that is expected to have above-average increases in revenues and earnings. Growth stocks often sell at high price-earnings ratios and are subject to wide swings in price. (Compare **Income stock**.)

uman capital: Intangible assets possessed by individuals, including knowledge, talent, skills, health and values.

centive: A factor that encourages people to do something. Often a monetary reward or the prospect of obtaining one — as in *Tax provisions in the new forest-management program give landowners an incentive to take good care of the trees on their property.*

come: Money received for work performed or from investments; may include salaries, wages, dividends, bonuses, interest, etc.

come fund: An investment company that concentrates on bonds, preferred stocks and common stocks that pay dividends, thus seeking to maximize current income (rather than growth) for its owners. (Compare **Growth fund.**)

Income stock: A stock that pays dividends regularly. Associated with firms that have stable earnings and operate in a mature industry. (Compare **Growth stock**.)

Index fund: A mutual fund that keeps a portfolio of securities designed to match the performance of the market as a whole. The market is represented by a market index such as the S&P 500.

Inflation: A general increase in the price level of goods and services.

Initial public offering (IPO): A company's first sale of stock to the public.

Insider trading: The illegal buying or selling of securities on the basis of information not available to the general public.

Institutional investor: A financial intermediary (a mutual fund or a pension fund, for example) that invests in the securities markets for clients.

Interest: Money paid by borrowers, at a particular rate (see **Interest rate**), for their use of the money they have borrowed. Also, money paid by financial institutions to depositors.

Interest rate: The price borrowers pay for using someone else's money; expressed as a percentage of the amount borrowed. Also, money paid by financial institutions to depositors.

Investing: A decision to forgo benefits today in an effort to increase future wealth or satisfaction over time. Investing is most often associated with purchasing stocks, bonds, mutual funds, real estate and other financial instruments or ventures. (See also **Investment, economic; Investment, financial; Investment, personal**.)

Investment bank: An institution that participates in the primary markets for the sale of newly issued stocks and corporate and government bonds.

Investment, economic: The purchase of capital goods such as machinery, technology and buildings used to increase the production of consumer goods and services in the future. Economic investment entails forgoing current benefits in anticipation of increasing the standard of living in the future. (See also **Investing**.)

Investment, financial: A decision to forego benefits today in an effort to increase future wealth or satisfaction over time. (See also **Investing**.)

Investment, personal: A decision by individuals to forgo benefits today in an effort to increase future wealth or satisfaction over time. This means setting aside income and using it for investing and other actions (saving, for example). (See also **Investing**.)

Junk bond: A high-risk, high-yield bond, unrated or rated lower than BBB.

Law of demand: An economic principle stating that consumers will purchase less of a good or service at higher prices and more at lower prices.

Law of supply: An economic principle stating that producers will provide more of a good or service at higher prices and less at lower prices.

Leading economic indicators: Measures of economic performance that tend to move ahead of GDP, thus indicating how the economy will perform in the months ahead. Examples include stock prices, the money supply and new business start-ups. (See also **Economic forecasting**.)

Limit order: An investor's order to a broker, instructing him or her to execute a transaction (to buy or sell a security) only at a specified price (the limit) or better.

Limited liability: The liability of a firm's owners (in the case of a lawsuit, for example) for no more money than they have invested in the business. Thus, a stockholder can lose no more than he or she has paid for shares of ownership regardless of the firm's financial obligations. Limited liability is one of the major advantages of organizing a company as a corporation. (See also **Corporation**.)

Liquidity: The ease with which an asset can be converted to cash. For example: money held in a checking account is a liquid asset; real estate is far less liquid

Load: A sales charge investors must pay to acquire certain assets — shares in many mutual funds, for example. Also called *front-end load or sales load*. (See also **Load fund**.)

Load fund: A mutual fund with shares sold at a price that includes a sales charge, or load — typically four to nine percent of the net amount invested. (See also **Load**.)

Margin requirement: The minimum portion of a new security purchase price that an investor must pay in cash. Margin requirements are determined by the Federal Reserve Board. (See also **Buying on margin**.)

Market: A place, institution or technological arrangement by means of which goods and services are bought and sold.

Market economy: An economy that relies on a system of interdependent market prices to allocate goods, services and productive resources and to coordinate the diverse plans of consumers and producers, all of them acting according their self-interest. (Compare **Command economy**.)

Market order: An investor's order to a broker for immediate execution of a trade at the best price available when the order reaches the marketplace. (Compare **Limit order**.)

Maturity: The date on which payment of a financial obligation is due. For a bond, the maturity date is the date on which the bond issuer must pay the face value of the bond to the bond holder.

Monetary policy: Changes in the supply of money and the availability of credit, initiated by a nation's central bank (in the United States, by the Fed) to promote price stability, full employment and economic growth. (See also **Federal Reserve**.)

Money market fund: A mutual fund company that sells shares of ownership and uses the proceeds to purchase short-term, high-quality securities such as Treasury bills and negotiable certificates of deposit. Income earned by shareholders is received in the form of additional shares of stock in the fund. (See also **Mutual fund**.)

Municipal bond: A bond issued by a city, county, state or other political entity. Interest paid on most municipal bonds is exempt from federal income taxes and often from state and local taxes as well. (Compare **Bond, Corporate bond, U.S. savings bond**.)

Mutual fund: A pool of money used by an a company to buy various assets — including stocks, bonds or money market instruments — on behalf of its shareholders. Mutual fund investments provide investors with diversification and professional management.

ASDAQ: An electronic marketplace enabling buyers and sellers to get together via computer and hundreds of thousands of miles of high-speed data lines to trade stocks.

et asset value per share (NAV): A valuation of an investment company's shares, calculated by subtracting any liabilities from the market value of the firm's assets and dividing the difference by the number of shares outstanding. In general, NAV is the price an investor would receive when selling shares back to a fund.

ew York Stock Exchange (NYSE): The oldest stock exchange in the United States, founded in 1792.

o-load fund: An investment company in which shares are sold directly to customers at net asset value, without a sales charge. (See also **Load** and compare **Load fund**.)

dd lot: A trading unit of fewer than 100 shares of stock. To buy one share or seven shares, for example, is to buy an odd lot. (Compare **Round lot**.)

pen market operations: The buying and selling of government bonds by the Federal Reserve to control bank reserves and the money supply; an important monetary policy tool. (See also **Monetary policy**.)

pportunity cost: The next-best alternative (or the value of that alternative) that a person gives up in making a choice.

ver-the-counter market (OTC): A widespread aggregation of dealers who make markets in many different securities, trading through telephone or computer negotiations between buyers and sellers. Virtually all government and municipal bonds and most corporate bonds are traded in the OTC market.

ver-the-counter stock: A stock not listed on an exchange and traded only in the OTC market.

artnership: A business owned by two or more people who share the firm's profits and losses. (Compare **Corporation, Sole proprietorship**.)

Paying yourself first: A principle of personal financial management that emphasizes making saving a priority over spending. Individuals "pay themselves first" when they save or invest some money from every paycheck before they buy consumer goods.

Peak: A high point in the expansion phase of the business cycle, and also a turning point. After the peak, the economy begins to contract. (See also **Business cycle**.)

Portfolio: A collection of savings and investments held by an individual or an institution. The more diversified the portfolio, the more likely it is that the investor will earn the same return as the market. (See also **Diversification**.)

Preferred stock: An ownership share with a guaranteed dividend that is paid before any dividends are paid on common stock. (Compare **Common stock**.)

Price: Regarding securities, the dollar amount at which a security trades.

Price earnings (P/E) ratio: The current price of a stock divided by the current (or sometimes the projected) earnings per share of the issuing firm. A high P/E ratio generally indicates that investors expect the firm's earnings to grow.

Primary market: The market in which new securities are sold. (Compare **Secondary market**.)

Principal: An original amount of money invested or lent.

Productive resources: Natural resources, human resources, capital resources and entrepreneurship used to make goods and services.

Prospectus: A document related to a new securities offering, intended to provide investors with information that will help them decide whether to buy the security. The prospectus will ordinarily describe the proposed business plan and related information, including financial data, a summary of the firm's business history, a list of its officers, a description of its operations and notification of any pending litigation.

Recession: An extended decline in national economic activity; often defined as a decline in real GDP for at least two consecutive quarters (i.e., six months). (See also **Contraction**.)

Return: Earnings from an investment, usually expressed as an annual percentage. (See also **Yield**.)

Revolving credit: Credit that is automatically renewed as debts are paid off or paid down.

Risk: The chance of losing money on an investment. Risk arises from variability in returns. The greater the potential variability (in stock prices, for example), the greater the risk. (See also **Risk-return relationship**.) Risk is sometimes classified according to the sources of variability:

- **Currency risk:** The risk that returns to be paid in foreign currency will be affected adversely by exchange-rate changes.
- **Inflation risk:** The risk that returns (on money deposited in a CD account, for example) will not keep pace with inflation
- **Interest-rate risk:** The risk that returns will not keep pace with rising interest rates.
- **Market risk:** The risk that forces of supply and demand might affect the value of an investment adversely.
- **Risk of principal:** The risk that some or all of an investor's original deposit or investment might be lost.

Risk-return relationship: A "goes together" relationship between risk and potential returns. Because investors generally are averse to risk, high-risk investment options (junk bonds, for example) must offer higher potential returns than low-risk options (index funds or CD accounts, for example). (See also **Risk**.)

Role of government: Regarding financial markets, the government's role is to protect the integrity of markets by enforcing property rights and correcting market failures.

Round lot: The standard unit of trading in a particular type of security. For stocks, a round lot is 100 shares or a multiple of 100 shares. (Compare **Odd lot**.)

Rule of 72: A mathematical rule used to approximate the number of years it will take for an investment to double in value when interest is compounded. The number of years is calculated by dividing 72 by the annual return. For example, savings deposited in an account paying interest at an annual rate of four percent will double in 72 /4, or 18 years.

S & P 500: The Standard & Poor's 500 Stock Index. An index made up of 500 stock prices to provide a broad indicator of stock price movements.

Save: To set money aside for future use.

Saving: Disposable income minus consumption.

Savings account: An interest-bearing account at a financial institution.

Scarcity: The lack of enough resources to satisfy human wants. Because scarcity is ever-present, individuals face an ever-present need to make choices. (See also **Choice**

Secondary market: A market in which stocks can be bought and sold once they are approved for public sale; for example, the New York Stock Exchange. (Compare **Primary market**.)

Securities and Exchange Commission (SEC): The federal agency that administers U.S. securities laws; established under the Securities Exchange Act of 1934.

Securities indexes: A statistical composite that measures changes in financial markets. The Dow Jones Industrial Average (DJIA) is the most commonly known securities index. (See also **DJIA**.)

Security: A certificate attesting to a stockholder's ownership shares in a firm or a bondholder's creditor relationship with a corporation or a governmental unit.

Selling short: To sell short, the buyer borrows shares he or she does not own from a broker. The buyer orders the shares to be sold and takes the money from the sale. Then the buyer waits for the stock price to fall. If the price does fall, the buyer buys the shares at the lower price, pays the broker's commission and any fees, and gains a profit. Selling short is risky; if the stock price increases, the buyer loses money.

Shareholder: An individual or organization that owns common stock or preferred stock. Also called a *stockholder*.

Shift in demand: A change in one or more of the determinants of demand including consumers' tastes, the number of consumers in the market, consumers' incomes, the prices of related goods, and consumer expectations. A change in demand causes the demand curve to shift to the right or left.

ift in supply: A change in one or more of the determinants of supply including resource prices, technology, taxes and subsidies, prices of other goods, price expectations and the number of sellers. A change in supply causes the supply curve to shift to the right or left.

ıortage: The situation that arises when the quantity demanded of a product exceeds the quantity supplied. Shortages generally occur when a price is set below the equilibrium price. (See also **Equilibrium price;** compare **Surplus**.)

mple interest: Interest paid on the initial investment only; calculated by multiplying the investment principal times the annual rate of interest times the number of years. (Compare **Compound interest**.)

ole proprietorship: A business owned by one person. The sole proprietor receives all the profits of the business and is responsible for all of its debts. Many businesses in the United States are sole proprietorships. They are usually small businesses — e.g., neighborhood barber shops, gift shops, family farms. (Compare **Corporation, Partnership**.)

pecialist: A member of a securities exchange who makes trades only in one or more designated securities; a "market maker" in the designated security or securities, assigned by the exchange to maintain an orderly market in his or her area of trading.

peculation: High-risk investment practices. Speculators take above-average risks — buying something on the basis of its potential selling price — in expectation of gaining above-average returns, generally during a short time period.

tock: An ownership share or shares in a corporation. (See also **Common stock, Preferred stock**.)

tock certificate: A document attesting to ownership of shares of stock.

tock market: A market in which the public buys and sells stock. To purchase stocks on a stock exchange, individuals work through a broker.

Stock market crash: A sudden, steep decline in stock prices, prompting many stockholders to sell their shares out of fear that prices will continue to fall. Examples include the crash of October 1929 and the crash of October 1987.

Stock split: The division of the outstanding number of shares into a higher number of shares. The market price per share drops proportionately.

Stock symbol: The letter or sequence of letters used to identify a security. The stock symbol for ExxonMobil, for example, is XOM.

Stockholder: An individual or organization that owns common stock or preferred stock. Also called a *shareholder*.

Supply: The quantity of a good or service that producers are willing and able to offer for sale at each possible price during a period of time.

Surplus: The situation that arises when the quantity supplied of a product exceeds the quantity demanded. Surpluses generally occur when a price is set above the equilibrium price. (See also **Equilibrium price;** compare **Shortage**.)

Technical analysis: The study of relationships among market variables to gain insight into the supply of and demand for securities. The market variables used include price levels, trading volume and price movements. (Compare **Fundamental analysis**.)

Ticker: An automated quotation system on which security transactions are reported after they occur on an exchange floor. (See also **Ticker tape**.)

Ticker tape: The narrow, continuous rolls of paper on which stock transactions were recorded before electronic technology made the old recording system obsolete. The term now refers to the flow of prices appearing on tickers out of brokerage firms. (See also **Ticker**.)

Trade deficit: A negative trade balance — that is, a balance in which a nation's imports are of greater value than its exports.

Trading volume: The number of shares of a stock traded on a given trading day, expressed in multiples of 100.

Treasury bonds: Longer-term (compared to treasury bills), interest-bearing bonds issued by the U.S. Treasury.

Trough: A low point in the business cycle, and also a turning point. After a trough, the economy begins to expand. (See also **Business cycle**.)

U.S. savings bonds: Securities issued by the U.S. Treasury in relatively small denominations for individual investors. (See also **Bond**.)

Venture capital: A pool of funds, typically contributed by large investors, from which allocations are made to young, small companies that have good growth prospects but are short of funds. (See **Venture capital fund**.)

Venture capital fund: An investment company that invests its shareholders' money in new business ventures that are risky but potentially very profitable.

Yield: Earnings from an investment, usually expressed as an annual percentage. (See also **Return**.)

Zero-coupon bond: A bond that pays all its interest and principal at the bond's maturity. An investor's income from a zero-coupon bond comes solely from the bond's appreciation in value.